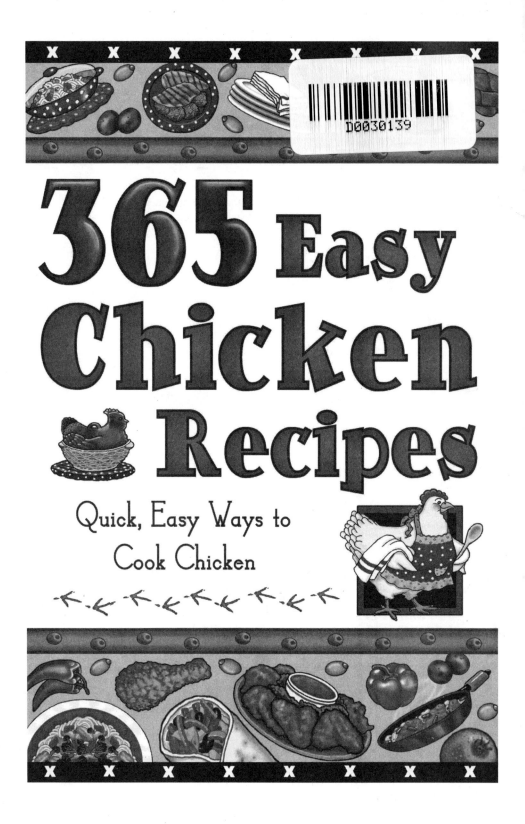

365 Easy Chicken Recipes

Quick, Easy Ways to Cook Chicken

365 Easy Chicken Recipes
Quick, Easy Ways to Cook Chicken

1st Printing - June 2006
2nd Printing - February 2007
3rd Printing - October 2007

International Standard Book No. 978-1-931294-98-0

Library of Congress No. 2006931921

Library of Congress Catalog Data
Main Title: 365 easy chicken recipes : quick, easy ways to cook chicken /
[illustrations by Nancy Bohanan].
Variant Title: Three hundred sixty-five easy chicken recipes
Description: 285 p. : ill. ; 23 cm.
Notes: Includes index.
Subjects: 1. Cookery (Chicken). 2. Quick and easy cookery.
TX750.5.C45 A1385 2006
641.6/65 22

Illustrations by Nancy Bohanan

Edited, Designed, Published and Manufactured in the United States of America
Cookbook Resources, LLC
541 Doubletree Drive
Highland Village, Texas 75077
Toll free 866-229-2665

www.cookbookresources.com

cookbook resources LLC
Bringing Family and Friends to the Table

Chicken Rules the Roost

Welcome to the world of chicken – where the bird is king and the possibilities are endless. From a succulent roasted chicken to a classic chicken pot pie, chicken has become a must-have kitchen staple with wonderful versatility. You can fry it, barbeque it, roast it, saute it or find it rotisserie or deli-style in your local grocery store. Whether you're counting calories, carbohydrates, fat grams, your hard-earned pennies or your blessings, chicken is a perfect choice 365 days a year because it's a simple, economical choice for healthy, hearty meals.

The National Chicken Council estimates that American consumers put about 26 billion pounds of chicken in their grocery carts in 2005. That's an amazing 87 pounds of bird for every man, woman and child in the U.S. People simply love chicken!

We bring you the ultimate chicken cookbook to give you a bird's eye view of the variety of ways to bring chicken to the table with numerous time-saving dishes perfect for a quick dinner for the family after a hectic day or a dinner party for family and friends. This book strives to give you more of what you want – **tasty and delectable chicken recipes that will save you time, effort and make your life simpler and more enjoyable.**

From skillets to wraps to exciting grilling ideas, *365 Easy Chicken Recipes* proves there's no limit to the delicious ways to cook the bird. Try **Chicken-Tortilla Dumplings**, a fun twist on traditional chicken and dumplings. Or how about serving up a skillet dish with **Crunchy Chip Chicken? Dad's Best Smoked Chicken** is also an excellent choice with its excellent 7-Up marinade with a kick. Many of our recipes have that special something like a great technique or a knockout sauce.

Along with abundant, mouth-watering recipe ideas, *365 Easy Chicken Recipes* offers Fowl Language to help you chat chicken and get your beak around poultry terms and phrases. Fowl Tips offer hints for safe poultry handling and Fowl Fun, fun fowl facts and jokes is about our friend, the chicken. If you love chicken as we do, you will now have 365 more reasons to crave leftovers.

Chicken: The Early Days

The chicken is believed to have originated at least 4,000 years ago in Asia, a region where some of the world's finest chicken recipes come from. There is evidence that centuries ago, people realized the value of chicken and raised chickens to provide meat and eggs as well. For example, chickens are depicted in Babylonian carvings as far back as 600 BC and mentioned by early Greek writers, such as the playwright Aristophanes in 400 BC. Indeed, the Romans considered chickens valuable and even sacred to Mars, the God of War.

In ancient Rome, people believed chickens had special powers and they used them to predict the future. They also had a great number of recipes that involved chicken and eggs. Romans had several breeds of chickens and ate every part of the chicken, including the livers, gizzards and stomach.

U.S. Chicken Industry History

The chicken industry in the United States is one of the most successful sectors in agriculture. In just 50 years, the U.S. broiler industry has evolved from fragmented, locally oriented businesses into a highly efficient, vertically integrated, progressive success story increasingly supplying customers nationwide and around the globe. The modern chicken industry produces nutritious, wholesome, high-quality products that become more affordable year after year.

During the late-1800s through the early 1900s, early poultry production consisted of many households having backyard flocks of dual-purpose chickens. These chickens supplied eggs and an occasional chicken for Sunday or holiday dinner. By the turn of the century, a few entrepreneurs began selling young chickens during the summer for meat as a sideline activity on their family farms.

By the 1960s, the commercial broiler industry began its economic boom. The specially bred meat chickens (broilers) surpassed farm chickens as the number one source of chicken meat in the United States. In the late 1960s and early 1970s, chicken-producing companies used television and print media to market chickens under brand names.

Chicken consumption surpassed beef consumption in the U.S. in 1992. Chicken had already surpassed pork consumption in 1985.

How to Use This Book

Throughout *365 Easy Chicken Recipes* you'll find some helpful hints and tidbits to help your flight from grocery cart to dinner plate be easy and fun. Our chickens will help guide your way.

Fowl Facts: Fowl facts will make your flight easier by offering helpful cooking hints and suggestions as well as safety measures for handling chicken, cooking utensils and materials (such as avoiding cross-contamination).

Fowl Language: Fowl Language will help you chat chicken and get your beak around poultry terms and phrases.

Fowl Fun: Fowl Fun offers fun facts and jokes about chickens, such as: What is the longest recorded flight of a chicken? Answer: 13 seconds.

CONTENTS

*What did the sick chicken say?
I have the people pox!*

Chicken: The Early Days 4
Bone up on your chicken history. Chickens have come a long way since they were depicted in Babylonian carvings in 600 BC and were believed to have had special powers.

Wings 'N Things 9
Quick, beak-watering chicken starters ranging from imaginative finger fare to hearty soups that will have your guests crowing for more.
Chicken Nibblers 10
Barnyard Soups & Stews...................16
Plucky, Clucky Chicken Salads...............23

Beak-Pleasing Casseroles...........................31
Please your flock with these simple, innovative chicken casseroles that are anything but ordinary. Each one is unique with its own distinct flavor, colorful combination of vegetables, cheeses and pastas. But all taste great!

Barnyard Bakes and Broils 107
From hearty to light, spicy to mild, these inventive chicken specialties will make you fly over the coop. Just add these wonderful ingredients together, put them in the oven – and stand back!

CONTENTS

In Gainesville, Georgia – the chicken capital of the world – it's illegal to eat chicken with a fork.

Birds of a Feather Frys, Grills and Sautes 181

Make your brood happy in a snap with these quick and easy chicken sautes and frys. Grilling never got any easier!

Slow Clucker 225

Pluck a little oregano here, stir in some veggies there, throw in some chicken and let your slow cooker do all the work! Over 60 savory chicken recipes allow you to add ingredients to the cooker, go about your busy day and come home to a warm, wonderful dinner surely to please your flock.

One Last Peep (Index).............276

Cookbook Resources Published Cookbooks 286

Order Form 287

Wings 'N Things

Q: Why can't a rooster ever get rich?
A: Because he works for chicken feed.

Chili-Honeyed Wings

¼ cup (½ stick) butter	60 ml
1 cup flour	240 ml
18 - 20 wing drummettes and wing portions	
⅔ cup honey	160 ml
⅔ cup chili sauce	160 ml
2 teaspoons minced garlic	10 ml

- Preheat oven to 325° (162° C). In large skillet, melt butter, press each wing in flour, mixed with a little salt mixture and cover well.

- Brown chicken wings over medium-high heat and place in greased 9 x 13-inch (23 x 33 cm) glass baking dish.

- In small bowl, combine honey, chili sauce and garlic and stir well. Spoon honey mixture over each wing and make sure some of sauce covers each wing. Cover and bake 1 hour.

Flautas de Pollo

Traditional flautas are filled with beef, chicken or pork and work as a main course, appetizer or side dish.

1 cup cooked, minced chicken	240 ml
12 flour tortillas	
Oil	
Guacamole	
Salsa	

- Spoon 1 rounded tablespoon (15 ml) chicken on center of each tortilla and roll into tight tube. Heat about 1-inch (2.5 cm) of oil to about 350° (176° C) in 4-quart (4 L) roaster or Dutch oven. Fry flautas in oil, turn once to brown on both sides and drain. Serve with choice of guacamole or salsa.

Chimichangas Con Pollo

Chimichangas are deep-fried stuffed tortillas. Tucson claims to be the birthplace of the chimichanga or chimi.

4 - 6 boneless, skinless chicken breast halves,
  cooked, shredded
3 - 4 New Mexico green chilies, roasted, peeled,
  chopped
2 tomatoes, peeled, seeded, chopped
1 onion, chopped finely
6 - 8 flour tortillas
1 (8 ounce) package shredded Mexican
  4-cheese blend   **227 g**
Red or green chile sauce

- Combine chicken, green chilies, tomatoes and onion and stir well to mix. Divide mixture evenly onto tortillas and top with cheese. Fold ends like envelope, roll and secure with toothpick.

- Place in deep fryer with oil heated to 350° (176° C) and fry until golden brown. Drain and serve with chile sauce.

Deluxe Dinner Nachos

Nachos:

1 (14 ounce) package tortilla chips, divided	396 g
1 (8 ounce) package shredded processed cheese, divided	227 g
1 (8 ounce) can chopped jalapenos, divided	227 g

Deluxe Nacho Topping:

1 (11 ounce) can mexicorn with liquid	312 g
1 (15 ounce) can jalapeno pinto beans, drained	425 g
2 cups skinned, chopped rotisserie chicken	480 ml
1 bunch fresh green onions, chopped	

- Place about three-quarters of tortilla chips in bottom of sprayed baking dish. Sprinkle half cheese and about 3 jalapenos on top. Heat at 400° (204° C) just until cheese melts.

- Combine mexicorn, beans and rotisserie chicken in saucepan. Heat over medium heat, stirring constantly, until mixture is hot. Spoon mixture over nachos, place dish in oven and heat for about 10 minutes.

- Sprinkle remaining cheese and green onions over top and serve immediately. Garnish with remaining jalapenos, remaining tortillas and salsa.

Turkey Jerky

One of the best things in South Texas is turkey jerky and it is found in many local grocery stores.

Turkey breasts, cooked

- Preheat oven to 175° (80° C).

- Slice turkey breasts across the grain in very thin slices about ¼-inch (.6 cm) thick.

- Place on baking sheet and sprinkle both sides lightly with salt and a lot of freshly ground black pepper.

- Cook in oven until turkey gets to the right consistency. It should be very dense, dark brown, but not burned. (The time is different with the size of pieces. Beef jerky takes 6 to 8 hours or more, but turkey jerky usually takes less time. Adjust time according to taste.)

 **Fowl Fun**

Wings Take Flight
Deep-fried chicken wings have long been a staple of southern cooking. The concept of cooking wings in peppery hot sauce was born in 1964 at the Anchor Bar in Buffalo, New York, when co-owner Teresa Bellissimo cooked leftover wings in hot sauce as a late-night snack for her son and his friends. The boys liked them so much that the Bellissimos put them on the menu the next day. Served with celery slices and bleu cheese sauce, "Buffalo Wings" were an instant hit.

Easy Crispy Chicken Tacos

Everybody goes for this classic. Crispy taco shells with chicken, beef or fish make great Southwest treats.

8 - 10 taco shells, warmed	
4 - 6 boneless, skinless chicken breast halves, cooked, chopped	
1 cup diced tomato, drained	240 ml
½ cup diced onion	120 ml
1 cup chopped lettuce	240 ml
1 (12 ounce) package shredded cheddar cheese	340 g
1 (8 ounce) jar spicy salsa	227 g

- Make tacos by filling each taco shell with chicken, tomato, onion, lettuce and cheese. Serve with salsa.

Turkey Tenders with Honey-Ginger Glaze

Oil	
1 pound turkey tenders	.5 kg
Glaze:	
⅔ cup honey	160 ml
2 teaspoons peeled grated fresh ginger	10 ml
1 tablespoon white wine Worcestershire sauce	15 ml
1 tablespoon soy sauce	15 ml
1 tablespoon lemon juice	15 ml
Rice	

- Place a little oil in heavy skillet and cook turkey tenders about 5 minutes on each side or until they brown.

- Combine all glaze ingredients, mix well and pour into skillet. Bring mixture to boil, reduce heat and simmer 15 minutes. Serve over hot cooked rice.

TIP: You might want to try the new packages of rice that can be microwaved for 90 seconds – and it's ready to serve.

Chicken for Lunch

4 cooked, thick chicken breast slices from deli
1 (3 ounce) package cream cheese, softened   84 g
3 tablespoons salsa   45 ml
2 tablespoons mayonnaise   30 ml

- Place chicken slices on serving platter.

- Use mixer to blend cream cheese, salsa and mayonnaise until smooth and creamy.

- Place heaping tablespoon cream cheese mixture on top of each chicken slice and serve cold.

Cracked-Pepper Turkey Breast

This is a delicious turkey breast that can be served many ways. Leftovers are great in turkey sandwiches and turkey casserole.

1 (2½ - 3 pound) refrigerated cooked, cracked
  pepper turkey breast   1.3 kg
1 (16 ounce) jar hot chipotle salsa   .5 kg
1 (8 ounce) package shredded 4-cheese blend   227 g

- Slice enough turkey for each person. Spoon 1 heaping tablespoon (15 ml) chipotle salsa over each slice and sprinkle a little cheese over top.

Northern Chili

2 onions, coarsely chopped
3 (15 ounce) cans great northern beans,
   drained   3 (425 g)
2 (14 ounce) cans chicken broth   2 (396 g)
2 tablespoons minced garlic   30 ml
1 (7 ounce) can chopped green chilies   198 g
1 tablespoon ground cumin   15 ml
3 cups cooked, finely chopped chicken breasts   710 ml
1 (8 ounce) package shredded Monterey
   Jack cheese   227 g

- In large, heavy pot with a little oil, cook onions, about 5 minutes, but do not brown.

- Place 1 can beans in shallow bowl and mash with fork. Add mashed beans, 2 remaining cans of beans, chicken broth, garlic, green chilies and cumin. Bring to boil and reduce heat.

- Cover and simmer 30 minutes.

- Add chopped chicken, stir to blend well and heat until chili is thoroughly hot.

- When serving, top each bowl with 3 tablespoons (45 ml) Jack cheese.

Chicken-Noodle Soup Supper

1 (3 ounce) package chicken-flavored ramen noodles, broken	84 g
1 (10 ounce) package frozen green peas, thawed	280 g
1 (4 ounce) jar sliced mushrooms, drained	114 g
3 cups cooked, cubed chicken	710 ml

• In large saucepan, heat 2¼ cups (540 ml) water to boiling. Add ramen noodles, contents of seasoning packet and peas. Heat to boiling, reduce heat to medium and cook about 5 minutes.

• Stir in mushrooms and chicken and continue cooking over low heat until all ingredients are hot. To serve, spoon into soup bowls.

Five-Can Soup Bowl

1 (14 ounce) can chicken broth	396 g
1 (10 ounce) can cream of chicken soup	280 g
1 (12 ounce) can chicken breast	340 g
1 (15 ounce) can ranch-style beans	425 g
1 (10 ounce) can tomatoes and green chilies	280 g
Tortilla chips, crushed coarsely	
Grated cheese	
Sour cream	

• In saucepan combine broth, soup, chicken, beans and tomatoes and green chilies and simmer 30 minutes. Serve over tortilla chips and top with cheese and sour cream.

Chicken-Vegetable Stew Pot

1 (16 ounce) package frozen, chopped onions and bell pepper	.5 kg
2 tablespoons minced garlic	30 ml
2 tablespoons chili powder	30 ml
3 teaspoons ground cumin	15 ml
2 pounds chicken cutlets, cubed	1 kg
2 (14 ounce) cans chicken broth	2 (396 g)
3 (15 ounce) cans pinto beans with jalapenos, divided	3 (425 g)

- Cook onions and bell peppers about 5 minutes, stirring occasionally, in skillet with a little oil. Add garlic, chili powder, cumin and cubed chicken and cook another 5 minutes.

- Stir in broth and a little salt. Bring to boil and reduce heat. Cover and simmer for 15 minutes.

- Place 1 can beans in shallow bowl and mash with fork. Add mashed beans and remaining 2 cans beans to pot. Bring to boil, reduce heat and simmer for 10 minutes.

Hearty 15-Minute Turkey Soup

1 (14 ounce) can chicken broth	396 g
3 (15 ounce) cans navy beans, rinsed, drained	3 (425 g)
1 (28 ounce) can diced tomatoes with liquid	794 g
2 - 3 cups small chunks white turkey meat	480 ml
2 teaspoons minced garlic	10 ml
¼ teaspoon cayenne pepper	1 ml
Freshly grated parmesan cheese for garnish	

- Mix all ingredients except cheese in saucepan and heat. Garnish with parmesan cheese before serving.

Day-After-Thanksgiving Turkey Chili

3 pounds ground turkey	1.3 kg
½ teaspoon garlic powder	2 ml
3 tablespoons chili powder	45 ml
1 (8 ounce) can tomato sauce	227 g
Shredded cheese	

- In large saucepan, add turkey and garlic powder with 1 cup (240 ml) water. Cook over medium heat until mixture begins to fry.
- Add chili powder and tomato sauce and simmer until meat is tender. Garnish with cheese.

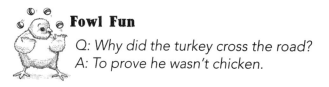

Fowl Fun

Q: Why did the turkey cross the road?
A: To prove he wasn't chicken.

Old-Fashioned Chicken and Dumplings

2 pounds boneless, skinless chicken breasts	1 kg
½ onion, chopped	
½ cup sliced celery	120 ml
1 carrot, sliced	
3 tablespoons shortening	45 ml
2 cups flour	480 ml

- In large kettle or soup pot, place chicken breasts and cover with water. Add onion, celery, carrot, 1 teaspoon (5 ml) salt and ½ teaspoon (2 ml) pepper. Cover and cook for 40 minutes or until chicken is tender. Remove chicken and break into bite-size pieces. Strain broth and return to large pot.

- In large bowl, cut shortening into flour and 1 teaspoon (5 ml) salt with pastry blender or fork until dough is pea-size. Add 9 tablespoons (115 ml) ice water one at a time and mix lightly with fork.

- On floured surface, roll dough very thinly and keep roller well floured. Cut into strips and layer on wax paper. Chill for 45 minutes.

- Bring broth and chicken pieces to boil. Drop strips into boiling broth and chicken pieces. Do not stir but jiggle or shake pot. (Stirring will break up dumplings.) Cook on medium heat for 30 minutes.

Hot Gobble Gobble Soup

This is spicy, but not too much, just right!

3 - 4 cups chopped turkey	710 ml
3 (10 ounce) cans condensed chicken broth	3 (280 g)
2 (10 ounce) cans diced tomatoes and green chilies	2 (280 g)
1 (16 ounce) can whole corn, drained	.5 kg
1 large onion, chopped	
1 (10 ounce) can tomato soup	280 g
1 teaspoon garlic powder	5 ml
1 teaspoon dried oregano	5 ml
3 tablespoons cornstarch	45 ml

- In large roaster, combine turkey, broth, tomatoes and green chilies, corn, onion, tomato soup, garlic powder and oregano.

- Mix cornstarch with 3 tablespoons (45 ml) water and add to soup mixture. Bring to boil, reduce heat and simmer, stirring occasionally, about 2 hours.

White Lightning Chili

1½ cups dried navy beans	360 ml
3 (14 ounce) cans chicken broth	3 (396 g)
2 tablespoons (¼ stick) butter	30 ml
1 onion, chopped	
1 clove garlic, minced	
3 cups chopped, cooked chicken	710 ml
1 (4 ounce) can chopped green chilies	114 g
½ teaspoon sweet basil	2 ml
1½ teaspoons ground cumin	7 ml
½ teaspoon dried oregano	2 ml
6 (8-inch) flour tortillas	6 (20 cm)
Grated Monterey Jack cheese	

- Wash beans and place in Dutch oven. Cover with water 2 inches (5 cm) above beans and soak overnight. Drain beans, add broth, butter, 1 cup (240 ml) water, onion and garlic and bring to boil. Reduce heat, cover and simmer 2 hours 30 minutes. Stir occasionally.

- With potato masher, mash half of beans several times. Add chicken, green chilies, basil, ½ teaspoon (2 ml) pepper, cumin and oregano. Bring to boil, reduce heat, cover and simmer another 30 minutes.

- With kitchen shears, make 4 cuts in each tortilla toward center, but not through center. Line serving bowls with tortillas and overlap cut edges. Spoon in chili and top with cheese.

  TIP: Some people like to add ⅛ teaspoon (.5 ml) each of cayenne pepper and ground cloves.

Cheesy Caesar Pizza

1 (12-inch/32 cm) Italian pizza crust	
2 cups shredded mozzarella cheese	480 ml
1 (6 ounce) package cooked chicken breast	
strips	168 g
2 cups shredded lettuce	480 ml
3 fresh green onions, sliced	
¾ cup shredded cheddar-Colby cheese	180 ml
½ (8 ounce) bottle Caesar dressing	½ (227 g)

- Preheat oven to 400° (204° C). Top pizza crust with mozzarella cheese and bake 8 minutes or until cheese melts.

- In bowl, combine chicken strips, lettuce, onions and cheese. Pour about half of Caesar dressing over salad and toss.

- Top hot pizza with salad and cut into wedges. Serve immediately.

Chicken-Waldorf Salad

1 pound boneless, skinless chicken breasts	
1 red and 1 green apple with peel, sliced	
1 cup sliced celery	240 ml
½ cup chopped walnuts	120 ml
2 (6 ounce) cartons orange yogurt	2 (168 g)
½ cup mayonnaise	120 ml
1 (6 ounce) package shredded lettuce	168 g

- Place chicken in large saucepan and cover with water. On high heat, cook about 15 minutes, drain and cool. Cut into 1-inch (2.5 cm) chucks, season with salt and pepper and place in large salad bowl.

- Add sliced apples, celery and walnuts. Stir in yogurt and mayonnaise and toss to mix well. (May be served room temperature or chilled several hours.) Serve over shredded lettuce.

After-Thanksgiving Salad

2 (10 ounce) packages prepared romaine lettuce 2 (280 g)
2½ – 3 cups cooked, sliced turkey   600 ml
1 (8 ounce) jar baby corn, quartered   227 g
2 tomatoes, chopped
1 (8 ounce) package shredded Colby cheese   227 g

Dressing:
⅔ cup mayonnaise   160 ml
⅔ cup prepared salsa   160 ml
¼ cup cider vinegar   60 ml
2 tablespoons sugar 30 ml

- In large salad bowl, combine romaine lettuce, turkey, baby corn, tomatoes and cheese.

- Combine all dressing ingredients. When ready to serve sprinkle a little salt and pepper, spoon dressing over salad and toss to coat well.

TIP: This is a wonderful salad just like this, but if you have some ripe olives, red onion, black beans or precooked bacon, throw it in the bowl. It will be even better.

Raisin-Rice Chicken Salad

3 cups instant brown rice	710 ml
¼ cup (½ stick) butter	60 ml
3 cups finely chopped, cooked chicken breasts	710 ml
½ cup golden raisins	120 ml
½ cup chopped red bell pepper	120 ml

Dressing:

2 tablespoons lemon juice	30 ml
1 tablespoon dijon-style mustard	15 ml
2 tablespoons honey	30 ml
1 teaspoon white wine vinegar	5 ml
¼ cup slivered almonds, toasted	60 ml

- Cook brown rice according to package directions. Add butter and salt and pepper to taste. While rice is still hot, stir in cubed chicken, raisins and chopped bell pepper. Transfer to serving bowl.

- Combine lemon juice, mustard, honey and wine vinegar in jar and shake until ingredients blend well. Drizzle over rice-chicken mixture and sprinkle with almonds.

TIP: Toasting brings out the flavors of nuts and seeds. Place nuts or seeds on baking sheet and bake at 225° (107° C) for 10 minutes. Be careful not to burn them.

Fowl Language

Foie gras is a French term that means "fat liver" for the fattened liver of a duck or goose. Foie gras is served either raw or sauteed and spread onto crisp toasts.

Chicken Medley Supreme

1 cup chopped onion	240 ml
1 cup chopped celery	240 ml
1 (6 ounce) package long grain-wild rice, cooked	168 g
1 (10 ounce) can cream of chicken soup	280 g
1 (4 ounce) jar chopped pimentos	114 g
1 (15 ounce) can French-style green beans, drained	425 g
½ cup slivered almonds	120 ml
1 cup mayonnaise	240 ml
3 cups lightly crushed potato chips	710 ml

- Preheat oven to 350° (176° C). Saute onion and celery in skillet with a little oil. In large bowl, combine all ingredients except potato chips. Season with a little salt and pepper.

- Butter deep 9 x 13-inch (23 x 33 cm) baking dish and spoon mixture into dish. Sprinkle crushed potato chips over casserole and bake for 35 minute or until chips are light brown.

Pasta-Turkey Salad Supper

1 (12 ounce) package tri-color spiral pasta	340 g
1 (4 ounce) can sliced ripe olives, drained	114 g
1 cup each fresh broccoli and cauliflower florets	240 ml
2 small yellow squash, sliced	
1 cup halved cherry tomatoes	240 ml
1 (8 ounce) bottle cheddar-parmesan ranch dressing	227 g
1½ pounds hickory-smoked cracked-pepper turkey breast, sliced	.7 kg

- Cook pasta according to package directions. Drain and rinse in cold water. Place in large salad bowl and add olives, broccoli, cauliflower, sliced squash and tomatoes. Toss with dressing. Place thin slices of turkey breast, arranged in rows, over salad. Serve immediately.

Barbecue-Chicken Salad

Dressing:
¾ cup ranch dressing	180 ml
3 tablespoons prepared barbecue sauce	45 ml
2 tablespoons salsa	30 ml

Salad:
3 grilled, boneless, skinless chicken breasts	
1 (9 ounce) package romaine lettuce, torn	255 g
1 (15 ounce) can seasoned black beans, rinsed, drained	425 g
12 - 15 cherry tomatoes	

• Combine all dressing ingredients, chill and set aside.

• Cut chicken breasts in strips and heat. Place chicken strips, romaine, black beans and cherry tomatoes in bowl and toss with enough dressing to lightly coat.

Bridge Club Luncheon Chicken

1 rotisserie-cooked chicken	
1 cup red or green grapes, halved	240 ml
2 cups chopped celery	480 ml
⅔ cup whole walnuts	160 ml
⅔ cup sliced fresh onion	160 ml

Dressing:
½ cup mayonnaise	120 ml
1 tablespoon orange juice	15 ml
2 tablespoons red wine vinegar	30 ml
1 teaspoon chili powder	5 ml
1 teaspoon paprika	5 ml

• Skin chicken, cut chicken breast in thin strips and place in bowl with lid. (Reserve dark meat for another use.) Add red or green grapes, celery, walnuts and sliced onions.

• Combine all dressing ingredients, add salt and pepper to taste and mix well. Spoon over salad mixture and toss.

Luscious Papaya-Chicken Salad

1 (10 ounce) package romaine lettuce, torn	280 g
2 ripe papayas, peeled, seeded, cubed	
1 large red bell pepper, seeded, sliced	
2 cups cooked, cubed chicken breasts	480 ml
⅓ cup pecan pieces, toasted	80 ml

Dressing:	
¼ cup lime juice	60 ml
¼ cup honey	60 ml
2 teaspoons minced garlic	10 ml
1 teaspoon dijon-style mustard	5 ml
3 tablespoons extra-virgin olive oil	45 ml

- In large salad bowl, combine lettuce, papayas and bell pepper. In small bowl, whisk lime juice, honey, garlic, mustard and a little salt to taste. Slowly add olive oil in thin stream and whisk dressing until it blends well.

- Pour dressing over salad, add cubed chicken and toss. To serve, sprinkle pecans over top of salad.

Chicken Rice Salad Supreme

2 (5 ounce) cans premium chunk chicken breast	2 (143 g)
2 (9 ounce) packages whole grain brown	
Ready Rice	2 (255 g)
⅔ cup sun-dried tomatoes	160 ml
2 ripe avocados, peeled, diced	
¾ cup dijon-style mustard vinaigrette dressing	180 ml

- Drain chicken, separate into chunks and save broth. Prepare 2 microwave rice pouches (ready in 90 seconds) according to package directions.

- Combine chicken, rice, tomatoes and avocado. Combine vinaigrette dressing and ½ teaspoon (2 ml) salt. Gently stir into chicken-rice mixture and refrigerate 2 hours before serving.

Strawberry-Chicken Salad

1 pound boneless, skinless chicken breast halves	.5 kg
1 (10 ounce) package spring greens mix	280 g
1 pint fresh strawberries, sliced	.5 kg
½ cup chopped walnuts	120 ml

Dressing:	
¾ cup honey	180 ml
⅔ cup red wine vinegar	160 ml
1 tablespoon soy sauce	15 ml
½ teaspoon ground ginger	2 ml

- Cut chicken into strips and place in large skillet with a little oil. Cook and stir on medium to high heat for about 10 minutes.

- While chicken cooks, combine all dressing ingredients and mix well. After chicken strips cook, pour ½ cup (120 ml) dressing into skillet with chicken and cook 2 minutes longer or until liquid evaporates.

- In salad bowl, combine spring greens mix, strawberries and walnuts. Pour in remaining dressing and toss. Top with chicken strips.

Chinese Chicken Salad

2 cups cooked, chopped chicken	480 ml
1 cup diced celery	240 ml
1 (11 ounce) can mandarin oranges, drained	312 g
⅓ cup toasted sliced almonds	80 ml
¾ cup whipped topping	180 ml
¾ cup Catalina dressing	180 ml
1 cup chow mein noodles	240 ml

- Mix chicken, celery, mandarin oranges and almonds in large bowl. In separate bowl mix whipped topping, dressing, noodles and ½ teaspoon (2 ml) salt.

- Combine dressing with salad and serve immediately.

TIP: You can make the salad in advance, but mix the dressing right before serving.

Beak-Pleasing Casseroles

Q: Why couldn't the chicken find her eggs?

A: Because she mislaid them.

3-Cheese Turkey Casserole

1 (8 ounce) package egg noodles	227 g
1 teaspoon oil	5 ml
3 tablespoons butter	45 ml
¾ cup chopped green bell pepper	180 ml
½ cup chopped celery	120 ml
½ cup chopped onion	120 ml
1 (10 ounce) can cream of chicken soup	280 g
½ cup milk	120 ml
1 (6 ounce) jar whole mushrooms	168 g
1 (12 ounce) carton small curd cottage cheese	340 g
4 cups diced turkey or chicken	1 L
1 (12 ounce) package shredded cheddar cheese	340 g
¾ cup freshly grated parmesan cheese	180 ml

- Preheat oven to 350° (176° C). In large soup pot, place noodles in 3 quarts (3 L) hot water, add 1 tablespoon (15 ml) salt and oil and cook according to package directions.

- Melt butter in skillet and saute bell pepper, celery and onion.

- In large bowl, combine noodles, bell pepper-onion mixture, chicken soup, milk, mushrooms, ½ teaspoon (2 ml) pepper, cottage cheese, turkey and cheddar cheese.

- Pour into sprayed 9 x 13-inch (23 x 33 cm) baking dish and top with parmesan cheese. Bake uncovered at 350° (176° C) for 40 minutes.

Chucky Clucky Casserole

1 (16 ounce) package frozen broccoli spears	.5 kg
3 cups cooked, diced chicken	710 ml
1 (10 ounce) can cream of chicken soup	280 g
2 tablespoons milk	30 ml
⅓ cup mayonnaise	80 ml
2 teaspoons lemon juice	10 ml
3 tablespoons butter, melted	45 ml
1 cup breadcrumbs or cracker crumbs	240 ml
⅓ cup shredded cheddar cheese	80 ml

- Preheat oven to 350° (176° C). Cook broccoli according to package directions and drain. Place broccoli in sprayed 9 x 13-inch (23 x 33 cm) glass baking dish. Sprinkle 1 teaspoon (5 ml) salt over broccoli and cover with diced chicken.

- In saucepan, combine soup, milk, mayonnaise, lemon juice and ¼ teaspoon (1 ml) pepper. Heat just enough to dilute soup a little and pour over chicken.

- Mix melted butter, breadcrumbs and cheese and sprinkle over soup mixture. Bake uncovered for 30 minutes or until mixture is hot and bubbly.

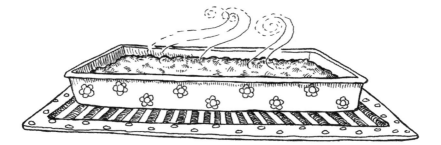

Easy Chicken Enchiladas

10 corn tortillas
1 (10 ounce) can golden mushroom soup   280 g
1 (10 ounce) can cream of chicken soup   280 g
1 cup milk   240 ml
1 small onion, chopped
2 (7 ounce) cans green chile salsa   2 (198 g)
4 - 5 boneless, skinless chicken breast halves,
   cooked
1 (12 ounce) package shredded cheddar cheese 340 g

- Preheat oven to 350° (176° C).

- Cut tortillas into 1-inch strips and lay half of them in
  sprayed, 9 x 13-inch (23 x 33 cm) baking dish. Mix
  mushroom soup, cream of chicken soup, milk, onion and
  salsa in saucepan and heat just enough to mix.

- Chop cooked chicken and place half on top of tortilla
  strips in baking dish. Pour half of sauce on top of chicken,
  repeat tortilla layer and sauce layer.

- Cover and bake for 45 minutes. Remove from oven, cover
  with cheese and bake another 10 minutes. Serve hot.

Busy Day Chicken Casserole

6 boneless, skinless chicken breast halves, cooked
1 (1 pint) carton sour cream   .5 kg
1 (7 ounce) package ready-cut spaghetti   198 g
2 (10 ounce) cans cream of chicken soup   2 (280 g)
1 (4 ounce) can mushrooms, drained   114 g
½ cup (1 stick) butter, melted   120 ml
1 cup fresh grated parmesan cheese   240 ml

- Preheat oven to 350° (176° C). Cut chicken into strips
  and combine all ingredients, except parmesan cheese with
  ⅛ teaspoon (.5 ml) pepper and mix well. Pour into sprayed
  9 x 13-inch (23 x 33 cm) baking dish and sprinkle cheese
  on top. Bake covered for 50 minutes.

Hot-n-Sour Chicky Casserole

1 (3 ounce) package chicken-flavored instant ramen noodles	84 g
1 (16 ounce) package frozen broccoli, cauliflower and carrots	.5 kg
⅔ cup sweet-and-sour sauce	160 ml
3 boneless, skinless chicken breast halves, cooked	

- In saucepan, cook noodles and vegetables in 2 cups (480 ml) boiling water for 3 minutes, stir occasionally and drain.

- Add contents of seasoning packet, sweet-and-sour sauce and a little salt and pepper to noodle mixture.

- Cut chicken in strips, add chicken to noodle mixture and heat thoroughly.

Turkey-Broccoli Bake

1 (16 ounce) package frozen broccoli spears, thawed	.5 kg
2 cups cooked, diced leftover turkey or chicken	480 ml

Sauce:

1 (10 ounce) can cream of chicken soup	280 g
½ cup mayonnaise	120 ml
2 tablespoons lemon juice	30 ml
⅓ cup grated parmesan cheese	80 ml

- Preheat oven to 350° (176° C). Arrange broccoli spears in greased 9 x 13-inch (23 x 33 cm) baking dish and sprinkle with diced turkey.

- Combine chicken soup, mayonnaise, lemon juice, cheese and ¼ cup (60 ml) water in saucepan. Heat just enough to mix well. Spoon over broccoli and turkey. Cover and bake for 20 minutes, uncover and continue baking for another 15 minutes.

Chicken-Tortilla Dumplings

*This is a great recipe and using tortillas is a lot easier
than making real dumplings!*

6 large boneless, skinless chicken breast halves,
  cooked, cubed
2 ribs celery, chopped
1 onion, chopped
2 tablespoons chicken bouillon granules   30 ml
1 (10 ounce) can cream of chicken soup   280 g
10 - 11 (8-inch) flour tortillas   10 (20 cm)

- Place chicken breasts, 10 cups (2 L) water, celery and onion in very large kettle or roasting pan. Bring to boil, reduce heat and cook about 30 minutes or until chicken is tender. Remove chicken and set aside to cool.

- Save broth in roasting pan (about 9 cups/2 L broth). Add chicken bouillon and taste to make sure it is rich and tasty. (Add more bouillon if needed and more water if you don't have 9 cups/2 L broth.) Add chicken soup to broth and bring to boil.

- Cut tortillas into 2 x 1-inch (5 x 2.5 cm) strips. Add strips, one at a time, to briskly boiling broth mixture and stir constantly.

- When all strips are in saucepan, pour in chicken, reduce heat to low and simmer 5 to 10 minutes. Stir well but gently to prevent dumplings from sticking.

- (The kettle of chicken and dumplings will be very thick.) Pour into very large serving bowl and serve hot.

Rule the Roost Casserole

1 (7 ounce) box chicken-flavored rice and macaroni	198 g
1 (10 ounce) can cream of mushroom soup	280 g
1 (10 ounce) can cream of celery soup	280 g
3 cups cooked, chopped chicken or turkey	710 ml
1 (10 ounce) package frozen peas, thawed	280 g
1 cup shredded cheddar cheese	240 ml

- Cook rice and macaroni according to package directions. Mix both soups with ½ cup (120 ml) water.

- Combine chicken, cooked rice and macaroni, both soups, peas and cheese and mix well.

- Pour into buttered 3-quart (3 L) baking dish and bake, covered, at 350° (176° C) for 40 minutes.

 Fowl Fun

If a rooster is not present in a flock of hens, a hen will often take the role, stop laying and begin to crow.

Cheesy Chicky Bake

8 boneless, skinless chicken breast halves
8 slices Swiss cheese
1 (10 ounce) can cream of chicken soup   280 g
1 (8 ounce) box chicken stuffing mix   227 g

- Flatten each chicken breast with rolling pin and place in greased 9 x 13-inch (23 x 33 cm) baking dish.
- Place cheese slices over chicken.
- Combine chicken soup and ½ cup (120 ml) water and pour over chicken.
- Prepare stuffing mix according to package directions and sprinkle over chicken.
- Bake, uncovered, at 325° (162° C) for 1 hour.

Chicken Breasts Supreme

6 boneless, skinless chicken breast halves	
¼ cup (½ stick) butter	60 ml
1 (10 ounce) can condensed cream of chicken soup	280 g
¾ cup sauterne or chicken broth	180 ml
1 (8.5 ounce) can sliced water chestnuts, drained	238 g
1 (4 ounce) can sliced mushrooms, drained	114 g
2 tablespoons chopped green peppers	30 ml
¼ teaspoon crushed thyme leaves	1 ml

- Preheat oven to 350° (176° C). In skillet, brown chicken breasts in butter on all sides. Arrange in ungreased 9 x 13-inch (23 x 33 cm) baking pan. Sprinkle with ½ teaspoon (2 ml) salt and dash of pepper.

- Add soup to butter in skillet and slowly stir in sauterne or broth. Add remaining ingredients and heat to boil.

- Pour soup mixture over chicken. Cover and bake for 45 minutes. Remove cover and bake 15 minutes longer.

Fowl Fact

When choosing a package of fresh chicken breasts, look for one that isn't too "juicy." Water is a sure sign of thawing. Look for medium-size, uniform breasts that will cook in the same amount of time.

Chicken Chow Mein

3½ cups cooked, cubed chicken breasts	830 ml
2 (10 ounce) cans cream of chicken soup	2 (280 g)
2 (15 ounce) cans chop suey vegetables,	
drained	2 (425 g)
1 (8 ounce) can sliced water chestnuts, drained	227 g
¾ cup chopped cashew nuts	180 ml
1 green bell pepper, chopped	
1 onion, chopped	
1 cup chopped celery	240 ml
¼ teaspoon hot sauce	1 ml
1¼ cups chow mein noodles	300 ml

- Combine chicken, soup, vegetables, water chestnuts, cashew nuts, green pepper, onion, celery and hot sauce in large bowl. Stir to mix well.

- Spoon into sprayed 9 x 13-inch (23 x 33 cm) baking dish. Sprinkle chow mein noodles over top of casserole.

- Bake uncovered at 350° (176° C) for 35 minutes or until it bubbles at edges of casserole. Let set 5 minutes before serving.

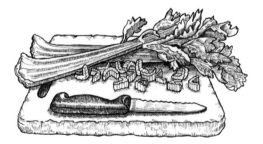

Chicken Dish, WOW!

1 (10 ounce) can cream of chicken soup	280 g
1 (10 ounce) can fiesta nacho cheese	280 g
1 (5 ounce) can evaporated milk	143 g
2 (15 ounce) cans French-style green beans,	
drained	2 (425 g)
1 teaspoon chicken bouillon granules	5 ml
4 cups cooked, cubed chicken breasts	1 L
1 sweet red bell pepper, chopped	
2 ribs celery, sliced	
¼ cup chopped onion	60 ml
1 cup chow mein noodles	240 ml
½ cup slivered almonds	120 ml
1 (3 ounce) can fried onion rings	84 g

- Combine soup, fiesta nacho cheese and evaporated milk and mix well.

- Fold in green beans, chicken bouillon, chicken, bell pepper, celery, onion, noodles, almonds, and ½ teaspoon (2 ml) each of salt and pepper.

- Spoon into buttered 9 x 13-inch (23 x 33 cm) baking dish.

- Bake covered at 350° (176° C) for 35 minutes. Remove from oven and sprinkle onion rings over casserole.

- Place back in oven and bake another 10 minutes.

TIP: This casserole may easily be made ahead of time and baked the next day. Just wait to add the onion rings until you put it in the oven.

Chicken Divan

2 (10 ounce) packages frozen broccoli	2 (280 g)
4 - 6 boneless, skinless chicken breast halves, cooked, sliced	
2 (10 ounce) cans cream of chicken soup	2 (280 g)
1 cup mayonnaise	240 ml
1 teaspoon lemon juice	5 ml
½ teaspoon curry powder or Worcestershire sauce	2 ml
1½ cups shredded sharp cheese, divided	360 ml
½ cup dry, seasoned breadcrumbs	120 ml
1 teaspoon butter, melted	5 ml

- Preheat oven to 350° (176° C). In saucepan, cook broccoli until tender and drain. Arrange broccoli in sprayed 9 x 13-inch (23 x 33 cm) baking dish. Place chicken slices on top.

- In bowl, combine soup, mayonnaise, lemon juice, curry or Worcestershire sauce and ¾ cup (180 ml) cheese and pour over chicken.

- In separate bowl, combine breadcrumbs and butter and layer over chicken. Sprinkle remaining cheese over top and bake for 25 to 30 minutes.

 **Fowl Fun**

There are more chickens than people in the world.

Manuel's Fiesta Chicken

½ cup (1 stick) butter	120 ml
5-6 boneless, skinless chicken breast halves	
2 cups finely crushed cheese crackers	480 ml
2 tablespoons taco seasoning mix	30 ml
1 bunch green onions with tops, chopped	
1 teaspoon chicken bouillon granules	5 ml
1 (1 pint) carton whipping cream	.5 kg
1 (8 ounce) package shredded grated	
Monterey Jack cheese	227 g
1 (4 ounce) can chopped green chilies, drained	114 g

- Preheat oven to 350° (176° C). Melt butter in 9 x 13-inch (23 x 33 cm) baking dish and set aside.

- Pound chicken breasts to ¼-inch (.6 cm) thick. Combine cracker crumbs and taco seasoning and mix well. Dredge chicken in mixture and make sure crumbs stick to chicken.

- Place chicken breasts in baking dish with butter. Remove several tablespoons melted butter from dish and place in saucepan. Add onions and saute. Reduce heat and add chicken bouillon.

- Stir well and add whipping cream, cheese and chopped green chilies. Pour mixture over chicken in baking dish and bake uncovered for 55 minutes.

Chicken Martinez

1 (10 ounce) can fiesta nacho cheese soup	280 g
1 (10 ounce) can cream of chicken soup	280 g
1 (8 ounce) carton sour cream	227 g
1 onion, chopped	
1 (10 ounce) can diced tomatoes and green chilies	280 g
1 (15 ounce) can black beans, rinsed, drained	425 g
1 (15 ounce) can whole kernel mexicorn, drained	425 g
1 teaspoon chili powder	5 ml
8 flour tortillas, cut into strips	
4 - 5 large boneless, skinless chicken breast halves, cooked, cut into strips	
1 (8 ounce) package shredded Mexican 4-cheese blend	227 g

- Combine both soups, sour cream, onion, tomatoes, black beans, corn and chili powder in large bowl and mix well.

- Spread small amount of soup-bean mixture over bottom of greased 9 x 13-inch (23 x 33 cm) baking dish.

- Arrange half of tortilla strips over soup-bean mixture. Make 1 layer of chicken, another layer of half soup-bean mixture, remaining tortilla strips and remaining chicken. Top with remaining soup-bean mixture.

- Bake covered 350° (176° C) for 45 minutes or until it bubbles.

- Uncover and spread shredded cheese over top of casserole. Return to oven for about 5 minutes, just until cheese melts.

Chicken Spaghetti

3 boneless, skinless chicken breasts, boiled	
1 (10 ounce) can tomatoes and green chilies	280 g
1 (10 ounce) can cream of mushroom soup	280 g
1 (8 ounce) package shredded cheddar cheese	227 g
1 (8 ounce) package shredded	
Velveeta® cheese	227 g
1 (12 ounce) package spaghetti	340 g

- Preheat oven to 350° (176° C).

- Shred cooked chicken into large bowl. Add tomatoes, soup, cheddar cheese and Velveeta® cheese. Boil spaghetti according to package directions and drain.

- Add to chicken mixture and mix well. Pour into 3-quart (3 L) baking dish, cover and bake for 35 minutes.

Chicken-Cheese Casserole

1 (10 ounce) can cream of chicken soup	280 g
3 cups cooked, chopped chicken or turkey	710 ml
1 (16 ounce) package frozen broccoli florets,	
thawed	.5 kg
⅔ cup mayonnaise	160 ml
1 cup shredded cheddar cheese	240 ml
1½ cups crushed cheese crackers	360 ml

- Preheat oven to 350° (176° C).

- Mix soup with ¼ cup (60 ml) water in large bowl. Add chicken, broccoli, mayonnaise and cheese and mix well.

- Pour into sprayed 3-quart (3 L) baking dish and spread cracker crumbs over top. Bake uncovered for 40 minutes.

Classic Chicken Marsala

5 - 6 boneless, skinless chicken breast halves	
3 eggs, beaten	
4 tablespoons oil	60 ml
Italian seasoned breadcrumbs	
1 (1 pound) fresh mushrooms, sliced	.5 kg
2 - 3 cloves garlic, minced	
1 (10 ounce) can chicken broth	280 g
½ cup marsala wine	120 ml
1 (4 ounce) package shredded	
mozzarella cheese	114 g

- Rinse chicken pieces, pat dry and flatten to about ¼-inch (.6 cm) thick with rolling pin. Dip chicken in beaten eggs and coat all sides.

- Marinate covered in refrigerator for several hours or overnight. Turn chicken occasionally.

- Preheat oven to 350° (176°C).

- Heat oil in large skillet over medium-high heat. Dip chicken in breadcrumbs, place in skillet and brown on all sides. Drain and place in sprayed 9 x 13-inch (23 x 33 cm) baking dish.

- Spread mushrooms over chicken. Mix garlic, broth and wine and pour over chicken. Bake and cover for 30 minutes. Remove cover and bake additional 25 minutes.

- Sprinkle cheese over top of chicken pieces and bake additional 5 minutes or until cheese melts.

Chicken Tetrazzini

½ cup (1 stick) butter	120 ml
6 tablespoons flour	90 ml
2 (14 ounce) cans chicken broth	2 (396 g)
1 (8 ounce) carton whipping cream	227 g
1 (16 ounce) package linguine, cooked, drained	.5 kg
5 - 6 boneless, skinless chicken breast halves, cooked, cubed	
1 cup sliced fresh mushrooms	240 ml
2 ribs celery, chopped	
1 green bell pepper, chopped	
1 (4 ounce) jar diced pimentos, drained	114 g
4 - 5 drops hot sauce	
½ cup grated parmesan cheese	120 ml

- Melt butter, add flour, a little salt and pepper in saucepan over medium heat and stir until smooth. Gradually add broth and bring to boil. Cook and stir constantly until it thickens.

- Remove from heat and stir in cream. If sauce seems too thick, add a little milk.

- Mix 2 cups (480 ml) sauce with cooked linguine, pour into buttered 9 x 13-inch (23 x 33 cm) baking dish and spread over casserole dish.

- To remaining sauce, add chicken, mushrooms, celery, bell pepper, pimentos and hot sauce and mix well. Pour over linguine and sprinkle with parmesan cheese.

- Cover and bake at 350° (176° C) for about 45 minutes. Uncover and bake another 10 minutes.

TIP: You may use leftover turkey instead of chicken as long as the turkey is not smoked turkey. The white meat of the turkey is better to use than the dark meat.

Blue Ribbon Chicken

3 large boneless, skinless chicken breast halves, cooked	
1 (8 ounce) can mild taco sauce	227 g
Garlic powder	
1 medium onion, chopped	
1 (8 ounce) carton sour cream	227 g
1 cup white sauce (recipe below)	
1 (7 ounce) package corn tortillas, torn	198 g
1½ cups shredded Monterey Jack cheese	360 ml
Sliced jalapenos	
Chili powder	

- Preheat oven to 350° (176° C). Shred chicken breasts and mix with taco sauce. Sprinkle with a little garlic powder, salt and pepper and set aside. Combine sour cream and white sauce and set aside.

- Place half of tortillas in sprayed 9 x 13-inch (23 x 33 cm) baking dish. Add chicken mixture and half of sour cream mixture. Sprinkle with remaining tortillas.

- Top with remaining sour cream mixture and sprinkle with cheese. Scatter jalapenos and chili powder over top.

- Bake for 20 to 30 minutes or until it is thoroughly hot. Serves 6 to 8.

White Sauce:	
2 tablespoons butter	30 ml
2 tablespoons flour	30 ml
1 cup milk, warmed	240 ml

- Melt butter in skillet over medium heat, add flour and stir constantly to mix well. (Make sure there are no lumps.) Heat and stir several minutes until paste-like mixture forms.

- Pour milk into mixture, stir constantly and bring to a boil. Reduce heat to simmer, continue to stir constantly and cook about 2 minutes. Stir in a little salt and pepper and remove from heat.

Chicken-Ham Lasagna

1 (4 ounce) can chopped mushrooms, drained	114 g
1 large onion, chopped	
¼ cup (½ stick) butter	60 ml
½ cup flour	120 ml
1 (14 ounce) can chicken broth	396 g
1 (1 pint) half-and-half cream	.5 kg
1 (3 ounce) package grated parmesan cheese	84 g
1 (16 ounce) package frozen broccoli florets	.5 kg
9 lasagna noodles, cooked, drained	
1½ cups cooked, finely diced ham, divided	360 ml
1 (12 ounce) package shredded Monterey Jack cheese, divided	340 g
2 cups cooked, shredded chicken breasts	480 ml

- Preheat oven to 350° (176° C).

- Saute mushrooms and onion in butter in large skillet. Stir in flour, 1 teaspoon (5 ml) salt and ¼ teaspoon (1 ml) pepper and stir until they blend well.

- Gradually stir in broth and cream, cook and stir for about 2 minutes or until it thickens. Stir in parmesan cheese.

- Cut broccoli florets into smaller pieces and add to cream mixture. Discard stems.

- Spread about ½ cup (120 ml) cream-broccoli mixture in sprayed 11 x 14-inch (30 x 36 cm) baking dish. Layer with 3 noodles, one-third of remaining broccoli mixture, ½ cup (120 ml) ham, 1 cup (240 ml) chicken and 1 cup (240 ml) Monterey Jack cheese.

- Top with 3 more noodles, one-third of broccoli mixture, 1 cup (240 ml) ham, 1 cup (240 ml) chicken and 1 cup (120 ml) Monterey Jack cheese. Pour in remaining noodles, chicken and cream-broccoli mixture.

- Bake covered for 50 minutes or until it bubbles. Sprinkle with remaining cheese. Let stand for 15 minutes before cutting into squares to serve.

Chicken-Ham Tetrazzini

½ cup slivered almonds, toasted	120 ml
1 (10 ounce) can cream of mushroom soup	280 g
1 (10 ounce) can cream of chicken soup	280 g
¾ cup milk	180 ml
2 tablespoons dry white wine	30 ml
1 (7 ounce) package spaghetti, cooked, drained	198 g
2½ cups cooked, diced chicken	600 ml
2 cups cooked, diced ham	480 ml
½ cup chopped green bell pepper	120 ml
½ cup halved, pitted ripe olives	120 ml
1 (8 ounce) package shredded cheddar cheese	227 g

- Preheat oven to 350° (176° C).

- Combine almonds, soups, milk and wine in bowl. Stir in spaghetti, chicken, ham, chopped pepper and pitted olives.

- Pour mixture into sprayed 9 x 13-inch (23 x 33 cm) baking dish. Sprinkle top of mixture with cheddar cheese and bake uncovered for 35 minutes or until hot and bubbly.

 **Fowl Fun**

Jay: Did you hear the joke about the broken egg?
Alfred: Yes, it cracked me up!

Chicken-Noodle Delight

This recipe is a hearty main dish and the bell peppers make it colorful as well. It's a great family supper.

2 ribs celery, chopped	
½ onion, chopped	
½ green and ½ red bell pepper, chopped	
6 tablespoons (¾ stick) butter, divided	90 ml
3 cups cooked, cubed chicken breasts	710 ml
1 (4 ounce) can sliced mushrooms, drained	114 g
1 (16 ounce) jar sun-dried tomato alfredo sauce	.5 kg
½ cup half-and-half cream	120 ml
1½ teaspoons chicken bouillon	7 ml
1 (8 ounce) package medium egg noodles, cooked, drained	227 g

Topping:	
1 cup corn flake crumbs	240 ml
½ cup shredded cheddar cheese	120 ml

- Combine celery, onion, bell peppers and 4 tablespoons (60 ml) butter in skillet or large saucepan and saute for about 5 minutes.

- Remove from heat and add chicken, mushrooms, alfredo sauce, cream, chicken bouillon and noodles and mix well.

- Pour into buttered 3-quart (3 L) baking dish. Combine topping ingredients and sprinkle over casserole. Bake uncovered at 325° (162° C) for 20 minutes or until casserole bubbles around edges.

Chicken-Orzo Florentine

4 boneless, skinless chicken breast halves	
¾ cup uncooked orzo	180 ml
1 (8 ounce) package fresh mushrooms, sliced	227 g
1 (10 ounce) package frozen spinach, thawed, well drained	280 g
1 (10 ounce) can golden mushroom soup	280 g
½ cup mayonnaise	120 ml
1 tablespoon lemon juice	15 ml
1 (8 ounce) package shredded Monterey Jack cheese	227 g
½ cup seasoned Italian breadcrumbs	120 ml

- Cook chicken in boiling water for about 15 minutes and reserve broth. Cut chicken in bite-size pieces and set aside. Pour broth through strainer and cook orzo in remaining broth.

- Saute mushrooms in large, sprayed skillet until tender. Remove from heat and stir in chicken, orzo, spinach, soup, mayonnaise, lemon juice and ½ teaspoon (2 ml) pepper. Fold in half cheese and mix well.

- Spoon into greased 9 x 13-inch (23 x 33 cm) baking dish and sprinkle with remaining cheese and breadcrumbs. Bake uncovered at 350° (176° C) for 35 minutes.

Chicken-Sausage Extraordinaire

1 (6 ounce) box long grain, wild rice	168 g
1 pound pork sausage	.5 kg
1 cup chopped celery	240 ml
2 onions, chopped	
1 (4 ounce) jar sliced mushrooms, drained	114 g
6 boneless, skinless, chicken breast halves, cooked, sliced	
4 tablespoons butter, divided	60 ml
¼ cup flour	60 ml
1 cup whipping cream	240 ml
1 (14 ounce) can chicken broth	396 ml
1 teaspoon poultry seasoning	5 ml
2 cups crushed crackers	480 ml

- Cook rice according to package directions and set aside.

- In skillet, brown sausage and remove with slotted spoon. Saute celery and onions in sausage fat until onion is transparent, but not brown. Drain.

- Stir in mushrooms and chicken and set aside. Melt 3 tablespoons (45 ml) butter in large saucepan, add flour and mix well.

- Over medium heat, slowly add cream, broth and poultry seasoning. Cook, stirring constantly, until mixture is fairly thick. Pour into large bowl.

- Add rice, sausage-onion mixture, chicken-mushroom mixture and ½ teaspoon (2 ml) each of salt and pepper. Spoon into 10 x 14-inch (25 x 36 cm) buttered baking dish.

- Mix 1 tablespoon (15 ml) melted butter, crushed crackers and sprinkle over casserole. Bake uncovered at 350° (176° C) for 40 minutes or until bubbles around edges.

TIP: This dish makes enough for about 12 to 14 people so it could easily be placed into 2 smaller baking dishes and freeze one.

Adobe Chicken

2 cups cooked brown rice	480 ml
1 (10 ounce) can chopped tomatoes and green	
chilies, drained	280 g
3 cups chopped, cooked chicken	710 ml
1 (8 ounce) package shredded Monterey Jack	
cheese, divided	227 g

- Combine rice, tomatoes and green chilies, chicken and half cheese.

- Spoon into buttered 7 x 11-inch (18 x 28 cm) baking dish and cook, covered, at 325° (162° C) for 30 minutes.

- Uncover, sprinkle with remaining cheese and return to oven for 5 minutes.

Alfredo Chicken

5 - 6 boneless, skinless chicken breast halves	
1 (16 ounce) package frozen broccoli florets,	
thawed	.5 kg
1 sweet red bell pepper, seeded, chopped	
1 (16 ounce) jar alfredo sauce	.5 kg

- Preheat oven to 325° (162° C). Brown and cook chicken breasts in large skillet with a little oil until juices run clear. Transfer to greased 9 x 13-inch (23 x 33 cm) baking dish.

- Microwave broccoli according to package directions and drain. Spoon broccoli and bell pepper over chicken.

- In small saucepan, heat alfredo sauce with ¼ cup (60 ml) water. Pour over chicken and vegetables. Cover and cook 15 to 20 minutes.

TIP: This chicken-broccoli dish can be "dressed up" a bit by sprinkling shredded parmesan cheese on the top after casserole comes out of the oven.

Chicken-Vegetable Medley

¼ cup (½ stick) plus 3 tablespoons butter	60 ml/45 ml
¼ cup flour	60 ml
1 pint half-and-half cream	.5 kg
½ cup cooking sherry	120 ml
1 (10 ounce) can cream of chicken soup	280 g
1 (10 ounce) package frozen broccoli spears, thawed	280 g
1 (10 ounce) package frozen cauliflower, thawed	280 g
1 red bell pepper, thinly sliced	
1 cup chopped celery	240 ml
1 cup cooked brown rice	240 ml
4 cups cooked, cubed chicken or turkey	1 L
1 (8 ounce) package shredded cheddar cheese	227 g
1 cup soft breadcrumbs	240 ml

- Melt ¼ cup (60 ml) butter in saucepan, add flour and stir until they blend.

- Slowly stir in cream and sherry and cook, stirring constantly, until mixture thickens. Blend in soup until mixture is smooth and set aside.

- Place broccoli, cauliflower, red bell pepper and celery into buttered 9 x 13-inch (23 x 33 cm) baking dish.

- Cover with rice, half sauce and top with chicken. Stir shredded cheese into remaining sauce and pour over chicken.

- Melt 3 tablespoons (45 ml) butter and combine breadcrumbs. Sprinkle over casserole. Bake uncovered at 350° (176° C) for about 40 minutes or until casserole is hot.

Chile-Chicken Casserole

3 boneless, skinless chicken breasts, cooked, cubed	
1 bell pepper, chopped	
1 onion, chopped	
1 (4 ounce) can chopped green chilies, drained	114 g
1 teaspoon oregano	5 ml
1 teaspoon dried cilantro leaves	5 ml
½ teaspoon garlic powder	2 ml
1 (7 ounce) can whole green chilies, drained	198 g
1½ cups grated Monterey Jack cheese	360 ml
1½ cups sharp cheddar cheese	360 ml
3 large eggs	
1 tablespoon flour	15 ml
1 cup half-and-half cream	240 ml

- Preheat oven to 350° (176° C). In skillet, combine chicken with bell pepper, onion, chopped green chilies, oregano, cilantro, garlic powder, ½ teaspoon (2 ml) each of salt and pepper.

- Seed whole chilies and spread on bottom of sprayed 9 x 13-inch (23 x 33 cm) baking dish. Cover with meat mixture and sprinkle with cheeses.

- Combine eggs and flour and beat with fork until fluffy. Add half-and-half cream, mix well and pour over top of meat in baking dish. Bake for 30 to 35 minutes or until light brown.

Chinese Chicken

3½ cups cooked chicken, cubed	830 ml
2 (10 ounce) cans cream of chicken soup	2 (280 g)
1 (16 ounce) can chop suey vegetables, drained	.5 kg
1 (8 ounce) can sliced water chestnuts, drained	227 g
¾ cup cashew nuts	180 ml
1 cup chopped green peppers	240 ml
1 bunch green onions with tops, sliced	
½ cup chopped celery	120 ml
⅓ teaspoon hot sauce	2 ml
¼ teaspoon curry powder	1 ml
1 (5 ounce) can chow mein noodles	143 g

- Preheat oven to 350° (176° C). In large bowl, combine chicken, soups, vegetables, water chestnuts, cashew nuts, green pepper, green onions, celery, hot sauce and curry powder. Stir to mix well.

- Spoon mixture into sprayed 9 x 13-inch (23 x 33 cm) glass baking dish and sprinkle chow mein noodles over casserole.

- Bake uncovered for 30 to 35 minutes or until bubbly at edges. Set aside for about 5 minutes before serving.

 Fowl Fun

Laid head to claw, KFC chickens consumed worldwide would stretch about 275,000 miles, circling the earth at the equator 11 times.

Chinese Garden

It is stretching a point to call this Chinese, but the combination of ingredients makes a great tasting casserole.

1 (6 ounce) package fried rice with almonds and oriental seasoning	168 g
2 tablespoons butter	30 ml
1 onion, chopped	
2 cups chopped celery	480 ml
1 (15 ounce) can Chinese vegetables, drained	425 g
1 (8 ounce) can sliced bamboo shoots	227 g
3½ cups cooked, chopped chicken	830 ml
1 (10 ounce) can cream of chicken soup	280 g
1 cup mayonnaise	240 ml
2 tablespoons soy sauce	30 ml
½ teaspoon garlic powder	2 ml
1 cup chop mein noodles	240 ml

- Cook rice according to package directions and set aside.

- Heat butter in large skillet and saute onion and celery. Add Chinese vegetables, bamboo shoots and chicken and mix well.

- In saucepan, heat chicken soup, mayonnaise, soy sauce, garlic powder and a little pepper just enough to mix well.

- In large bowl, combine rice, vegetable-chicken mixture and soup mixture and mix well. Transfer to greased 3-quart (3 L) baking dish.

- Sprinkle chow mein noodles over casserole. Bake uncovered at 350° (176° C) for 35 minutes.

Comfort Chicken Plus

1 (6 ounce) box chicken stuffing mix	168 g
1 bunch fresh broccoli, cut into florets	
1 cup chopped celery	240 ml
1 cup chopped red bell pepper	240 ml
2 tablespoons butter	30 ml
1 (8 ounce) can whole kernel corn, drained	227 g
2½ cups finely chopped chicken or	
leftover turkey	600 ml
1 (1 ounce) envelope hollandaise sauce mix	28 g
1 (3 ounce) can french-fried onions	84 g

- Prepare chicken stuffing mix according to package directions.

- Place broccoli, celery, bell pepper, butter and ¼ cup (60 ml) water in microwave-safe bowl. Cover with wax paper and microwave on HIGH for 1½ minutes.

- Add broccoli-celery mixture, corn and chicken to stuffing and mix well. Spoon into buttered 8 x 12-inch (20 x 32 cm) baking dish.

- Prepare hollandaise sauce according to package directions, but use 1¼ cups (300 ml) water instead of 1 cup (240 ml) water as directed.

- Pour hollandaise sauce over casserole and sprinkle top with onions. Bake uncovered at 325° (162° C) for 25 minutes.

Creamed Chicken and Rice

4 cups cooked instant rice	1 L
6 tablespoons (¾ stick) butter, divided	90 ml
¼ cup flour	60 ml
2 cups milk	480 ml
2 teaspoons chicken bouillon granules	10 ml
1 teaspoon parsley flakes	5 ml
½ teaspoon celery salt	2 ml
4 cups cooked, cubed chicken	1 L
1 (16 ounce) box processed cheese, cubed	.5 kg
1 (8 ounce) carton sour cream	227 g
1½ cups round, buttery cracker crumbs	360 ml

- Spread cooked rice in buttered 9 x 13-inch (23 x 33 cm) baking dish and set aside.

- In large saucepan melt 4 tablespoons (½ stick/60 ml) butter, stir in flour and mix until smooth. Gradually add milk, bouillon, seasonings and ½ teaspoon (2 ml) salt.

- Cook, stirring constantly, on medium heat for about 2 minutes or until sauce thickens.

- Reduce heat and add chicken, cheese and sour cream and stir until cheese melts.

- Spoon over rice in baking dish. Melt remaining 2 tablespoons (¼ stick/30 ml) butter and toss with cracker crumbs. Sprinkle over casserole.

- Bake uncovered at 325° (162° C) for 35 minutes or until hot.

Curried Chicken Casserole

1 (10 ounce) box chicken-flavored Rice-a-Roni	280 g
1 teaspoon curry powder	5 ml
2 (5 ounce) cans chunk white chicken with juice	2 (143 g)
⅓ cup raisins, optional	80 ml

- Preheat oven to 350° (176° C).

- In saucepan, prepare rice according to package directions.

- Add curry powder and chicken with juice and raisins and mix well.

- Pour into greased 7 x 11-inch (18 x 28 cm) baking pan. Cover and bake for 15 minutes.

So Simple Chicken and Rice

4 – 6 boneless, skinless chicken breast halves
Seasoning salt
1 cup rice
1 (1 ounce) packet onion soup mix

- Preheat oven to 350° (176°C).

- Sprinkle chicken with seasoning salt and a little pepper. Place rice in sprayed 9 x 13-inch baking dish and place chicken on top.

- Mix 1½ cups water with onion soup mix and pour over chicken. Cover and bake for 1½ hours. Serves 4 to 6.

Fluffy Chicken Souffle

16 slices white bread, crusts removed	
5 boneless, skinless, chicken breast halves,	
cooked, thinly sliced diagonally	
½ cup mayonnaise	120 ml
1 cup shredded cheddar cheese, divided	240 ml
5 large eggs	
2 cups milk	480 ml
1 (10 ounce) can cream of mushroom soup	280 g

- Butter 9 x 13-inch (23 x 33 cm) baking dish and line bottom with 8 slices of bread, buttered on 1 side. Cover with sliced chicken.

- Spread chicken slices with mayonnaise and sprinkle with ½ cup (120 ml) cheese. Top with remaining 8 slices bread.

- Beat eggs, milk, ½ teaspoon (2 ml) each of salt and pepper and pour over entire casserole. Refrigerate all day or overnight.

- When ready to bake, spread mushroom soup with back of large spoon over top of casserole. Bake covered at 350° (176° C) for 45 minutes.

- Uncover, sprinkle with remaining ½ cup (120 ml) cheddar cheese, return to oven and bake for another 15 minutes.

TIP: You could use deli-sliced chicken instead of cooking chicken breasts to save time.

Spicy Chicken-Enchilada Casserole

1 onion, chopped	
2 tablespoons oil	30 ml
1 (15 ounce) can stewed tomatoes with juice	425 g
1 (8 ounce) can tomato sauce	227 g
1 (4 ounce) can chopped green chilies	114 g
1 (1 ounce) package enchilada sauce mix	28 g
1 clove garlic, minced	
3 - 4 cups cooked, boned, shredded chicken	710 ml
12 corn tortillas	
2 (2 ounce) cans sliced black olives	2 (57 g)
1 (16 ounce) package grated Monterey Jack cheese	.5 kg

- Preheat oven to 350° (176° C).

- In large roaster or kettle, saute onion in oil until translucent, but not brown. Add tomatoes, tomato sauce, green chilies, enchilada sauce mix, garlic, ½ teaspoon (2 ml) salt and chicken. Bring to boil, turn heat down and simmer 15 minutes.

- In greased 9 x 13-inch (23 x 33 cm) baking pan, place 4 tortillas and spread evenly with one-third chicken mixture over top. Add one-third olives and cheese and spread evenly. Repeat layers twice, but reserve final layer of cheese.

- Cover and bake for 35 minutes. Remove cover from dish and sprinkle remaining cheese over top. Return to oven for 5 minutes.

Easy Chicken and Dumplings

3 cups cooked, chopped chicken	710 ml
2 (10 ounce) cans cream of chicken soup	2 (280 g)
3 teaspoons chicken bouillon granules	15 ml
1 (8 ounce) can refrigerated buttermilk biscuits	227 g

- Combine chopped chicken, both cans of soup, chicken bouillon granules and 4½ cups (1.1 L) water in large soup pot or Dutch oven. Boil mixture and stir to mix well.

- Separate biscuits and cut in half, cut again making 4 pieces out of each biscuit. Drop biscuit pieces, 1 at a time, into boiling chicken mixture and stir gently.

- When all biscuits are in pot, reduce heat to low, simmer and stir occasionally for about 15 minutes.

TIP: Deli turkey will work just fine in this recipe. It's a great time-saver!

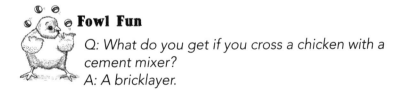

Fowl Fun

Q: What do you get if you cross a chicken with a cement mixer?
A: A bricklayer.

Family Chicken Bake

This is a great, basic "meat-and-potato" dish that all families love.

¼ cup (½ stick) butter	60 ml
1 red bell pepper, chopped	
1 onion, chopped	
2 ribs celery, chopped	
1 (8 ounce) carton sour cream	227 g
1½ cups half-and-half cream	360 ml
1 (7 ounce) can chopped green chilies, drained	198 g
1 teaspoon chicken bouillon granules	5 ml
½ teaspoon celery salt	2 ml
3 - 4 cups cooked, cubed chicken	710 ml
1 (16 ounce) package shredded cheddar cheese, divided	.5 kg
1 (2 pound) package frozen hash brown potatoes, thawed	1 kg

- Preheat oven to 350° (176° C).

- Melt butter in saucepan and saute bell pepper, onion and celery. In large bowl, combine sour cream, half-and-half, green chilies, seasonings and about ½ teaspoon (2 ml) each of salt and pepper.

- Stir in bell pepper mixture, chicken and half of cheese. Fold in hash brown potatoes. Spoon into greased 9 x 13-inch (23 x 33 cm) baking dish.

- Bake uncovered for 45 minutes or until casserole is bubbly. Remove from oven and sprinkle remaining cheese over top of casserole. Return to oven for about 5 minutes.

TIP: For a change of pace, heat some hot, thick, chunky salsa to spoon over the top of each serving.

Family Night Spaghetti

This recipe has a little different twist on the ever-popular chicken spaghetti. This is a wonderful casserole to serve to family or for company. It has great flavor with chicken, pasta and colorful vegetables all in one dish. It's a winner, I promise!

1 bunch fresh green onions with tops, chopped	
1 cup chopped celery	240 ml
1 red bell pepper, chopped	
1 yellow or orange bell pepper, chopped	
¼ cup (½ stick) butter	60 ml
1 tablespoon dried cilantro leaves	15 ml
1 teaspoon Italian seasoning	5 ml
1 (8 ounce) package thin spaghetti, cooked, drained	227 g
4 cups cooked, chopped chicken or turkey	1 L
1 (8 ounce) carton sour cream	227 g
1 (16 ounce) jar creamy alfredo sauce	.5 kg
1 (10 ounce) box frozen green peas, thawed	280 g
1 (8 ounce) package shredded mozzarella cheese, divided	227 g

- Saute onions, celery and bell peppers in butter in large skillet. In large bowl combine onion-pepper mixture, cilantro, Italian seasoning, spaghetti, chicken, sour cream and alfredo sauce and mix well.

- Sprinkle a little salt and pepper in mixture. Fold in peas and half mozzarella cheese. Spoon into greased 10 x 14-inch (25 cm x 36 cm) deep baking dish and bake covered at 350° (176° C) for 45 minutes. Remove from oven and sprinkle remaining cheese over casserole. Return to oven for about 5 minutes.

TIP: If you want a little twist, just use chopped, cooked ham instead of chicken.

Garden Chicken

This colorful, delicious casserole is not only flavor packed, but it is also a sight to behold! You can't beat this bountiful dish for family or company.

4 boneless, skinless chicken breasts halves, cut into strips	
1 teaspoon minced garlic	5 ml
5 tablespoons butter, divided	75 ml
1 small yellow squash, thinly sliced	
1 small zucchini, thinly sliced	
1 red bell pepper, thinly sliced	
4 tablespoons flour	60 ml
2 teaspoons pesto seasoning	10 ml
1 (14 ounce) can chicken broth	396 g
1 cup half-and-half cream	240 ml
1 (8 ounce) package angel hair pasta, cooked al dente, drained	227 g
⅓ cup shredded parmesan cheese	80 ml

- Saute chicken and garlic in butter in large skillet over medium heat for about 15 minutes. Remove ingredients and set aside.

- With butter in skillet, saute squash, zucchini and bell pepper and cook just until tender-crisp.

- In small saucepan, melt 3 tablespoons (45 ml) butter and add flour, pesto seasoning and ½ teaspoon (2 ml) each of salt and pepper. Stir to form smooth paste.

- Over medium high heat, gradually add broth, stirring constantly, until thick. Stir in cream and heat thoroughly.

- In large bowl, combine chicken, vegetables, broth-cream mixture and drained pasta. Transfer to greased 9 x 13-inch (23 x 33 cm) baking dish.

- Cover and bake at 350° (176° C) for 30 minutes.

- Uncover and sprinkle parmesan cheese over top of casserole and return to oven for another 5 minutes.

Great Crazy Lasagna

Chicken never got mixed up with any better ingredients!

1 tablespoon butter	15 ml
½ onion, chopped	
1 cup sliced fresh mushrooms	240 ml
1 (10 ounce) can cream of chicken soup	280 g
1 (16 ounce) jar alfredo sauce	.5 kg
1 (4 ounce) jar diced pimentos, drained	114 g
⅓ cup dry white wine	80 ml
1 (10 ounce) package frozen chopped spinach, thawed	280 g
1 (15 ounce) carton ricotta cheese	425 g
⅓ cup grated parmesan cheese	80 ml
1 egg, beaten	
9 lasagna noodles, cooked	
3 - 4 cups cooked shredded chicken	1 L
1 (16 ounce) package shredded cheddar cheese, divided	.5 kg

- Melt butter and saute onion and mushrooms in large skillet. Stir in soup, alfredo sauce, pimentos and wine. Reserve one-third sauce for top of lasagna.

- Drain spinach well. Combine spinach, ricotta, parmesan and egg and mix well.

- Place 3 noodles in sprayed 10 x 15-inch (25 x 38 cm) baking dish.

- Layer each with half of remaining sauce, spinach-ricotta mixture and chicken. (The spinach-ricotta mixture will be fairly dry.)

- Sprinkle with 1½ cups (360 ml) cheddar cheese. Repeat layering. Top with last 3 noodles and reserved sauce.

- Cover and bake at 350° (176° C) for 45 minutes. Remove from oven and sprinkle remaining cheese on top.

- Return to oven uncovered and bake another 5 minutes. Let casserole stand 10 minutes.

Green Chile-Chicken Enchilada Casserole

*This classic casserole is good for all occasions. If you don't want to cook
a whole chicken, use 6 to 8 boneless, skinless chicken breasts halves.
It will save you some time.*

1 whole chicken	
1 large onion, chopped	
3 ribs celery, chopped	
1 tablespoon butter	15 ml
1 (7 ounce) can chopped green chilies	198 g
1 cup milk	240 ml
1 (10 ounce) can cream of chicken soup	280 g
1 (10 ounce) can cream of mushroom soup	280 g
10 corn tortillas, cut into strips	
1 (12 ounce) package shredded cheddar cheese	340 g

- Preheat oven to 350° (176° C).

- Bake chicken in covered baking pan with 1½ cups (360 ml) water, onion, celery, butter, salt and pepper for 1 hour or until juices run clear.

- Remove from oven, remove chicken to platter to cool and reserve 1 cup (240 ml) chicken stock. When chicken cools, remove meat from bone.

- Combine green chilies, milk, reserved chicken stock, cream of chicken soup and cream of mushroom soup in saucepan and heat just enough to mix.

- In sprayed, 9 x 13-inch (23 x 33 cm) baking dish, place half of tortillas in bottom of dish, cover with half chicken and half soup mixture and repeat layers.

- Cover and bake for about 30 minutes. Sprinkle cheese on top of casserole and bake another 5 minutes.

Sizzling Chicken Pepe

2 (10 ounce) cans cream of chicken soup	2 (280) g
1 cup milk	240 ml
1 (1 ounce) envelope taco seasoning	28 g
1 (4 ounce) can chopped green chilies	114 g
1 (10 ounce) package corn tortillas or chips	280 g
5 - 6 boneless, skinless chicken breasts, cooked, cubed	
1 (16 ounce) package shredded Monterey Jack cheese	.5 kg

- Preheat oven to 325° (162° C). Combine soups, milk, taco seasoning and green chilies.

- In 9 x 13-inch (23 x 33 cm) glass baking dish, make 2 layers of following ingredients: chips, chicken, soup mixture and cheese. Bake uncovered for 1 hour.

Jazzy Turkey and Dressing

1 (8 ounce) package stuffing	227 g
3 cups diced, cooked turkey	710 ml
1 (15 ounce) can golden hominy, drained	425 g
1 (4 ounce) can chopped green chilies, drained	114 g
½ cup chopped red bell pepper	120 ml
2 tablespoons dried parsley flakes	30 ml
1 (10 ounce) can cream of chicken soup	280 g
1 (8 ounce) carton sour cream	227 g
2 tablespoons (¼ stick) butter, melted	30 ml
2 teaspoons ground cumin	10 ml
1 cup shredded mozzarella cheese	240 ml

- Preheat oven to 350° (176° C). In large mixing bowl, combine all ingredients except cheese with ½ cup (120 ml) water and ½ teaspoon (2 ml) salt and mix well.

- Pour into greased 9 x 13-inch (23 x 33 cm) baking dish and cover with foil. Bake at 350° (176° C) for 35 minutes.

- Uncover, sprinkle with cheese and bake 5 minutes.

Jalapeno Chicken Bark

This one barks a little to get your attention, but it sure is good.

6 boneless, skinless chicken breast halves	
¼ cup oil	60 ml
¼ cup white wine	60 ml
1 pint sour cream	.5 kg
1 tablespoon flour	15 ml
1 clove garlic, minced	
½ teaspoon ground cumin	2 ml
1 (7 ounce) can whole jalapeno peppers	198 g
1 (12 ounce) package Monterey Jack cheese	340 g
1 onion, sliced in rounds	

- Preheat oven to 325° (162° C).

- Brown chicken on both sides in oil. Place in 9 x 13-inch (23 x 33 cm) baking dish. In blender, combine wine, sour cream, flour, garlic, ½ teaspoon (2 ml) salt, ¼ teaspoon (1 ml) pepper, cumin and peppers.

- Blend until smooth to make sauce. Pour sauce over chicken breasts, sprinkle with cheese and top with onion rings. Bake, covered, for 1 hour.

TIP: If you like it extra hot, leave the seeds in the jalapenos. If you take the seeds out, rubber gloves will protect your hands from the juices.

Jalapeno Chicken

Even if you are not a spinach fan, you will find this to your liking!

2 cups chopped onion	480 ml
2 tablespoons (¼ stick) butter	30 ml
1 (10 ounce) package frozen spinach, cooked, drained	280 g
6 jalapenos or 1 (7 ounce) can green chilies, drained	198 g
1 (8 ounce) carton sour cream	226 g
2 (10 ounce) cans cream of chicken soup	2 (280 g)
4 green onions with tops, chopped	
1 (12 ounce) package corn tortilla chips, slightly crushed	340 g
4 cups diced turkey or chicken	1 L
1 (8 ounce) package shredded Monterey Jack cheese	227 g

- Preheat oven to 350° (176° C). Saute onion in butter and blend in spinach, peppers, sour cream, soups, onion tops and ½ teaspoon (2 ml) salt.

- In large 15 x 10-inch (38 x 25 cm) baking dish or 2 9 x 9-inch (23 x 23 cm) dishes, layer chips, chicken, spinach mixture and cheese. Repeat process with cheese on top. Bake for 35 minutes.

TIP: Squeeze spinach in paper towels to drain completely.

Fowl Language

The term "cull" refers to removing a bird from the flock because of productivity, age, health or personality issues.

Jolly Ole Chicken

*With this casserole, you have the chicken and
cranberry sauce all in one dish.*

1 (6 ounce) package long grain, wild rice with seasonings	168 g
1 (16 ounce) can whole berry cranberry sauce	.5 kg
⅓ cup orange juice	80 ml
3 tablespoons butter, melted	45 ml
½ teaspoon curry powder	2 ml
6 - 8 boneless, skinless chicken breast halves	
⅔ cup slivered almonds	160 ml

- Cook rice according to package directions and pour into greased 9 x 13-inch (23 x 33 cm) baking dish.

- Combine cranberry sauce, orange juice, butter and curry powder in saucepan and heat just enough to mix ingredients well.

- Place chicken breasts over rice and pour cranberry-orange juice mixture over chicken.

- Bake covered at 325° (162° C) for about 10 to 15 minutes.

- Uncover, sprinkle almonds over casserole and return to oven for about 10 to 15 minutes, just until chicken browns lightly.

King Ranch Chicken

The King Ranch is the largest ranch in the U.S. and was established in 1852 by a Spanish land grant. Today the ranch covers more than 800,000 acres in South Texas with additional holdings in Brazil and 3 states in the U.S.

8 (8-inch) corn tortillas, divided	8 (20 cm)
Chicken broth	
2 tablespoons butter	30 ml
1 onion, chopped	
1 green bell pepper, chopped	
1 (14 ounce) can cream of chicken soup	396 g
1 (14 ounce) can cream of mushroom soup	396 g
1 tablespoon chili powder	15 ml
3 - 4 pound fryer, cooked, boned, diced	1.3 kg
1 (12 ounce) package shredded cheese	340 g
1 (10 ounce) can chopped tomatoes and green chilies	280 g

- Preheat oven to 350° (176° C).

- Dip half of tortillas in hot chicken broth just long enough to soften and place in 10 x 14-inch (25 x 36 cm) sprayed baking dish.

- In skillet with butter, saute onion and bell pepper. Stir in soups, chili powder and diced chicken.

- Pour layer of half soup-chicken mixture over tortillas and half cheese. Repeat layers and pour tomatoes and green chilies over casserole.

- Bake for 40 to 45 minutes or until hot and bubbly.

Don't Be Chicken Casserole

2 cups tortilla chips, crushed	480 ml
4 boneless, skinless chicken breast halves, cooked	
1 (15 ounce) can garbanzo beans, drained	425 g
1 (15 ounce) can pinto beans, drained	425 g
1 (15 ounce) can whole kernel corn, drained	425 g
1 (16 ounce) jar hot salsa	.5 kg
1 chopped red onion	
2 teaspoons cumin	10 ml
1 teaspoon dried cilantro leaves	5 ml
1 green bell pepper, diced	
2 teaspoons minced garlic	10 ml
1 (8 ounce) package shredded Monterey Jack cheese	227 g
1 (8 ounce) package shredded sharp cheddar cheese	227 g

- Grease 9 x 13-inch (23 x 33 cm) baking dish and scatter crushed tortilla chips evenly in dish.

- Cut chicken breasts in thin slices. In large bowl, combine chicken, beans, corn, salsa, onion, cumin, cilantro leaves, bell pepper, garlic and 1 teaspoon (5 ml) salt and mix well.

- Spoon half of mixture evenly over chips.

- Combine cheeses and sprinkle half over mixture. Cover with remaining half of chicken-bean mixture and remaining cheese.

- Bake uncovered at 350° (176° C) for 35 minutes. Let stand 10 minutes before serving. Garnish with tomato slices, sour cream and chopped fresh onions, if you like.

Mexican-Turkey Fiesta

If you use leftover turkey, all you have to do to have a delicious casserole is to cut up your turkey, an onion and a bell pepper. The rest is opening cans and a bag of chips!

4 cups deli chopped turkey	
1 onion, chopped	
1 (12 ounce) package shredded cheddar cheese	340 g
1 green bell pepper, chopped	
1 teaspoon chili powder	5 ml
½ teaspoon ground cumin	2 ml
2 (10 ounce) cans cream of chicken soup	2 (280 g)
1 (10 ounce) can diced green chilies and tomatoes	280 g
1 (10 ounce) bag tortilla chips	280 g

- Preheat oven to 300° (148° C). In large pan, combine all ingredients except tortilla chips. Add ½ teaspoon (2 ml) each of salt and pepper and mix well. Spray 9 x 13-inch (23 x 33 cm) baking dish, pour two-thirds tortilla chips into baking dish and crush slightly with hand.

- Pour all turkey-cheese mixture over crushed tortilla chips and spread out. Crush remaining tortilla chips in baggie and spread over casserole. Bake uncovered for 40 minutes.

Chicken Cashew Bake

⅓ cup minced onion	80 ml
1 cup minced celery	240 ml
1 tablespoon butter, melted	15 ml
1 (10 ounce) can cream of mushroom soup	280 g
½ cup chicken broth	120 ml
1 tablespoon soy sauce	15 ml
3 drops hot sauce	
2 cups cooked, diced chicken	480 ml
1 cup chow mein noodles	240 ml
½ cup chopped cashew nuts	120 ml

- Preheat oven to 350° (176° C).

- Saute onion and celery in butter. Add soup and chicken broth. Stir in soy sauce, hot sauce and chicken and simmer for about 5 minutes.

- Pour into 1-quart (1 L) baking dish. Sprinkle noodles and nuts on top.

- Bake for 20 minutes or until thoroughly hot. Serves 4 to 6.

Fowl Fact

Do not reuse any marinades that have been in contact with uncooked chicken.

Not JUST Chicken

This is a great recipe for leftover ham or turkey. It is really a "quick fix" for the family.

3 cups cooked, cubed chicken or turkey	710 ml
3 cups fully cooked, cubed ham	710 ml
1 (8 ounce) package shredded cheddar cheese	227 g
1 (15 ounce) can English peas, drained	425 g
1 onion, chopped	
3 ribs celery, chopped	
¼ cup (½ stick) butter	60 ml
1 tablespoon flour	80 ml/15 ml
1 pint half-and-half cream	.5 kg
½ cup milk	120 ml
1 teaspoon dillweed	5 ml
Hot, cooked instant brown rice	

- Preheat oven to 350° (176° C).

- Combine chicken, ham, cheese and English peas in large bowl.

- In very large saucepan, saute onion and celery in butter until tender. Add flour and stir to make a paste.

- Gradually add cream, milk, dillweed and 1 teaspoon (5 ml) salt. Heat, stirring constantly, until mixture thickens.

- Add thickened cream mixture to chicken-ham mixture and mix well.

- Spoon into sprayed 4-quart (4 L) baking dish that you can take to the table.

- Cover and bake for 20 minutes. Spoon chicken and ham casserole over hot brown rice.

Old-Fashioned Chicken Spaghetti

This is a great recipe for leftover turkey.

8 - 10 ounces spaghetti	227 g
1 bell pepper, chopped	
1 onion, chopped	
1 cup chopped celery	240 ml
½ cup (1 stick) butter	120 ml
1 (10 ounce) can tomato soup	280 g
1 (10 ounce) can diced tomatoes and	
green chilies	280 g
1 (4 ounce) can chopped mushrooms	114 g
½ teaspoon garlic powder	2 ml
3 teaspoons chicken bouillon granules	15 ml
4 - 5 cups chopped chicken or turkey	1 L
1 (8 ounce) package cubed, Velveeta® cheese	227 g
1 (8 ounce) package shredded cheddar cheese	227 g

- Preheat oven to 325° (162° C). Cook spaghetti according to package directions and drain.

- In medium saucepan, saute bell pepper, onion and celery in butter.

- Add soup, tomatoes, mushrooms, garlic powder, bouillon and ½ cup (120 ml) water and mix well.

- In large mixing bowl, mix spaghetti, soup, tomato mixture, chicken and cheese. Place in 2 (2-quart/2 L) sprayed baking dishes.

- Bake one dish covered for 40 to 50 minutes. Freeze the other dish for later. To cook frozen dish, thaw first.

Orange-Spiced Chicken

⅔ cup flour	160 ml
½ teaspoon dried basil	2 ml
¼ teaspoon leaf tarragon	1 ml
2 - 3 tablespoons oil	30 ml
6 large boneless, skinless, chicken breast halves	
1 (6 ounce) can frozen orange juice, thawed	168 g
½ cup white wine vinegar	120 ml
⅔ cup packed brown sugar	160 ml
1 (6 ounce) box long grain and wild rice, cooked	168 g

- Preheat oven to 350° (176° C). Mix flour, 1 teaspoon (5 ml) salt, ½ teaspoon (2 ml) pepper and spices in baggie. Pour oil into large skillet and heat. Coat chicken in flour mixture and brown both sides of chicken.

- In small bowl, mix orange juice, ¼ cup (60 ml) water, vinegar and brown sugar. When chicken breasts brown, place in sprayed baking dish, cover with orange juice mixture and bake uncovered for 1 hour. Serve chicken and orange sauce over rice.

Poppy Seed Chicken

8 boneless, skinless chicken breast halves	
1 (10 ounce) can cream of chicken soup	280 g
1 (8 ounce) carton sour cream	227 g
½ cup dry white wine or cooking wine	120 ml
1½ cups (1 stack) round buttery crackers	360 ml
1 cup chopped almonds, toasted	240 ml
½ cup (1 stick) butter, melted	120 ml
2 - 3 tablespoons poppy seeds	30 ml

- Preheat oven to 350° (176° C). Place chicken in sprayed 9 x 13-inch (23 x 33 cm) baking pan and set aside. In saucepan, combine soup, sour cream and wine and heat just until it mixes. Pour soup mixture over chicken.

- Combine cracker crumbs, almonds and butter and sprinkle over casserole. Sprinkle with poppy seeds and bake for 45 minutes. Serve over rice or noodles.

Pollo Delicioso

4 fresh jalapeno chilies, seeded, diced	
1 onion, chopped	
1 bell pepper, chopped	
1 clove garlic, minced	
2 tablespoons oil	30 ml
1 teaspoon ground cumin	5 ml
½ teaspoon chili powder	2 ml
1 (10 ounce) can cream of chicken soup	280 g
1 (10 ounce) package frozen spinach, thawed	280 g
1 (1 pint) carton sour cream	.5 kg
4 large boneless, skinless chicken breasts halves, cooked, cubed	
1 (13 ounce) package corn chips	370 g
1 (16 ounce) packages grated Monterey Jack cheese	.5 kg

- Preheat oven to 325° (162° C).

- In large skillet saute chilies, onion, bell pepper and garlic in oil. Stir in cumin, chili powder and chicken soup.

- Squeeze thawed spinach in paper towels to drain thoroughly. Fold spinach, ½ teaspoon (2 ml) salt, sour cream and chicken into mixture. Heat, stirring constantly, but do not boil.

- In buttered 9 x 13-inch (23 x 33 cm) baking dish, layer one-third corn chips, one-third cheese and one-half chicken mixture. Repeat layering and top with last layer of corn chips and cheese.

- Bake for 40 minutes or until casserole is hot and bubbly.

TIP: Be sure to wear rubber gloves when you take the seeds out of the jalapenos. If you like it hot, leave the seeds in.

Pow Wow Chicken

3 onions, chopped	
3 bell peppers, chopped	
1 teaspoon garlic powder	5 ml
Oil	
2 (10 ounce) cans chopped tomatoes and green chilies	2 (280 g)
1 (16 ounce) package cubed Velveeta® cheese	.5 kg
1 (12 ounce) package shredded cheddar cheese	340 g
6 cups cooked, chopped chicken	1.5 L
1 (1 pint) carton sour cream	.5 kg
1 (4 ounce) jar pimentos	114 g
Cooked rice	
Tortilla chips, crushed	

- Cook onion, bell peppers and garlic in a little oil. Add tomatoes and green chilies and bring to boil. Reduce heat and simmer about 15 to 20 minutes or until slightly thick.

- Add cheeses, stir constantly and heat slowly until cheeses melt. Add chicken, sour cream and pimentos. Heat until hot, but do not boil.

- To serve, place rice on individual plate and top with a few crushed chips. Spoon chicken-cheese mixture over rice and chips. Serve immediately.

Fowl Fun

A chicken can travel up to 9 miles an hour.

Red Rock Taco Chicken

This is a great recipe for leftover chicken.

3 cups cooked, chopped chicken	710 ml
1 (1 ounce) packet taco seasoning	28 g
1 cup white rice	240 ml
2 cups chopped celery	480 ml
1 red bell pepper, seeded, chopped	
2 (15 ounce) cans Mexican-stewed tomatoes	2 (425 g)
1 (6 ounce) can fried onion rings	168 g

- Preheat oven to 325° (162° C).

- Combine cooked chicken, taco seasoning, rice, ½ cup (120 ml) water, celery, bell pepper and tomatoes in large bowl. Transfer to sprayed 9 x 13-inch (23 x 33 cm) baking dish.

- Cover and bake for 25 minutes, remove cover and sprinkle onion rings over casserole. Return to oven for 15 minutes.

Chicky Chicken with Red Peppers

1 (14 ounce) can chicken broth	396 g
1 (8 ounce) can whole kernel corn, drained	227 g
2 cups cooked, cubed chicken breasts	480 ml
1 cup roasted red bell peppers	240 ml
¼ cup pine nuts, toasted	60 ml

- Preheat oven to 325° (162° C).

- In saucepan over medium-high heat, combine chicken broth, corn, chicken and roasted bell peppers. Cover and simmer about 10 minutes.

- Spoon into sprayed 7 x 11-inch (18 x 28 cm) baking dish, top with pine nuts and bake 15 minutes.

Sassy Chicken over Tex-Mex Corn

2 teaspoons garlic powder	10 ml
1 teaspoon ground cumin	5 ml
⅔ cup flour	160 ml
4 boneless, skinless chicken breast halves	

Tex-Mex Corn:

1 (10 ounce) can chicken broth	280 g
1½ cups hot salsa	360 ml
1 (11 ounce) can mexicorn	312 g
1 cup instant rice	240 ml

- Combine garlic powder, cumin, flour and ample salt in shallow bowl. Dip chicken in flour mixture and coat each side of chicken.

- Place a little oil in heavy skillet over medium to high heat. Cut each chicken breast in half lengthwise. Brown each piece on both sides, reduce heat and add 2 tablespoons (30 ml) water to skillet.

- Cover and simmer for 15 minutes. Transfer chicken to foil-lined baking pan and place in oven at 250° (121° C).

- Use same unwashed skillet, combine broth, salsa and corn and cook about 10 minutes. Stir in rice and let stand 10 minutes or until rice is tender.

- To serve, spoon Tex-Mex Corn on platter and place chicken breasts over corn.

 Fowl Fun

Q: Why did the horse cross the road?
A: Because the chicken needed a day off.

Sour Cream Chicken Enchiladas

4 - 5 boneless, skinless chicken breast halves	
1 onion, chopped	
2 tablespoons butter	30 ml
1 (4 ounce) can chopped green chilies	114 g
1 (12 ounce) package shredded cheddar cheese	340 g
2 teaspoons chili powder, divided	10 ml
1 (16 ounce) carton sour cream, divided	.5 kg
10 - 12 flour tortillas	
¼ cup flour	60 ml
¼ cup (½ stick) butter, melted	60 ml
1 (12 ounce) package shredded Monterey Jack cheese, divided	340 g

- Cook chicken in enough water in saucepan to cover chicken, drain and reserve 1½ cups (360 ml) broth. Allow chicken to cool and chop into small pieces.

- Saute onion in butter, add chicken, green chilies, cheddar cheese, 1 teaspoon (5 ml) chili powder and 1 cup (240 ml) sour cream and mix well.

- Microwave tortillas on high for about 1 minute or until softened. Spoon chicken-cheese mixture onto tortillas and roll up to enclose filling.

- Place seam-side down in greased, 10 x 15-inch (25 x 38 cm) baking pan. In saucepan, combine flour and melted butter, mix well and add reserved broth. Cook, stirring constantly, until thick and bubbly.

- Fold in one-half cheese, remaining 1 cup (240 ml) sour cream and remaining chili powder. Spoon over enchiladas.

- Bake at 350° (176° C) for 30 minutes. Remove from oven and sprinkle with remaining cheese.

Chicken-Broccoli Deluxe

½ cup (1 stick) butter	120 ml
½ cup flour	120 ml
1 (14 ounce) can chicken broth	396 g
1 (1 pint) carton half-and-half cream	.5 kg
1 (16 ounce) package shredded cheddar cheese, divided	.5 kg
1 (5 ounce) package grated parmesan cheese	143 g
2 tablespoons lemon juice	30 ml
2 tablespoons dried parsley	30 ml
¾ cup mayonnaise	180 ml
2 (10 ounce) boxes frozen broccoli florets, slightly cooked	2 (280 g)
5 boneless, skinless chicken breast halves, cooked, sliced	
1 (12 ounce) box vermicelli	340 g

- Preheat oven to 325° (162° C).

- Melt butter in very large saucepan or roasting pan. Add flour and mix. Over low to medium heat, gradually add chicken broth and cream, stirring constantly, until it thickens.

- Add half cheddar cheese, parmesan cheese, lemon juice, dried parsley, 1 teaspoon (5 ml) salt and ½ teaspoon (2 ml) pepper. Heat on low until cheeses melt. Remove from heat and add mayonnaise.

- Punch small holes in broccoli boxes and microwave 4 minutes. Gently add broccoli and chicken slices to sauce.

- Cook vermicelli according to package directions, drain and pour into sprayed 10 x 15-inch (25 x 38 cm) baking dish. Spoon sauce and chicken mixture over vermicelli.

- Bake covered for 40 minutes. Uncover and spread remaining cheese over top. Return to oven for another 5 minutes.

Eggxellent Chicken Pie

1 (12 ounce) package shredded cheddar cheese, divided	340 g
1 (10 ounce) package frozen, chopped broccoli, thawed	280 g
2 cups cooked, finely diced chicken breasts	480 ml
½ cup finely chopped onion	120 ml
½ cup finely chopped red bell pepper	120 ml
1⅓ cups half-and-half cream	320 ml
3 eggs	
¾ cup baking mix	180 ml

- Combine 2 cups (480 ml) cheddar cheese, broccoli, chicken, onion and bell pepper in bowl. Spread into buttered, 10-inch (25 cm) deep-dish pie plate.

- In mixing bowl, beat cream, eggs, baking mix and salt and pepper to taste. Slowly pour cream-egg mixture over broccoli-chicken mixture, but do not stir.

- Bake covered at 375° (190° C) for 35 minutes. Uncover and sprinkle remaining cheese over top. Return to oven for about 5 minutes or just until cheese melts.

Sour Cream Chicken Casserole

5 boneless, skinless chicken breast halves, cooked, cubed	
2 (8 ounce) cartons sour cream	2 (227 g)
1 (7 ounce) package uncooked, ready-cut spaghetti	198 g
2 (10 ounce) cans cream of chicken soup	2 (280 g)
1 (4 ounce) can mushrooms, drained	114 g
½ cup (1 stick) butter, melted	120 ml
1 (8 ounce) package fresh, grated parmesan cheese	227 g

- Preheat oven to 325° (162° C). Combine all ingredients with ⅛ teaspoon (.5 ml) pepper. Pour into greased 9 x 13-inch (23 x 33 cm) baking dish. Sprinkle cheese on top. Bake, covered, for 50 minutes.

Spicy Orange Chicken Over Noodles

1 pound boneless, skinless chicken tenders	.5 kg
2 tablespoons oil	30 ml
2 tablespoons soy sauce	30 ml
1 (16 ounce) package frozen stir-fry vegetables, thawed	.5 g

Sauce:
⅔ cup orange marmalade	160 ml
1 tablespoon oil	15 ml
1 tablespoon soy sauce	15 ml
1½ teaspoons lime juice	7 ml
½ teaspoon minced ginger	2 ml
½ teaspoon cayenne pepper	2 ml
1 (6 ounce) package chow mein noodles	168 g

- Lightly brown chicken tenders in oil in large skillet over medium to high heat. Add 2 tablespoons (30 ml) soy sauce and cook another 3 minutes.

- Add stir-fry vegetables and cook about 5 minutes or until vegetables are tender-crisp.

- In saucepan, combine marmalade, oil, 1 tablespoon (15 ml) soy sauce, lime juice, minced ginger and cayenne pepper and mix well.

- Heat and pour over stir-fry chicken and vegetables. Serve over chow mein noodles.

Stampede Chicken Enchiladas

*This classic enchilada dish will make your herd excited.
Get ready for the stampede.*

3 cups cooked, shredded chicken	710 ml
1 (4 ounce) can chopped green chilies	114 g
1 (7 ounce) can green chile salsa	198 g
1 onion, minced	
6 chicken bouillon cubes	
1 (1 pint) carton whipping cream	.5 kg
Oil	
10 corn tortillas	
1 (16 ounce) package shredded Monterey	
Jack cheese	.5 kg
1 (8 ounce) carton sour cream	227 g

- Preheat oven to 350° (176° C).

- Combine chicken, green chilies, green chile salsa and onion. Place bouillon cubes, ½ teaspoon (2 ml) salt and cream in saucepan and heat until bouillon dissolves, but do not boil.

- Heat oil in skillet and dip each tortilla into oil for about 5 seconds to soften. Drain on paper towels. Dip each tortilla into saucepan with cream and coat each side. Fill each tortilla with chicken mixture.

- Roll and place seam-side down in sprayed 9 x 13-inch (23 x 33 cm) baking dish. Pour remaining cream over enchiladas and sprinkle with cheese. Bake uncovered for 30 to 35 minutes. When ready to serve, top with dollops of sour cream.

Supper-Ready Chicken

You will have one skillet and one saucepan to wash and within 20 minutes you will have creamy chicken plus vegetables ready to go in the oven. And the kids will love the crunchy topping.

6 boneless, skinless chicken breast halves	
2 tablespoons oil	30 ml
1 cup chopped celery	240 ml
2 cups (½-inch/1.2 cm) thick slices zucchini	480 ml
1 (16 ounce) package baby carrots	.5 kg
½ onion, chopped	
¼ cup (½ stick) plus 2 tablespoons butter	60 ml/30 ml
1 (10 ounce) can cream of chicken soup	280 g
1 (10 ounce) can fiesta nacho cheese soup	280 g
1 cup milk or half-and-half cream	240 ml
½ teaspoon dillweed	2 ml
1 teaspoon dried basil	5 ml
1½ cups soft breadcrumbs or cracker crumbs	360 ml
½ cup chopped walnuts	120 ml

- Brown chicken in skillet with oil. Place chicken breasts in greased 9 x 13-inch (23 x 33 cm) baking dish and set aside.

- In saucepan, cook celery, zucchini, carrots and onion for about 10 minutes in ¼ cup (60 ml) butter and very little water and drain.

- In saucepan, combine soups, milk, dill weed, basil and ½ teaspoon (2 ml) pepper and heat just enough to mix well.

- Spoon about ¾ cup (180 ml) soup mixture over chicken. Combine remaining soup mixture and drained vegetables. Spoon over chicken and soup mixture.

- Combine 2 tablespoons (30 ml) butter, breadcrumbs and walnuts and sprinkle over casserole. Bake uncovered at 375° (190° C) for 35 to 40 minutes or until topping browns lightly.

Sweet-and-Sour Chicken & Veggies

1 (3 ounce) package chicken-flavored Ramen noodles	10 g
1 (16 ounce) package frozen broccoli, cauliflower and carrots	.5 kg
3 boneless, skinless, cooked chicken breast halves, cut in strips	
⅔ cup sweet-and-sour sauce	160 ml
1 tablespoon soy sauce	15 ml

- In large saucepan, cook noodles and vegetables in 2 cups (480 ml) water (reserve seasoning packet) for 3 minutes or until liquid absorbs.

- Add seasoning packet, chicken (or turkey) sweet-and-sour sauce, soy sauce and a little salt and pepper. Heat on low to medium heat, stirring until all is thoroughly heated.

Swiss Chicken

4 boneless, skinless chicken breasts	
4 slices Swiss cheese	
1 (10 ounce) can cream of chicken soup	280 g
¼ cup dry white wine	60 ml
½ cup herb-seasoned stuffing	120 ml
¼ cup (½ stick) butter, melted	60 ml

- Preheat oven to 350°. (176°)

- Arrange chicken in greased 9 x 13-inch (23 x 33 cm) pan. Top with cheese. Combine soup and wine and stir well.

- Spoon evenly over chicken and sprinkle with stuffing mix. Drizzle butter over crumbs. Bake uncovered at 350° (176° C) for 45 to 55 minutes.

Sweet Pepper Chicken

6 - 8 boneless, skinless chicken breasts halves	
2 tablespoons oil	30 ml
⅓ cup cornstarch	80 ml
⅔ cup sugar	160 ml
½ cup packed brown sugar	120 ml
1 teaspoon chicken bouillon granules	5 ml
1 (15 ounce) can pineapple chunks with juice	425 g
1½ cups orange juice	360 ml
½ cup vinegar	120 ml
¼ cup ketchup	60 ml
2 tablespoons soy sauce	30 ml
¼ teaspoon ground ginger	1 ml
1 red bell pepper, thinly sliced	

- Brown chicken breasts in large skillet with oil. Place in buttered 10 x 14-inch (25 x 36 cm) baking dish.

- In large saucepan, combine cornstarch, sugar, brown sugar and bouillon granules and mix well.

- Drain pineapple and save juice. Add pineapple juice, orange juice, vinegar, ketchup, soy sauce and ginger to cornstarch mixture in saucepan and mix well.

- Cook on high heat, stirring constantly, until mixture thickens. Pour sauce over chicken breasts.

- Bake uncovered at 325° (162° C) for 45 minutes.

- Remove from oven, add pineapple chunks and thinly sliced bell peppers and bake another 15 minutes.

Taco Casserole

1 (10 ounce) cream of mushroom soup	280 g
1 (10 ounce) can cream of chicken soup	280 g
1 cup milk	240 ml
1 (1 ounce) package taco seasoning	28 g
1 onion, chopped	
1 (4 ounce) can chopped green chilies, drained	114 g
5 - 6 boneless, skinless chicken breast halves, cooked	
1 (16 ounce) package shredded Monterey Jack cheese	.5 kg
1 (16 ounce) bag corn tortillas	.5 kg

- Preheat oven to 325° (162° C). Combine soups, milk, taco seasoning, onion and green chilies. Cut chicken breasts into bite-size pieces. In 9 x 13-inch (23 x 33 cm) glass dish, layer one-half chips, chicken, soup mixture and cheese. Repeat layers in same order. Cheese will be on top. Bake uncovered for 1 hour.

Tortilla-Chip Chicken

1 (10 ounce) package tortilla chips, divided	280 g
1 onion, chopped	
3 ribs celery, chopped	
1 (10 ounce) can cream of chicken soup	280 g
2 (10 ounce) cans tomatoes and green chilies	2 (280 g)
1 (16 ounce) package cubed processed cheese	.5 kg
4 - 5 boneless, skinless chicken breast halves, cooked, cubed	

- Preheat oven to 350° (176° C). Place half chips in sprayed 9 x 13-inch (23 x 33 cm) baking dish, crush a few chips with your hand.

- In large saucepan, combine onion, celery, chicken soup, tomatoes and green chilies and cheese. On medium heat, stir until cheese melts. Add chicken and pour over chips.

- Crush remaining chips in plastic bag; sprinkle over chicken mixture. Bake about 35 minutes.

Chicken Run Casserole

1 onion, chopped	
1 cup sliced celery	240 ml
3 tablespoons butter	45 ml
4 cups diced, cooked chicken	1 L
1 (6 ounce) package long grain, wild rice with seasoning packet, cooked	168 g
1 (10 ounce) can cream of celery soup	280 g
1 (10 ounce) can cream of chicken soup	280 g
1 (4 ounce) jar pimentos, drained	114 g
2 (15 ounce) cans French-style green beans, drained	2 (425 g)
1 cup slivered almonds	240 ml
1 cup mayonnaise	240 ml
2½ cups crushed potato chips	600 ml

- Preheat oven to 350° (176° C).

- In large saucepan, saute onion and celery in butter. Add chicken, rice, soups, pimentos, green beans, almonds, mayonnaise, ½ teaspoon (2 ml) salt and 1 teaspoon (5 ml) pepper and heat enough to mix.

- Pour into sprayed 10 x 15-inch (25 x 38 cm) baking dish. (This recipe needs a very large baking dish.)

- Sprinkle crushed potato chips over casserole and bake uncovered for 35 minutes or until potato chips are light brown.

Tempting Chicken and Veggies

1½ pounds chicken breast tenderloins	.7 kg
½ cup (1 stick) butter, divided	120 ml
1 (6 ounce) box fried rice with seasoning packet	168 g
⅛ teaspoon cayenne pepper	.5 ml
¼ cup chopped sweet red bell pepper	60 ml
1 (10 ounce) package frozen broccoli spears, thawed	280 g
1 (10 ounce) package frozen corn, thawed	280 g

- Preheat oven to 350° (176° C).

- In skillet, brown chicken tenderloins in about 3 tablespoons (45 ml) butter. Remove chicken to large mixing bowl.

- Saute rice until light brown in same skillet with remaining butter and spoon into bowl with chicken. Add 2½ cups (600 ml) water, cayenne pepper, bell pepper, broccoli spears and corn and mix well.

- Spoon into sprayed 9 x 13-inch (23 x 33 cm) baking dish. Cover and bake for 25 minutes or until rice and vegetables are tender.

Fowl Fun

Q: Why did the chicken cross the road, roll in the mud and cross the road again?
A: Because he was a dirty double-crosser.

Cheesy, Cheesy Chicken

Cheese lovers dig in! This is a real winner!

1 onion, chopped	
1 red and ½ green bell peppers, chopped	
½ cup (1 stick) butter, divided	120 ml
1 (10 ounce) can cream of chicken soup	280 g
1 (4 ounce) can sliced mushrooms	114 g
½ teaspoon dried cilantro	2 ml
½ teaspoon dried basil	2 ml
1 teaspoon celery salt	5 ml
½ teaspoon garlic pepper	2 ml
1 (8 ounce) package egg noodles, cooked	
al dente, drained	227 g
4 - 5 boneless, skinless chicken breast halves,	
cooked, cubed	
1 (15 ounce) carton ricotta cheese	425 g
1 (16 ounce) package shredded cheddar cheese	.5 kg
⅓ cup grated parmesan cheese	80 ml
1 cup breadcrumbs	240 ml

- Saute onion and bell peppers with 5 tablespoons (75 ml) butter in skillet. Remove from heat and stir in soup, mushrooms, cilantro, basil, celery salt, garlic pepper and a little salt.

- In large bowl combine noodles, chicken, cheeses and soup-mushroom mixture. Mix well.

- Spoon into buttered 9 x 13-inch (23 x 33 cm) baking dish.

- Melt 3 tablespoons (45 ml) butter and combine with breadcrumbs. Sprinkle over casserole.

- Bake covered at 350° (176° C) for 45 minutes.

The Chicken Takes the Artichoke

6 boneless, skinless chicken breast halves	
7 tablespoons butter, divided	98 ml
1 (14 ounce) jar water-packed artichoke hearts, drained	396 g
1 (8 ounce) can sliced water chestnuts, drained	227 g
¼ cup flour	60 ml
⅛ teaspoon ground nutmeg	.5 ml
1 teaspoon summer savory	5 ml
1 teaspoon dried thyme	5 ml
1 (14 ounce) can chicken broth	396 g
½ cup whipping cream	120 ml
1 cup grated Swiss cheese	240 ml
1 cup seasoned breadcrumbs	240 ml

- Brown chicken breasts in 2 tablespoons (30 ml) butter in skillet. Place chicken breasts in greased 9 x 13-inch (23 x 33 cm) baking dish.

- Cut each artichoke heart in half and place artichokes and water chestnuts around chicken.

- In saucepan, melt 3 tablespoons (45 ml) butter and stir in flour, ½ teaspoon (2 ml) pepper, nutmeg, summer savory and thyme until smooth and mix well.

- On medium to high heat, gradually stir in broth and cook, stirring constantly, until broth thickens. Remove from heat and stir in cream and cheese.

- Blend until cheese melts and pour over chicken, artichokes and water chestnuts.

- Combine breadcrumbs and 2 tablespoons (30 ml) melted butter and sprinkle over top of casserole. Bake uncovered at 350° (176° C) for 35 minutes.

Three-Cheers for Chicken

8 boneless, skinless chicken breast halves	
6 tablespoons (¾ stick) butter	90 ml
1 onion, chopped	
½ bell pepper, chopped	
1 (4 ounce) jar chopped pimentos, drained	114 g
1 cup uncooked rice	240 ml
1 (10 ounce) can cream of chicken soup	280 g
1 (10 ounce) can cream of celery soup	280 g
2 soup cans water	
1 (8 ounce) can sliced water chestnuts	227 g
1 cup grated cheddar cheese	240 ml

- Preheat oven to 350° (176° C).

- Salt and pepper chicken and place in large 11 x 14-inch (30 x 36 cm) glass baking dish.

- Melt butter and add onion, bell pepper, pimentos, rice, soups, water and water chestnuts and pour over chicken.

- Bake for 15 minutes, reduce oven temperature to 325° (162° C) and cook for 1 hour more. Add cheese 5 minutes before dish is done and return to oven for last 5 minutes.

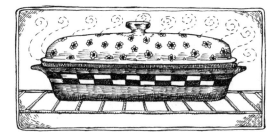

Tomatillo-Chicken Enchiladas

2 (13 ounce) cans tomatillos, drained	2 (370 g)
1 (7 ounce) can chopped green chilies	198 g
2 tablespoons oil	30 ml
1 onion, chopped	
1 clove garlic, minced	
1 (14 ounce) can chicken broth	396 g
¼ cup oil	60 ml
12 corn tortillas	
3 cups shredded, cooked chicken	710 ml
1 (12 ounce) packages shredded Monterey	
Jack cheese	340 g
1 (8 ounce) carton sour cream	227 g

- Preheat oven to 350° (176° C).

- Combine tomatillos and green chilies in blender and process. In large skillet, heat 2 tablespoons (30 ml) oil, add onion and garlic and cook until onion is translucent.

- Stir in puree and chicken broth. Simmer uncovered until sauce reduces to consistency of canned tomato sauce.

- In another skillet, heat ¼ cup (60 ml) oil and cook tortillas about 3 seconds on each side. Dip softened tortilla into tomatillo mixture. Lay sauced tortilla on plate. Place ¼ cup (60 ml) chicken and 2 tablespoons (30 ml) cheese across tortilla and roll to close.

- Place enchilada, seam-side down in 15 x 10-inch (38 x 25 cm) baking pan. Repeat until all tortillas are filled. Spoon remaining sauce over enchiladas and reserve remaining cheese.

- Cover and bake for about 30 minutes. Uncover and top with reserved cheese. Bake another 10 minutes, uncovered. When ready to serve, top each enchilada with spoonful sour cream.

Tootsie's Chicken Spectacular

This is a great recipe for leftover chicken or turkey.

2 cups cooked, diced chicken	480 ml
1 (15 ounce) can green beans, drained	425 g
1 cup cooked white rice	240 ml
1 (10 ounce) can cream of celery soup	280 g
½ cup mayonnaise	120 ml
½ cup sliced water chestnuts	120 ml
2 tablespoons chopped pimento	30 ml
2 tablespoons chopped onion	30 ml

- Preheat oven to 350° (176° C).

- In bowl, combine all ingredients with ¼ teaspoon (1 ml) salt and a dash of pepper and mix well.

- Place in 1½-quart (1.5 L) baking dish and bake for 25 to 30 minutes.

TIP: For a change, substitute cream of mushroom soup or cream of chicken soup.

Fowl Fact

A boneless chicken breast will cook in less than 10 minutes in a steamer. After you remove the chicken, let it sit uncut for 2 to 3 minutes, and any slight pinkness on the interior will gently finish cooking in the chicken's own steam.

Zesty Orange Chicken

½ cup white wine	120 ml
½ cup orange juice concentrate	120 ml
½ cup orange marmalade	120 ml
½ teaspoon ground ginger	120 ml
½ teaspoon cinnamon	120 ml
1 large chicken, quartered	
2 (11 ounce) cans mandarin oranges, drained	2 (312 g)
½ cup green grapes, halved	120 ml
1½ cups instant brown rice, cooked	360 ml

- Preheat oven to 325° (162° C). Combine wine, orange juice concentrate, marmalade, ginger and cinnamon in greased 9 x 13-inch (23 x 33 cm) baking dish. Add chicken quarters and turn to coat chicken.

- Bake uncovered, basting occasionally, for 40 minutes. Add oranges and grapes to dish during the last 5 minutes of cooking.

- Serve over hot cooked, buttered rice.

Easy Chicken Casserole

1 cup chopped celery	240 ml
1 red bell pepper, seeded, chopped	
1 large onion, chopped	
3 tablespoons oil	45 ml
1 (3 - 4 pound) chicken, cooked, boned, chopped	1.3 kg
1 (8 ounce) box macaroni, cooked, drained	227 g
1 (10 ounce) cream of mushroom soup	280 g
1 (8 ounce) package shredded American cheese, divided 227 g	

- Preheat oven to 350° (176° C).

- Saute celery, red pepper and onion in oil. Combine remaining ingredients except 1 cup (240 ml) cheese and mix well.

- Spoon into sprayed 9 x 13-inch (23 x 33 cm) baking dish. Top with remaining 1 cup (240 ml) cheese. Bake for 20 minutes or until cheese melts. Serves 6 to 8.

Gobble Gobble Casserole

1 (7 ounce) package herb-seasoned stuffing	198 g
1 cup whole cranberry sauce	240 ml
1 (12 ounce) can turkey	340 g
1 (10 ounce) can turkey gravy	280 g

- Prepare stuffing according to package directions.

- Combine prepared stuffing and cranberry sauce in medium bowl and set aside.

- Place turkey in buttered, 2-quart (2 L) baking dish. Pour gravy over turkey and spoon stuffing mixture over casserole.

- Bake uncovered at 375° (190° C) for 15 to 20 minutes.

Gobbler Supreme

1 onion, chopped	
1 cup sliced celery	240 ml
3 tablespoons butter	45 ml
4 cups diced, cooked turkey	1 L
1 (6 ounce) package long grain, wild rice, cooked	168 g
Seasoning packet in rice package	
2 (10 ounce) cans cream of chicken soup	2 (280 g)
1 (4 ounce) jar pimentos, drained	114 g
2 (15 ounce) cans French-style green beans, drained	2 (425 g)
1 cup slivered almonds	240 ml
1 cup mayonnaise	240 ml
2½ cups crushed potato chips	600 ml

- Preheat oven to 350° (176° C).

- In large saucepan saute onion and celery in butter.

- Add turkey, rice, seasoning packet, soup, pimentos, green beans, almonds, mayonnaise, ½ teaspoon (2 ml) salt and 1 teaspoon (5 ml) pepper and stir.

- Pour into greased 9 x 13-inch (23 x 33 cm) baking dish. (This needs a very large casserole dish.) Sprinkle crushed potato chips over casserole.

- Bake uncovered at 350° (176° C) for 35 minutes or until potato chips brown slightly.

TIP: If you want to make in advance and freeze, add potato chips when ready to cook casserole.

Turkey Perky Dinner

1 (2 pound) lemon-garlic seasoned, turkey tenderloin	1 kg

Vegetables and Gravy:
12 - 14 medium new potatoes, halved	
2 (14 ounce) cans chicken broth, divided	2 (396 g)
½ cup (1 stick) butter, divided	120 ml
5 - 6 medium yellow squash, sliced	
¼ cup cornstarch	60 ml

- Preheat oven to 325° (162° C). Place turkey tenderloin in 9 x 13-inch (23 x 33 cm) baking dish lined with foil. Sprinkle lots of pepper over turkey and bake uncovered for 1 hour 30 minutes.

- After tenderloin cooks 1 hour 10 minutes, place new potatoes in large saucepan and add 1 can chicken broth and ¼ cup (60 ml) butter. Cook 15 to 20 minutes or until tender.

- While potatoes cook, place squash in second saucepan and add remaining can broth and remaining ¼ cup (60 ml) butter. Cook about 10 minutes or until squash is just barely tender. Place tenderloin on large platter and use slotted spoon to place potatoes and squash around sliced tenderloin.

- Combine cornstarch and about ½ cup (120 ml) cooking broth and mix well. Combine broth into 1 saucepan, bring to boil and stir in cornstarch mixture. Add about 1 teaspoon (5 ml) pepper (and salt if you like) and cook, stirring constantly, until liquid thickens. Serve in gravy boat with tenderloin and vegetables.

Crispy Chicky Chicken

1 (6 ounce) box long grain, wild rice with herbs and seasonings	168 g
2 cups chopped celery	480 ml
1 onion, chopped	
1 cup coarsely chopped walnuts	240 ml
2 tablespoons butter	30 ml
2 cups mayonnaise	480 ml
1 (8 ounce) carton sour cream	227 g
1 tablespoon lemon juice	15 ml
4 cups cooked, cubed chicken	1 L
1 cup crushed potato chips	240 ml
1 (3 ounce) can fried onion rings, crushed	84 g

- Cook rice according to package directions.

- In skillet, lightly saute celery, onion and walnuts in butter. Add mayonnaise, sour cream, lemon juice, ¾ teaspoon (4 ml) salt and chicken and mix well.

- Fold in cooked rice and transfer to greased 9 x 13-inch (23 x 33 cm) baking dish.

- Combine potato chips and crushed onion rings and sprinkle over top of casserole.

- Bake uncovered at 325° (162° C) for 25 minutes.

Quickie Russian Chicken

This is great when you don't have time to cook.

6 boneless, skinless chicken breast halves
1 (8 ounce) bottle Russian salad dressing   **227 g**
1 (5 ounce) jar apricot preserves   **143 g**
1 (1 ounce) packet dry onion soup mix   **28 g**

- Preheat oven to 350° (176° C). Place chicken breasts in sprayed, shallow baking dish.

- Combine dressing, apricot preserves, onion soup mix and ¼ cup (60 ml) water in saucepan and bring to slow boil. Remove from heat and pour over chicken.

- Cover dish with foil and bake for 1 hour. Remove foil, baste with sauce and bake uncovered for 30 minutes more. Serve immediately.

 **Fowl Fun**

Chicken/Egg Debate Finally Resolved
According to National Geographic, scientists have settled the old dispute over which came first – the chicken or the egg? They say that reptiles were laying eggs thousands of years before chickens appeared, and the first chicken came from an egg laid by a bird that was not quite a chicken. Clearly, the egg came first.

Barnyard Bakes
and
Broils

Q: Why do hens lay eggs?
A: If they drop them, they'll break.

Apache Trail Drum-Sticks

⅔ cup fine, dry breadcrumbs	160 ml
⅔ cup finely crushed corn chips	160 ml
1 (1 ounce) package taco seasoning mix	28 g
1 (16 ounce) jar taco sauce, divided	.5 kg
2 pounds chicken drum-sticks, skinned	1 kg

- Combine breadcrumbs, crushed corn chips and dry taco seasoning mix. Place ½ cup (120 ml) taco sauce in flat bowl.

- Dip drum-sticks in taco sauce, one at a time, then dredge in crumb mixture. Discard taco sauce used for dipping.

- Place on lightly greased baking sheet and bake at 375° (190° C) for 30 to 35 minutes. Serve with remaining taco sauce.

Apricot-Ginger Chicken

2 teaspoons ground ginger	10 ml
½ cup Italian dressing	120 ml
4 boneless, skinless chicken breast halves	
⅔ cup apricot preserves	160 ml

- Combine ginger and Italian dressing and place in large plastic bag. Add chicken to bag, marinate in refrigerator overnight and turn occasionally.

- When ready to cook, remove chicken and reserve ¼ cup (60 ml) marinade. Place chicken in shallow baking dish.

- Pour ¼ cup (60 ml) marinade in saucepan, bring to boil and cook 1 minute. Remove from heat, stir in preserves and set aside. Bake chicken at 350° (176° C) for 45 minutes and brush with marinade mixture last 10 minutes of cooking.

Aztec Creamy Salsa Chicken

6 boneless, skinless chicken breast halves	
1 (1 ounce) packet dry taco seasoning mix	28 g
1 (16 ounce) jar salsa	.5 kg
1 (8 ounce) carton sour cream	227 g

- Preheat oven to 350° (176° C).

- Brown chicken breasts in skillet and transfer to sprayed 9 x 13-inch (23 x 33 cm) baking dish. Sprinkle taco seasoning over chicken and top with salsa.

- Cover and bake for 35 minutes.

- Remove chicken to serving plates. Add sour cream to juices in pan, stir well and microwave on HIGH for about 2 minutes. Stir pan juices and sour cream for sauce to serve over chicken.

Bacon-Wrapped Chicken

6 boneless, skinless chicken breast halves	
1 (8 ounce) carton cream cheese	
with onion and chives	227 g
Butter	
6 bacon strips	

- Preheat oven to 375° (190° C).

- Flatten chicken to ½-inch (1.2 cm) thickness and spread 3 tablespoons (45 ml) cream cheese over each piece.

- Dot with butter and sprinkle with a little salt, roll and wrap each with 1 bacon strip.

- Place seam-side down in sprayed 9 x 13-inch (23 x 33 cm) baking dish and bake uncovered for 40 to 45 minutes or until juices run clear. To brown, broil 6 inches (15 cm) from heat for about 3 minutes or until bacon is crisp.

Baked Chicken Poupon

2 tablespoons dijon-style mustard	30 ml
2 tablespoons oil	30 ml
1 teaspoon garlic powder	5 ml
½ teaspoon Italian seasoning	2 ml
4 boneless, skinless chicken breast halves	

- Mix dijon-style mustard, oil, garlic powder and seasoning in plastic bag, add chicken breasts and marinate for 15 minutes.

- Place chicken in sprayed shallow baking pan.

- Bake uncovered at 375° (190° C) for 35 minutes.

Easy Baked Chicken

6 boneless, skinless chicken breast halves	
½ cup (1 stick) butter, melted	120 ml
Cornbread stuffing mix with seasoning, crushed	

- Dip chicken breast in melted butter.

- Roll in cornbread stuffing mix to coat.

- Bake uncovered at 350° (176° C) for 45 minutes.

Fowl Fun

Q: What is a haunted chicken?
A: A poultry-geist.

Finger Lickin' BBQ Chicken

1 (2 pound) chicken, quartered	1 kg
½ cup ketchup	120 ml
¼ cup (½ stick) butter, melted	60 ml
2 tablespoons sugar	30 ml
1 tablespoon prepared mustard	15 ml
½ teaspoon minced garlic	2 ml
¼ cup lemon juice	60 ml
¼ cup white vinegar	60 ml
¼ cup Worcestershire sauce	60 ml

- Preheat oven to 325° (162° C).

- Sprinkle chicken quarters with salt and pepper and brown in skillet. Place in large greased baking pan.

- Combine ketchup, butter, sugar, mustard, garlic, lemon juice, vinegar and Worcestershire. Pour over chicken, cover and bake for 50 minutes.

Best-Ever Turkey Loaf

2 pounds ground turkey	1 kg
1 (6 ounce) package stuffing mix for beef plus seasoning packet	168 g
2 eggs, beaten	
½ cup ketchup, divided	120 ml

- Combine ground turkey, stuffing mix, eggs and ¼ cup (60 ml) ketchup and mix well.

- Shape meat in oval loaf into center of 9 x 13-inch (23 x 33 cm) baking dish.

- Spread remaining ¼ cup (60 ml) ketchup on top of loaf.

- Bake at 350° (176° C) for 1 hour.

Catalina Chicken

6 boneless, skinless chicken breast halves
1 (8 ounce) bottle Catalina dressing   227 g
1½ cups crushed cracker crumbs   360 ml

- Preheat oven to 350° (176° C).

- Marinate chicken breasts in Catalina dressing for 3 to
  4 hours and discard marinade. Combine 1 teaspoon (5 ml)
  pepper and cracker crumbs.

- Dip each chicken breast in crumbs and place in sprayed,
  9 x 13-inch (23 x 33 cm) baking dish.

- Bake uncovered for 1 hour.

Cheesy Crusted Chicken

¾ cup mayonnaise (not light)   180 ml
½ cup grated parmesan cheese   120 ml
5 - 6 boneless, skinless chicken breast halves
1 cup Italian breadcrumbs   240 ml

- Preheat oven to 375° (190° C).

- Combine mayonnaise and cheese. Place chicken
  breasts on sheet of wax paper and spread mayonnaise-
  cheese mixture over chicken. Sprinkle heavily with dry
  breadcrumbs on both sides.

- Place chicken on sprayed, 9 x 13-inch (23 x 33 cm)
  baking pan so pieces do not touch. Bake 20 minutes
  (25 minutes if chicken pieces are fairly large). Chicken
  pieces can be sliced and placed on serving platter.

Chicken and Beef Collide

1 (4 ounce) jar sliced dried beef, separated   114 g
6 strips bacon
6 boneless, skinless chicken breast halves
1(10 ounce) can cream of chicken soup   280 g

- Place dried beef in greased 9 x 13-inch (23 x 33 cm) baking dish. Wrap bacon strip around each chicken breast and place over beef.

- In saucepan, heat chicken soup and ¼ cup (60 ml) water and pour over chicken.

- Bake covered at 325° (162° C) 1 hour 10 minutes.

Chicken Crunch

4 - 6 boneless, skinless chicken breast halves
½ cup Italian salad dressing   120 ml
½ cup sour cream   120 ml
2½ cups crushed corn flakes   600 ml

- Place chicken in locking plastic bag and add salad dressing and sour cream. Seal and refrigerate 1 hour. Remove chicken from marinade and discard marinade.

- Dredge chicken in corn flakes and place in 9 x 13-inch (23 x 33 cm) non-stick sprayed baking dish.

- Bake uncovered at 375° (190° C) for 45 minutes.

Parmesan Chicken Breasts

6 boneless, skinless chicken breast halves	
1½ cups dry breadcrumbs	360 ml
½ cup grated parmesan cheese	120 ml
1 teaspoon dried basil	5 ml
½ teaspoon garlic powder	2 ml
1 (8 ounce) carton sour cream	227 g

- Flatten chicken to ½-inch (1.2 cm) thickness. Combine breadcrumbs, parmesan cheese, basil and garlic powder in shallow dish.

- Dip chicken in sour cream, coat with crumb mixture and place (so chicken breasts do not touch) in 10 x 15-inch (25 x 38 cm) greased baking dish.

- Bake uncovered at 325° (162° C) for 50 to 60 minutes or until golden brown.

Chicken Diablo

6 boneless, skinless chicken breast halves	
1 (8 ounce) package cream cheese, softened	227 g
1 (16 ounce) jar salsa	.5 kg
2 teaspoons cumin	10 ml
1 bunch fresh green onions with tops, chopped	

- Preheat oven to 350° (176° C).

- Pound chicken breasts to flatten. In mixing bowl, beat cheese until smooth; add salsa, cumin and onions.

- Place heaping spoonful of cream cheese mixture on each chicken breast and roll. (There will be leftover cream cheese mixture.)

- Place in greased 7 x 11-inch (18 x 28 cm) baking dish. Spoon remaining cream cheese mixture over chicken rolls. Cover and bake 30 minutes, uncover and continue cooking until chicken rolls are light brown.

Chicken Dipping

1½ cups cornbread stuffing mix with seasoning packet	360 ml
4 tablespoons oil	60 ml
4 boneless, skinless chicken breast halves	
Dipping sauce	

- Place stuffing mix in plastic bag and crush with rolling pin.
- Add oil to center of 9 x 13-inch (23 x 33 cm) baking pan and spread around entire pan.
- Cut chicken breasts into 3 or 4 pieces, dip in stuffing mix and place in baking pan. Arrange chicken in pan without touching.
- Bake at 350° (176° C) uncovered for 25 minutes. Remove from oven, turn pieces over and bake another 15 minutes or until brown.

Dipping Sauce:

4 tablespoons honey	60 ml
3 tablespoons spicy brown mustard	45 ml

- To serve, dip chicken in dipping sauce and enjoy.

Chicken Oriental

1 (6 ounce) jar sweet-and-sour sauce	168 g
1 (1 ounce) package dry onion soup mix	28 g
1 (16 ounce) can whole cranberry sauce	.5 kg
6 - 8 boneless, skinless chicken breast halves	

• In bowl combine sweet-and-sour sauce, onion soup mix and cranberry sauce.

• Place chicken breasts in sprayed 9 x 13-inch (23 x 33 cm) shallow baking dish. Pour cranberry mixture over chicken breasts.

• Bake covered at 325° (162° C) for 30 minutes. Uncover and bake 25 minutes longer.

 Fowl Fun
Americans eat an average of 80 pounds of chicken annually.

Chicken Parmesan

1½ cups biscuit mix	360 ml
⅔ cup grated parmesan cheese	160 ml
6 - 8 boneless, skinless chicken breast halves	
½ cup (1 stick) butter, melted	120 ml

- Combine biscuit mix and parmesan cheese in shallow bowl.

- Dip chicken in butter and in biscuit-cheese mixture.

- Place in large buttered, baking dish. Bake uncovered at 325° (162° C) for 1 hour or until light brown.

Chicken Parmesan and Spaghetti

1 (14 ounce) package frozen, cooked, breaded chicken cutlets, thawed 396 g	
1 (28 ounce) jar spaghetti sauce	794 g
2 (5 ounce) packages grated parmesan cheese, divided	2 (143 g)
1 (8 ounce) package thin spaghetti, cooked	227 g

- Preheat oven to 400° (204° C). Place cutlets in buttered 9 x 13-inch (23 x 33 cm) baking dish and top each with about ¼ cup (60 ml) spaghetti sauce and 1 heaping tablespoon (15 ml) parmesan. Bake 15 minutes.

- Place cooked spaghetti on serving platter and top with cutlets. Sprinkle remaining cheese over cutlets. Heat remaining spaghetti sauce and serve with chicken and spaghetti.

Apricot Chicken

1 cup apricot preserves	240 ml
1 (8 ounce) bottle Catalina dressing	227 g
1 (1 ounce) packet onion soup mix	28 g
6 boneless, skinless chicken breast halves	

- Preheat oven to 325° (162° C).

- Combine apricot preserves, dressing and soup mix.

- Place chicken breasts in sprayed, 9 x 13-inch (23 x 33 cm) baking dish and pour apricot mixture over chicken.

- Bake uncovered for 1 hour 20 minutes. Serve over hot rice.

TIP: For a change of pace, use Russian dressing instead of Catalina.

Chicken Breast Eden Isle

1 (8 ounce) carton sour cream	227 g
1 (3 ounce) cream cheese, softened	84 g
1 (10 ounce) can cream of chicken soup	280 g
1 (2.5 ounce) jar dried beef	70 g
6 boneless, skinless chicken breast halves	
6 bacon strips	
Fluffy rice	

- Preheat oven to 325° (162° C).

- Beat sour cream, cream cheese and soup. Line bottom of baking dish with dried beef. Place chicken breasts, wrapped with bacon strips, onto dried beef.

- Spoon sour cream mixture over chicken. Cover and bake for 2 hours. Uncover last few minutes to brown. Serve over rice.

Chicken Pockets

1 (3 ounce) package cream cheese, softened	84 g
1 (12 ounce) can chicken	340 g
3 tablespoons butter, softened	45 ml
2 tablespoons milk	30 ml
1 tablespoon chopped chives	15 ml
1 (8 ounce) can crescent rolls	227 g
Parmesan cheese	
Breadcrumbs	

- Blend cream cheese with chicken and butter. Add, milk and chives plus ⅛ teaspoon (.5 ml) salt. Separate dough into 4 rectangles and press seams together.

- Spoon mixture into center of dough. Pull 4 corners up and twist together. Seal sides by pinching together.

- Sprinkle top with parmesan cheese and breadcrumbs. Bake on ungreased cookie sheet at 350° (176° C) for 20 to 25 minutes.

Fruited Chicken

6 large boneless, skinless chicken breast halves	
½ cup (1 stick) butter, melted	120 ml
⅔ cup flour	160 ml
Paprika	
1 (15 ounce) can chunky fruit cocktail with juice	425 g

- Dip chicken in butter and flour. Place in 9 x 13-inch (23 x 33 cm) shallow baking dish. Sprinkle with a little salt, pepper and paprika.

- Bake, uncovered, at 350° (176° C) for 45 minutes.

- Pour fruit and half juice over chicken. Bake another 20 minutes.

Chicken Pot Pie

1 (15 ounce) package refrigerated piecrust	425 g
1 (19 ounce) can cream of chicken soup	538 g
2 cups diced chicken breasts	480 ml
1 (10 ounce) package frozen mixed vegetables, thawed	280 ml

- Preheat oven to 325° (162° C). Line 1 layer piecrust in 9-inch (23 cm) pie plate. Fill with chicken soup, chicken and mixed vegetables.

- Cover with second layer of piecrust, fold edges under and crimp. With knife, cut 4 slits in center of piecrust. Bake uncovered for 1 hour 15 minutes or until crust is golden brown.

   TIP: *When you're too busy to cook a chicken, get rotisserie chicken from the grocery store. They are great.*

Chicken Quesadillas

3 boneless, skinless chicken breast halves, cubed	
1 (10 ounce) can cheddar cheese soup	280 g
⅔ cup chunky salsa	160 ml
10 flour tortillas	

- Cook chicken in skillet until juices evaporate and stir often. Add soup and salsa and heat thoroughly.

- Spread about ⅓ cup (80 ml) soup mixture on half tortilla to within ½-inch (1.2 cm) of edge. Moisten edge with water, fold over and seal. Place tortillas on 2 baking sheets.

- Bake at 400° (204° C) for 5 to 6 minutes.

Chicken Salsa

Chicken:
6 boneless, skinless chicken breast halves
1 tablespoon cornstarch   15 ml

Marinade:
1 (16 ounce) jar salsa   .5 kg
¾ cup honey   180 ml
½ cup light soy sauce   120 ml
2 tablespoons oil   30 ml
½ teaspoon dried ginger   2 ml

- Preheat oven to 350° (176° C). Wash and dry each chicken piece with paper towels.

- In bowl, combine all marinade ingredients and mix well. Pour 1½ cups (360 ml) marinade into locking plastic bag, add chicken and refrigerate 2 to 3 hours. Cover and refrigerate remaining marinade.

- Place drained chicken (discard chicken marinade) in buttered 9 x 13-inch (23 x 33 cm) baking dish. Top with remaining refrigerated marinade and bake, uncovered for 25 to 30 minutes or until juices run clear.

- Remove chicken and keep warm. In small saucepan, combine cornstarch with 2 tablespoons (30 ml) water and stir in pan juices.

- Bring to boiling and cook about 2 minutes, stirring constantly, until it thickens. To serve, pour sauce over chicken.

Chicken Scarborough Fair

For best results, make early in the day and refrigerate or prepare 1 hour before serving.

3 boneless, skinless chicken breast halves	
½ cup (1 stick) butter, softened, divided	120 ml
3 slices mozzarella cheese	
½ cup flour	
1 egg	
1 cup seasoned breadcrumbs	240 ml
2 tablespoons chopped parsley	30 ml
¼ teaspoon dried sage, rosemary and thyme	1 ml
½ cup dry white wine	120 ml

- Preheat oven to 350° (176° C). Flatten chicken breasts between sheets of wax paper and spread half of butter over each piece. Season with salt and pepper and place 1 slice cheese on each piece.

- Roll chicken with ends tucked in. Beat egg with 1 (15 ml) tablespoon water. Coat chicken lightly with flour, dip in egg and roll in breadcrumbs. Arrange rolls seam-side down in sprayed 7 x 11-inch (18 x 28 cm) baking dish and refrigerate for 1 hour.

- When ready to bake, remove from refrigerator, melt remaining butter and add parsley, sage, rosemary and thyme. Cover and bake for 30 minutes and baste with butter mixture.

- Remove from oven and pour wine over chicken. Bake for additional 20 minutes and baste with pan juices.

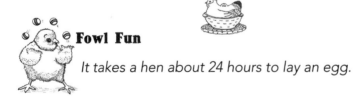

Fowl Fun

It takes a hen about 24 hours to lay an egg.

Barnyard Supper

5 boneless, skinless chicken breast halves
5 slices onion
5 potatoes, peeled, quartered
1 (10 ounce) can cream of celery soup   **280 g**

- Place chicken breasts in 9 x 13-inch (23 x 33 cm) greased baking dish. Top chicken with onion slices and place potatoes around chicken.

- Heat soup with ¼ cup (60 ml) water just enough to pour soup over chicken and vegetables.

- Bake covered at 325° (162° C) for 1 hour 10 minutes.

Chicken-Broccoli Bake

2 bags Success white rice
1 (8 ounce) package cubed processed cheese   227 g
1 (16 ounce) package frozen broccoli florets,
**   thawed   .5 kg**
3 cups cooked, cubed chicken or turkey   710 ml
1 cup cracker or breadcrumbs   240 ml

- Preheat oven to 325° (162° C).

- Cook rice in large saucepan according to package directions. Stir in cheese and ¼ cup (60 ml) water, stir and mix until cheese melts.

- Cook broccoli according to package directions. Add broccoli and chicken to rice-cheese mixture and mix well. Spoon into greased 9 x 13-inch (23 x 33 cm) greased baking dish. Top with cracker or seasoned breadcrumbs and bake for 15 minutes.

Chicken-Cheese Enchiladas

1 (1 ounce) package taco seasoning	28 g
2 tablespoons oil, divided	30 ml
4 - 5 large boneless, skinless chicken breast halves, cubed	
1 (16 ounce) jar chunky salsa, divided	.5 kg
1 (12 ounce) package shredded Monterey Jack cheese, divided	340 ml
1 (15 ounce) carton ricotta cheese	425 g
1 (4 ounce) can chopped green chilies	114 g
1 egg	
1 teaspoon dried cilantro	5 ml
1 (10 ounce) package flour tortillas	280 g
Sour cream	

- Combine ¼ cup (60 ml) water, taco seasoning and 1 tablespoon (15 ml) oil in shallow bowl and mix well. Place seasoning mixture in plastic bag. Add chicken, seal and refrigerate for 1 to 2 hours.

- Cook chicken in remaining oil over medium high heat for about 15 minutes.

- Combine ½ cup (120 ml) salsa and ¼ cup (60 ml) water and spoon into greased 9 x 13-inch (23 x 33 cm) baking dish. Spread evenly over bottom of dish.

- Combine 2½ cups (600 ml) Monterey Jack cheese, ricotta cheese, green chilies, egg, cilantro and ½ teaspoon (2 ml) salt.

- Spoon ⅓ cup (80 ml) cheese mixture down center of each tortilla, top with chicken and roll. Place tortillas, seam-side down, over salsa mixture in dish.

- Drizzle remaining salsa over enchiladas and sprinkle with remaining ½ cup (120 ml) Monterey Jack cheese.

- Bake uncovered at 350° (176° C) for 25 minutes. To serve, top with a dab of sour cream.

Almond-Crusted Chicken

1 egg	
¼ cup seasoned breadcrumbs	60 ml
1 cup sliced almonds	240 ml
4 boneless, skinless chicken breast halves	
1 (5 ounce) package grated parmesan cheese	143 g

Sauce:	
1 teaspoon minced garlic	5 ml
⅓ cup finely chopped onion	80 ml
2 tablespoons oil	30 ml
1 cup white wine	240 ml
¼ cup teriyaki sauce	60 ml

- Preheat oven to 350° (176° C).

- Place egg and 1 teaspoon (5 ml) water in shallow bowl and beat. In another shallow bowl, combine breadcrumbs and almonds. Dip each chicken breast in egg, then in almond mixture and place in greased 9 x 13-inch (23 x 33 cm) baking pan.

- Bake uncovered for 20 minutes. Remove chicken from oven and sprinkle parmesan cheese over each breast. Cook another 15 minutes or until almonds and cheese are golden brown.

- In saucepan, saute garlic and onion in oil. Add wine and teriyaki sauce and bring to boil. Reduce heat and simmer about 10 minutes or until mixture reduces by half. When serving, divide sauce among 4 plates and place chicken breasts on top.

Chicken-Taco Bake

12 tortillas	
Oil	
1 onion, chopped	
2 tablespoons butter	30 ml
2 cups tomato juice	480 ml
1 (4 ounce) can chopped green chilies	114 g
1 (12 ounce) package shredded cheddar cheese	340 g
1 (8 ounce) carton whipping cream	227 g
5 boneless, skinless chicken breast halves, boiled, cubed	

- Preheat oven to 350° (176° C).

- Quarter tortillas and fry in oil until crisp. Drain and set aside.

- Saute onion in butter, add tomato juice, ½ teaspoon (2 ml) each of salt and pepper and green chilies. Simmer for 30 minutes.

- Add cheese, cream and chicken and heat until cheese melts.

- Alternate layers of chicken-cheese mixture and tortillas in sprayed 9 x 13-inch (23 x 33 cm) baking dish.

- Bake for 30 to 35 minutes.

Chile Pepper Chicken

5 boneless, skinless chicken breast halves
1 (1 ounce) package hot and spicy recipe
   Shake 'N Bake coating mixture   28 g
1 (4 ounce) can chopped green chilies   114 g
Chunky salsa

- Dredge chicken in coating mixture and place in greased 9 x 13-inch (23 x 33 cm) baking dish.

- Bake at 375° (190° C) for 25 minutes. Remove from oven, spread green chilies over 5 chicken breasts and return to oven for 5 minutes. Serve with salsa over each chicken breast.

Chile-Chicken Roll-Ups

8 boneless, skinless chicken breast halves
2 (4 ounce) cans diced green chilies   2 (114 g)
1 (8 ounce) package shredded cheddar cheese 227 g
½ cup (1 stick) butter, melted   120 ml
2 cups crushed tortilla chips   480 ml

- Place each chicken breast on wax paper, flatten to about ¼-inch (.6 cm) thickness with rolling pin or mallet and season with 1 teaspoon (5 ml) salt and ½ teaspoon (2 ml) pepper.

- Place diced green chilies and a little cheese evenly in center of each chicken breast. Carefully roll each chicken breast so no chilies or cheese seep out and secure with toothpicks.

- Place each chicken in small casserole dish and chill several hours or overnight. When ready to bake, roll each chicken breast in melted butter and crushed tortilla chips.

- Preheat oven to 350° (176° C) and bake for about 25 to 30 minutes or until tender.

Chilly Night's Turkey Bake

1 (6 ounce) package stuffing mix for chicken, divided	168 g
1½ pounds deli turkey	.7 kg
1 (10 ounce) can cream of chicken soup	280 g
½ cup sour cream	120 ml
1 (16 ounce) bag frozen mixed vegetables, thawed, drained	.5 kg

- Preheat oven to 375° (190° C). Sprinkle ½ cup (120 ml) dry stuffing mix evenly over bottom of greased 9 x 13-inch (23 x 33 cm) baking dish. Set aside.

- In bowl, combine remaining stuffing and 1 cup (240 ml) water and stir just until moist. Set aside.

- Slice turkey into 1-inch (2.5 cm) strips and place over dry stuffing mix in baking dish. In bowl, mix soup, sour cream and vegetables, spoon over turkey strips and top with prepared stuffing. Bake uncovered for 25 minutes.

Chip Chicken

2 cups crushed potato chips	480 ml
¼ teaspoon garlic powder	2 ml
5 - 6 boneless, skinless chicken breast halves	
½ cup (1 stick) butter, melted	120 ml

- Combine potato chips and garlic powder and mix well.

- Dip chicken breasts in butter and roll in potato chip mixture.

- Place in greased, shallow baking dish and bake, uncovered, at 350° (176° C) for 55 minutes.

Lemon Chicken Breeze

4 - 6 frozen, boneless, skinless chicken breast halves	
½ cup (1 stick) butter	120 ml
2 - 3 tablespoons oil	30 ml
2 - 3 tablespoons flour	30 ml
½ cup dry, white wine	120 ml
¼ cup lemon juice	60 ml
4 tablespoons chopped parsley	60 ml

- Preheat oven to 350° (176°C).

- While chicken is slightly frozen, slice each into 3 thin slices. Melt butter in skillet with oil, dredge chicken in flour and brown on all sides. Drain chicken on paper towels.

- Add wine, lemon juice, parsley and a little salt and pepper to skillet and mix. Place chicken breasts in sprayed 9 x 13-inch (23 x 33 cm) baking dish and pour lemon mixture over chicken.

- Bake for 15 minutes or until sauce seeps into chicken.

Snazzy Chicken

4 boneless, skinless chicken breast halves	
¼ cup lime juice	60 ml
1 (1 ounce) packet Italian salad dressing mix	28 g
¼ cup (½ stick) butter, melted	60 ml

- Preheat oven to 325° (162° C).

- Season chicken with salt and pepper and place in sprayed, 7 x 11-inch (18 x 28 cm) baking dish.

- Mix lime juice, salad dressing mix and melted butter and pour over chicken.

- Cover and bake for 1 hour. Remove cover for last 15 minutes of cooking time.

Cilantro-Chicken Breasts

6 boneless, skinless chicken breast halves	
3 teaspoons snipped cilantro, divided	15 ml
1¼ teaspoons cumin, divided	6 ml
2 cups breadcrumbs	480 ml
Oil	
3 tablespoons butter	45 ml
¼ cup flour	60 ml
2 cups milk	480 ml
⅓ cup dry white wine	80 ml
1 (8 ounce) grated Monterey Jack cheese	227 g

- Preheat oven to 350° (176° C).

- Pound chicken breast halves to ¼-inch thick with mallet or rolling pin. Mix 1 teaspoon (5 ml) each of salt and pepper, 2 teaspoons (10 ml) cilantro and 1 teaspoon (5 ml) cumin. Sprinkle seasonings over chicken cutlets and dip in breadcrumbs.

- Pour oil into large skillet and brown chicken on both sides. Remove to 9 x 13-inch (23 x 33 cm) greased baking dish.

- In saucepan, melt butter, blend in flour, ½ teaspoon (2 ml) salt, 1 teaspoon (5 ml) cilantro and ¼ teaspoon (1 ml) cumin. Add milk, stir constantly and cook until sauce thickens.

- Remove from heat and stir in wine. Pour sauce over chicken and bake, covered, for 45 minutes. Remove from oven, sprinkle cheese on top of each piece of chicken and return to oven for 5 minutes.

Cola Chicken

4 - 6 boneless, skinless chicken breast halves
1 cup ketchup   240 ml
1 cup cola   240 ml
2 tablespoons Worcestershire sauce   30 ml

- Place chicken in 9 x 13-inch (23 x 33 cm) baking dish and sprinkle with salt and pepper.
- Mix ketchup, cola and Worcestershire sauce and pour over chicken.
- Cover and bake at 350° (176° C) for 50 minutes.

Company's Coming Chicken

2 chickens, quartered
2 (10 ounce) cans cream of mushroom soup   2 (280 g)
1 pint sour cream   .5 kg
1 cup sherry   240 ml

- Place chickens in large shallow baking dish.
- In saucepan, combine soup, sour cream and sherry. Pour mixture over chicken.
- Bake covered at 300° (148° C) for 1 hour and 15 minutes. Serve over rice.

TIP: A little paprika on top makes this dish look great.

Cranberry Chicken

6 boneless, skinless chicken breast halves	
1 (16 ounce) can whole cranberry sauce	.5 kg
1 large tart apple, peeled, chopped	
⅓ cup chopped walnuts	80 ml
1 teaspoon curry powder	5 ml

- Place chicken in sprayed 9 x 13-inch (23 x 33 cm) baking pan and bake uncovered at 350° (176° C) for 20 minutes.

- Combine cranberry sauce, apple, walnuts and curry powder and spoon over chicken.

- Bake uncovered 25 minutes longer or until chicken juices run clear.

Cranberry-Glazed Cornish Hens

6 Cornish hens, thawed	
1 (16 ounce) can whole cranberry sauce	.5 kg
¼ cup (½ stick) butter	60 ml
¼ cup frozen orange juice concentrate	60 ml
2 teaspoons grated orange rind	10 ml

- Preheat oven to 375° (190° C). Wash hens and pat dry with paper towels. Season inside and out with a little salt and pepper. Place hens in shallow pan without rack and bake for 35 minutes.

- In saucepan, heat cranberry sauce, butter, orange juice and orange rind. Pour mixture over hens.

- Lower temperature to 325° (162° C) and continue to bake for additional 30 minutes. Baste often with cranberry sauce until it browns well.

Creamy Chicken Bake

1 (8 ounce) package egg noodles	227 g
1 (16 ounce) package frozen broccoli florets, thawed, trimmed	.5 kg
¼ cup (½ stick) butter, melted	60 ml
1 (8 ounce) package shredded cheddar cheese	227 g
1 (10 ounce) can cream of chicken soup	280 g
1 cup half-and-half cream	240 ml
¼ teaspoon ground mustard	1 ml
3 cups cooked, cubed chicken breasts	710 ml
⅔ cup slivered almonds	160 ml

- Preheat oven to 325° (162° C).

- Cook noodles according to package directions, drain and keep warm.

- Combine noodles and broccoli in large bowl. Add butter and cheese and stir until cheese melts.

- Stir in chicken soup, cream, mustard, chicken and 1 teaspoon (5 ml) each of salt and pepper. Spoon into sprayed 3-quart (3 L) baking dish.

- Bake covered for about 25 minutes. Remove from oven, sprinkle with slivered almonds and cook an additional 15 minutes.

Creamy Turkey Enchiladas

2 tablespoons butter	30 ml
1 onion, finely chopped	
3 green onions with tops, chopped	
½ teaspoon garlic powder	2 ml
1 (7 ounce) can chopped green chilies, drained	198 g
2 (8 ounce) packages cream cheese, softened	2 (227 g)
3 cups diced turkey or chicken	710 ml
8 (8 inch) flour tortillas	8 (20 cm)
2 (8 ounce) cartons whipping cream	2 (227 g)
1 (16 ounce) package shredded Monterey Jack cheese	.5 kg

- Preheat oven to 350° (176° C). In large skillet, add butter and saute onions.

- Add garlic powder, ½ teaspoon (2 ml) salt and green chilies and stir in cream cheese. Heat, stir until cream cheese melts and add diced turkey.

- Lay out 8 tortillas and spoon about 3 heaping tablespoons (45 ml) turkey mixture on each tortilla. Roll tortillas and place seam-side down in lightly greased 9 x 13-inch (23 x 33 cm) baking dish.

- Pour whipping cream over enchiladas and sprinkle cheese over enchiladas. Bake uncovered for 35 minutes.

Fowl Fun

Chickens and turkeys are known to cross-breed and are known as "turkins."

Crispy Herb-Seasoned Chicken

Marinade:
2 cups buttermilk	480 ml
1 (2½ - 3 pound) chicken cut into quarters	1.3 kg

Stuffing Mixture:
1 (9 ounce) package herb-seasoned stuffing mix	255 g
¼ cup grated parmesan cheese	60 ml
A scant ½ teaspoon cayenne pepper	2 ml
½ cup (1 stick) butter, melted	120 ml

- Place buttermilk in large plastic container with lid and add chicken quarters, turning several times to coat. Marinate in buttermilk in refrigerator for 8 hours. Discard marinade.

- Preheat oven to 350° (176° C). In food processor, process stuffing mix, parmesan cheese and cayenne pepper until they blend well. Dip chicken pieces in melted butter and roll in stuffing mixture until they coat well. Place chicken on greased baking sheet and bake 1 hour 10 minutes.

Crispy Nutty Chicken

⅓ cup minced dry-roasted peanuts	80 ml
1 cup corn flake crumbs	240 ml
½ cup ranch-style, buttermilk salad dressing	120 ml
6 boneless, skinless chicken breast halves	

- Combine peanuts and corn flake crumbs on wax paper. Pour dressing into pie pan, dip each piece of chicken in dressing and roll chicken in crumb mixture to coat.

- Arrange chicken in shallow 9 x 13-inch (23 x 33 cm) baking dish. Bake, uncovered, at 350° (176° C) for 50 minutes or until light brown.

Curry-Glazed Chicken

3 tablespoons butter	45 ml
⅓ cup honey	80 ml
2 tablespoons dijon-style mustard	30 ml
1½ teaspoons curry powder	7 ml
4 boneless, skinless chicken breast halves	
2 cups instant rice, cooked	480 ml

- Place butter in 9 x 13-inch (23 x 33 cm) baking pan, preheat oven to 375° (190° C) and melt butter.

- Mix honey, mustard and curry powder in pan with butter.

- Add chicken to pan and turn until chicken coats with butter mixture.

- Bake, uncovered, for 50 minutes, baste twice and serve over rice.

Glazed Drumsticks

1 (20 ounce) package frozen chicken drum sticks	567 g
Sauce:	
½ cup hoisin sauce	120 ml
2 tablespoons light soy sauce	30 ml
1 teaspoon minced garlic	5 ml

- Preheat broiler. Place drum sticks in a single layer, in greased 9 x 13-inch (23 x 33 cm) baking dish and broil for 10 minutes. Turn drumsticks and broil another 10 minutes. Reduce heat to 325° (162° C).

- In bowl, combine hoisin sauce, soy sauce and garlic, mixing well. Brush chicken drumsticks lightly with sauce and bake for 25 minutes. During baking time, remove from oven and brush with remaining sauce and continue cooking until glaze bubbles and browns.

E Z Chicken

6 - 8 boneless, skinless chicken breast halves
1 (10 ounce) can cream of chicken soup   280 g
1 (3 ounce) package cream cheese   84 g
1 (8 ounce) carton sour cream   227 g
2 cups instant rice, cooked   480 ml

- Place chicken breasts in shallow 9 x 13-inch (23 x 33 cm) baking dish.

- In saucepan, combine soup, cream cheese and sour cream and heat on low just until cream cheese melts and ingredients mix well.

- Pour soup mixture over chicken breasts and sprinkle with lemon pepper. Cover and bake at 300° (148° C) for 1 hour.

- Uncover, bake another 15 minutes and serve over cooked rice.

Easy-Oven Chicken

One step does all!

6 tablespoons (¾ stick) butter   90 ml
1 cup uncooked rice   240 ml
1 (1 ounce) package dry onion soup mix   28 g
1 cup chopped celery   240 ml
1 (14 ounce) can chicken broth   396 g
1 (10 ounce) can cream of chicken soup   280 g
8 boneless, skinless chicken breast halves

- Preheat oven to 325° (162° "C).

- Melt butter in 9 x 13-inch (23 x 33 cm) glass baking dish. Add all remaining ingredients, except chicken, add 2 cups (480 ml) water.

- Lay chicken breasts in rice and liquid mixture and cover with foil. Bake 1 hour 10 minutes.

El Pronto Chicken

⅔ cup dry, seasoned breadcrumbs	160 ml
½ cup grated parmesan cheese	120 ml
Garlic powder	
4 boneless, skinless chicken breast halves	
½ cup (1 stick) butter, melted	120 ml

- Combine breadcrumbs and cheese with some garlic powder, salt and pepper and mix well.

- Dip chicken in butter, roll in breadcrumb mixture and place in greased 9 x 13-inch (23 x 33 cm) baking dish.

- Cover and bake at 350° (176° C) for 55 minutes. Serve over rice.

Elegant Chicken

3 cups cooked shredded chicken	710 ml
1 (6 ounce) package long grain wild rice, cooked	168 g
1 (10 ounce) can cream of celery soup	280 g
1 (4 ounce) jar pimentos	114 g
1 cup mayonnaise	240 ml
1 (15 ounce) can French-style green beans, drained	425 g
1 (28 ounce) can fried onion rings	794 g

- Combine all ingredients except onion rings. Pour into greased 3-quart (3 L) baking dish. Bake at 350° (176° C) for 15 to 20 minutes. Top with onion rings and cook additional 10 minutes.

Family-Secret Chicken and Noodles

This is a great recipe to prepare ahead of time and freeze.

¼ cup (½ stick) butter	60 ml
½ cup flour	120 ml
½ teaspoon basil	2 ml
½ teaspoon parsley	2 ml
2 cups milk	480 ml
1 (4 ounce) can sliced mushrooms, drained	114 g
1 (10 ounce) can cream of mushroom soup	280 g
1 (2 ounce) jar diced pimentos	57 g
2 pounds boneless, skinless chicken breast halves, cooked, diced	1 kg
1 (14 ounce) can chicken broth	396 g
1 (16 ounce) package medium egg noodles	.5 kg
1 cup shredded cheddar or American cheese	240 ml

- Preheat oven to 350° (176° C). In saucepan over medium heat, melt butter and add flour, seasonings and ½ teaspoon (2 ml) salt. Add milk slowly and stir constantly until thick.

- Add mushrooms, mushroom soup, pimentos, diced chicken and chicken broth. Cook noodles according to package directions and drain.

- Mix noodles with sauce and stir gently. Pour mixture into 11 x 14-inch (30 x 36 cm) baking dish. Sprinkle with cheese, cover and chill until baking time. Bake for 20 to 30 minutes until it heats thoroughly.

Fowl Language

Pecking order is the social hierarchy of chickens.

Happy Chicken Bake

8 boneless, skinless chicken breast halves	
1 (8 ounce) bottle Catalina dressing	227 g
1 (1 ounce) envelope dry onion soup mix	28 g
1 (12 ounce) jar apricot preserves	340 g
1 tablespoon lime juice	15 ml
Cooked rice	

- Preheat oven to 325° (162° C).

- Place chicken breasts in greased 9 x 13-inch (23 x 33 cm) baking dish.

- In saucepan, combine Catalina dressing, soup mix, apricot preserves and lime juice. Heat just enough to mix.

- Pour over chicken breasts and bake, covered, for 1 hour 10 minutes. Serve over hot rice.

 **Fowl Fun**

Q: Why did the chicken cross the basketball court?
A: He heard the referee calling fowls.

Fiesta Chicken

½ cup (1 stick) butter	120 ml
2 cups finely crushed cheese crackers	480 ml
1 (1 ounce) packet taco seasoning mix	28 g
5 - 6 boneless, skinless chicken breast halves, flattened	
1 bunch fresh green onions with tops, chopped	
1 teaspoon dry chicken bouillon granules	5 ml
1 (1 pint) carton whipping cream	.5 kg
1 (8 ounce) package shredded Monterey Jack cheese	227 g
1 (4 ounce) can chopped green chilies	114 g

- Preheat oven to 350° (176° C).

- Melt butter in large baking dish and set aside. Combine cracker crumbs and taco mix. Dredge chicken in crumb mixture and pat mixture well to use all cracker crumbs.

- Place chicken breasts in sprayed 9 x 13-inch (23 x 33 cm) baking dish with melted butter. Take out several tablespoons melted butter and place in saucepan. Add onions and saute.

- Turn heat off, add chicken bouillon and stir. Add whipping cream, cheese, chopped green chilies and mix well. Pour over chicken in baking dish.

- Bake uncovered for 55 minutes.

Golden Chicken

6 boneless, skinless chicken breast halves	
¼ cup (½ stick) butter	60 ml
1 (10 ounce) can golden mushroom soup	280 g
½ cup sliced almonds	120 ml

- Preheat oven to 350° (176° C).

- Place chicken breasts in sprayed 9 x 13-inch (23 x 33 cm) baking pan.

- In saucepan, combine butter, soup, almonds and ¼ cup (60 ml) water. Heat and mix just until butter melts. Pour mixture over chicken. Cover and bake for 1 hour.

Four-Legged Chicken

4 boneless, skinless chicken breast halves	
4 boneless, skinless thighs	
4 legs, skinned	
¾ cup honey	180 ml
½ cup prepared mustard	120 ml
½ cup (1 stick) butter, melted	120 ml
1 teaspoon curry powder	5 ml
1 teaspoon minced cilantro	5 ml

- Preheat oven to 350° (176° C).

- In sprayed 9 x 13-inch (23 x 33 cm) baking dish, arrange all chicken pieces. In bowl, mix honey, mustard, butter, 1 teaspoon (5 ml) salt, curry powder and cilantro.   Spread evenly over chicken pieces.

- Bake for 30 minutes, remove from oven and baste chicken with pan juices. Return to oven and bake additional 30 minutes or until chicken is golden brown.

Fowl Fun

A chicken can have 4 or 5 toes on each foot.

Ginger Orange-Glazed Cornish Hens

1 cup fresh orange juice	240 ml
2 tablespoons plus ½ teaspoon peeled, minced fresh ginger	30 ml/2 ml
1 tablespoon soy sauce	15 ml
3 tablespoons honey	45 ml
2 (1½ pounds) cornish hens, halved	2 (.7 kg)

- Preheat oven to 400° (204° C). Combine orange juice, 2 tablespoons (30 ml) minced ginger, soy sauce and honey in saucepan and cook on high heat, stirring constantly, for 3 minutes or until thick and glossy.

- Place hens in sprayed 9 x 13-inch (23 x 33 cm) baking pan and sprinkle ½ teaspoon (2 ml) ginger and ½ teaspoon (2 ml) each of salt and pepper over birds. Spoon glaze mixture over hens and bake 25 minutes. Brush glaze over hens several times during cooking.

Honey-Baked Chicken

2 whole chickens, quartered	
½ cup (1 stick) butter, melted	120 ml
⅔ cup honey	160 ml
¼ cup dijon-style mustard	60 ml
1 teaspoon curry powder	5 ml

- Place chicken pieces skin side up in large, shallow baking dish and sprinkle with a little salt.

- Combine butter, honey, mustard and curry powder and pour over chicken.

- Bake uncovered at 350° (176° C) for 1 hour 5 minutes and baste every 20 minutes.

Herb-Roasted Turkey

Dry Rub:

2 tablespoons poultry seasoning	30 ml
2 teaspoons paprika	10 ml
2 teaspoons garlic powder	10 ml
½ teaspoon ground nutmeg	2 ml

Turkey:

1 (12 pound) turkey, thawed	5.4 kg
1 large onion, cut into wedges	
2 tablespoons oil	30 ml

- Preheat oven to 325° (176° C). Combine all dry rub seasonings with 2 tablespoons (30 ml) salt and 1 teaspoon (5 ml) pepper in small bowl.

- Rinse turkey under cold water and pat dry. Place onion wedges in turkey cavity and rub about half of rub ingredients inside.

- Place turkey, breast side up on shallow roasting pan lined with heavy foil and spread oil over outside of turkey. Sprinkle remaining rub mixture over outside and add ½ cup (120 ml) water to roaster.

- Cover loosely with heavy foil and bake about 3½ hours or until meat thermometer inserted in breast reaches 175° (80° C). Let stand about 15 minutes before carving. Reserve pan juices for gravy.

Turkey Gravy:

1 package dry turkey gravy mix	
3 tablespoons flour	45 ml
1 cup pan drippings or canned turkey broth	240 ml
½ cup cooked chopped turkey giblets, optional	120 ml

- Combine dry gravy mix and flour in saucepan. Slowly stir in pan drippings and 1 cup (240 ml) water and stir constantly. Bring to boil, reduce heat and stir constantly until mixture thickens. Add turkey giblets if desired.

Home-Style Southwest Chicken

2 cups fine breadcrumbs	480 ml
1 tablespoon cumin	15 ml
2 teaspoons chili powder	10 ml
½ teaspoon oregano	2 ml
4 eggs	
½ cup prepared green chile salsa	120 ml
2 cloves garlic, minced	
3 tablespoons butter	45 ml
3 - 4 pounds boneless, skinless chicken	
breast halves	1.3 kg
Iceberg lettuce	
Sour cream	
1 avocado	
1 lime	
Green onions with tops, chopped	

- Preheat oven to 350° (176° C).

- Combine breadcrumbs, cumin, chili powder, ½ teaspoon (2 ml) salt and oregano in large, shallow bowl and set aside. In separate bowl, beat eggs with salsa and garlic.

- Melt butter in 9 x 13-inch (23 x 33 cm) baking dish in oven. Dip chicken pieces into egg bowl and coat with breadcrumb mixture. Place pieces in baking dish and turn each piece in butter. Bake, uncovered, for about 35 to 40 minutes or until chicken is done.

- Place several leaves of iceberg lettuce on plate and serve chicken on top. Garnish with sour cream, avocado slices, lime slices and chopped green onion.

Creamy Soup Chicken

6 - 8 boneless, skinless chicken breast halves
1 (10 ounce) can golden mushroom soup   280 g
1 cup white wine or white cooking wine   240 ml
1 (8 ounce) carton sour cream   227 g
Hot cooked rice

- Place chicken breasts in large, sprayed, shallow baking pan, sprinkle with a little salt and pepper and bake uncovered at 350° (176° C) for 30 minutes.

- In saucepan, combine soup, wine and sour cream and heat enough to mix well.

- Remove chicken from oven and cover with sour cream mixture.

- Reduce heat to 300° (148° C) and return to oven for another 30 minutes. Baste twice.

- Serve over rice.

 **Fowl Fun**

Chicken, U.S.A.
*Four cities in the United States have the word "chicken" in their names: **Chicken**, Alaska; **Chicken Bristle**, Illinois; **Chicken Bristle**, Kentucky; and **Chicken Town**, Pennsylvania. According to lore, Chicken, Alaska got its name because the locals wanted to honor the state bird, the Ptarmigan, by naming their town Ptarmigan, Alaska. But they couldn't spell Ptarmigan. However, they could spell chicken. Chicken, Alaska currently has a population of about 2,200 and an average household income of around $48,000.*

Honey-Mustard Chicken

⅓ cup dijon-style mustard	80 ml
½ cup honey	120 ml
2 tablespoons dried dill	30 ml
4 chicken quarters	

- Combine mustard, honey and dill. Arrange chicken quarters in 9 x 13-inch (23 x 33 cm) baking dish.

- Pour mustard mixture over chicken. Turn chicken over and make sure mustard mixture covers chicken.

- Bake covered at 350° (176° C) for 35 minutes. Uncover and bake another 10 minutes.

Flakey Chicken

8 boneless, skinless chicken breast halves	
¾ cup mayonnaise	180 ml
2 cups crushed corn flakes	480 ml
½ cup grated parmesan cheese	120 ml

- Sprinkle chicken with salt and pepper. Dip chicken in mayonnaise and spread mayonnaise over chicken with brush.

- Combine corn flake crumbs and cheese and dip chicken in corn flake mixture until it completely coats chicken.

- Place chicken in sprayed 9 x 13-inch (23 x 33 cm) glass baking dish and bake, uncovered, at 325° (162° C) for 1 hour.

Lemon-Almond Chicken

Asparagus, lemon juice, curry powder and almonds give a flavorful twist to an otherwise ordinary chicken dish.

2 (14 ounce) cans cut asparagus, well drained	2 (396 g)
4 boneless, skinless chicken breast halves	
3 tablespoons butter	45 ml
1 (10 ounce) can cream of asparagus soup	280 g
⅔ cup mayonnaise	160 g
¼ cup milk	60 ml
1 red bell pepper, cut in strips	
2 tablespoons lemon juice	30 ml
1 teaspoon curry powder	5 ml
¼ teaspoon ground ginger	1 ml
½ cup sliced almonds, toasted	120 ml

- Place asparagus in buttered 7 x 11-inch (18 x 28 cm) baking dish and set aside. Sprinkle chicken with ½ teaspoon (2 ml) salt. In large skillet, saute chicken in butter for about 15 minutes.

- Spoon chicken strips over asparagus. In skillet, combine asparagus soup, mayonnaise, milk, bell pepper, lemon juice, curry powder, ginger and ¼ teaspoon (1 ml) pepper and heat just enough to mix well.

- Spoon over chicken and sprinkle almonds over top of casserole. Bake uncovered at 350° (176° C) for 35 minutes.

Lemon-Herb Chicken

8 boneless, skinless chicken breast halves
½ cup (1 stick) butter, melted   120 ml
1 cup flour   240 ml

Lemon-Herb Sauce:
¼ cup lemon juice   60 ml
½ teaspoon lemon pepper   2 ml
½ teaspoon garlic powder   2 ml
2 tablespoons brown sugar   30 ml
½ teaspoon oregano   2 ml
½ teaspoon crushed rosemary   2 ml
1 teaspoon lemon peel   5 ml
Hot cooked rice

- Preheat oven to 350° (176° C).

- Dip each chicken breast in butter and flour and place in sprayed 9 x 13-inch (23 x 33 cm) baking dish. Cover with foil and bake for 30 minutes.

- While chicken is cooking, add Lemon-Herb Sauce ingredients to mixing bowl with remaining butter, ½ teaspoon (2 ml) salt and ½ cup (120 ml) hot water and mix well.

- After chicken cooks for 30 minutes, remove foil and pour Lemon-Herb Sauce over chicken. Bake another 25 minutes and serve over cooked white rice.

 **Fowl Fun**
The largest chicken egg on record measured 12 inches and weighed 12 ounces.

Lemonade Chicken

6 boneless, skinless chicken breast halves
1 (6 ounce) can frozen lemonade, thawed   168 g
⅓ cup soy sauce   80 ml
1 teaspoon garlic powder   5 ml

- Place chicken in greased 9 x 13-inch (23 x 33 cm) baking dish.

- Combine lemonade, soy sauce and garlic powder and pour over chicken.

- Cover with foil and bake at 350° (176° C) for 45 minutes. Uncover, pour juices over chicken and cook another 10 minutes uncovered.

Montezuma Celebration Chicken

6 boneless, skinless chicken breast halves
1 green bell pepper, seeded, cut in rings
1 (16 ounce) jar hot salsa   .5 kg
⅔ cup packed brown sugar   160 ml
1 tablespoon prepared mustard   15 ml

- Preheat oven to 350° (176° C).

- Place chicken breasts covered with bell pepper rings in greased 9 x 13-inch (23 x 33 cm) baking dish without breasts touching each other. Combine salsa, brown sugar, mustard and ½ teaspoon (2 ml) salt and spoon over each piece of chicken.

- Cover and bake for 35 to 40 minutes. Uncover and continue cooking for another 10 to 15 minutes to let chicken breasts brown slightly.

Mozzarella Chicken

4 boneless, skinless chicken breast halves
1 cup dry Italian-seasoned breadcrumbs   240 ml
1 cup prepared spaghetti sauce   240 ml
4 slices mozzarella cheese

- Preheat oven to 350° (176° C).

- Pound each chicken breast to flatten slightly. Coat chicken well in breadcrumbs and arrange in sprayed 9 x 13-inch (23 x 33 cm) baking dish.

- Spread quarter of sauce over each portion. Place 1 slice cheese over each and garnish with remaining breadcrumbs. Bake uncovered for 45 minutes.

Nacho Chicken

1 chicken, quartered
2 (10 ounce) cans fiesta nacho cheese soup   2 (280 g)
¾ cup milk   180 ml
3 tablespoons white wine Worcestershire sauce   45 ml

- Preheat oven to 350° (176° C).

- Place chicken quarters in sprayed 9 x 13-inch (23 x 33 cm) baking pan with sides.

- In saucepan, combine soup, milk and Worcestershire and heat just enough to mix well. Spread over chicken.

- Cover and bake for 1 hour.

One-Dish Chicken Bake

1 (1 ounce) package vegetable soup-dip mix	28 g
1 (6 ounce) package chicken stuffing mix	168 g
4 boneless, skinless chicken breast halves	
1 (10 ounce) can cream of mushroom soup	280 g
⅓ cup sour cream	80 ml

• Toss contents of vegetable-seasoning packet, stuffing mix and 1⅔ cups (400 ml) water and set aside.

• Place chicken in greased 9 x 13-inch (23 x 33 cm) baking dish.

• Mix soup and sour cream in saucepan over low heat just enough to pour over chicken. Spoon stuffing evenly over top.

• Bake uncovered at 375° (176° C) for 40 minutes.

Onion-Sweet Chicken

2 chickens, quartered	
1 (16 ounce) can whole cranberry sauce	.5 kg
1 (8 ounce) bottle Catalina salad dressing	227 g
1 (1 ounce) packet dry onion soup mix	28 g

• Place chicken quarters in well greased large, shallow baking dish. Combine cranberry sauce, salad dressing and soup mix, blend well and pour over chicken.

• Cover and bake at 350° (176° C) for 1 hour 10 minutes. Before last 10 minutes, uncover chicken and place back in oven to brown.

Oregano Chicken

¼ cup (½ stick) butter, melted	60 ml
1 (1 ounce) packet dry Italian salad dressing mix	28 g
2 tablespoons lemon juice	30 ml
4 boneless, skinless chicken breast halves	
2 tablespoons dried oregano	30 ml

- Preheat oven to 350° (176° C).

- Combine butter, salad dressing mix and lemon juice. Place chicken in unsprayed 9 x 13-inch (23 x 33 cm) baking pan and spoon butter mixture over chicken.

- Cover and bake at 350° for 45 minutes. Uncover, baste with pan drippings and sprinkle with oregano. Bake additional 15 minutes or until chicken juices run clear.

Oven-Fried Chicken

⅔ cup fine dry breadcrumbs	160 ml
⅓ cup grated parmesan cheese	80 ml
½ teaspoon garlic salt	2 ml
6 boneless, skinless chicken breast halves	
½ cup Italian salad dressing	120 ml

- Preheat oven to 350° (176° C).

- Combine breadcrumbs, cheese and garlic salt in shallow bowl. Place salad dressing in second shallow bowl. Dip chicken in salad dressing and dredge in crumb mixture.

- Place chicken in 9 x 13-inch (23 x 33 cm) sprayed baking pan.

- Bake uncovered for 50 minutes.

Oven-Fried Ranch Chicken

1 medium chicken, cut into serving pieces	
1 (1 ounce) envelope ranch buttermilk salad	
dressing mix	28 g
1 cup buttermilk*	240 ml
½ cup mayonnaise	120 ml
2 - 3 cups crushed corn flakes	480 ml

- Preheat oven to 350° (176° C). Pat chicken pieces dry and place on paper towels.

- In shallow bowl, combine ranch dressing mix, buttermilk and mayonnaise and mix well. Dip chicken pieces in dressing and cover well.   Roll each piece in corn flakes and coat all sides well.

- Arrange pieces so they do not touch in sprayed 9 x 13-inch (23 x 33 cm) baking dish. Bake for 1 hour.

   TIP: To make buttermilk, mix 1 cup (240 ml) milk with 1 tablespoon (15 ml) lemon juice or vinegar and let milk sit about 10 minutes.

Oven-Fried Turkey

1 - 1½ pounds turkey tenderloins, thawed	.5
1 (5.5 ounce) package baked chicken	
coating mix	155 g

- Preheat oven to 400° (204° C). Place all tenderloin strips on several pieces of paper towels to partially dry. Pour chicken coating mix into shallow bowl and press both sides of each piece of turkey into seasoned coating.

- Place in sprayed 9 x 13-inch (23 x 33 cm) baking pan so pieces do not touch. Bake 20 to 30 minutes or until turkey is light brown.

Oven-Glazed Chicken

4 boneless, skinless chicken breast halves
1 (10 ounce) can Italian tomato soup   280 g
2 tablespoons white wine Worcestershire sauce   30 ml
2 tablespoons packed brown sugar   30 ml

- Preheat oven to 350° (176° C).

- Place chicken breasts in sprayed 7 x 11-inch (18 x 28 cm) baking dish.

- In small bowl, combine tomato soup, Worcestershire and brown sugar and mix well. Spoon over chicken.

- Bake for 1 hour.

Oven-Herb Chicken

2 cups crushed corn flakes   480 ml
½ cup grated parmesan cheese   120 ml
1 tablespoon rosemary   15 ml
1 tablespoon thyme leaves   15 ml
1 teaspoon oregano   5 ml
1 tablespoon parsley flakes   15 ml
½ teaspoon garlic powder   2 ml
½ cup (1 stick) butter, melted   120 ml
5-6 boneless, skinless chicken breast halves or
   1 chicken, quartered

- Preheat oven to 325° (162° C). In medium bowl, combine corn flakes, parmesan cheese, rosemary, thyme, oregano, parsley, garlic powder, ½ teaspoon (2 ml) salt and 1 teaspoon (5 ml) pepper.

- Melt butter in small bowl in microwave. Dip chicken breasts in butter and corn flake mixture; coat well.

- Place chicken in shallow, sprayed 9 x 13-inch (23 x 33 cm) baking dish. (Do not crowd pieces.) Bake uncovered for 1 hour.

Parmesan-Crusted Chicken

1 egg white, beaten	
1½ cups dry breadcrumbs	360 ml
1 teaspoon dried parsley	5 ml
½ cup grated parmesan cheese	120 ml
4 small boneless, skinless chicken breast halves	

Sage-Butter Sauce:

¼ cup minced shallots	60 ml
½ cup dry white wine	120 ml
½ cup whipping cream	120 ml
½ cup chicken broth	120 ml
¼ cup (½ stick) butter, cubed	60 ml
¾ teaspoon dried sage	4 ml

- Preheat oven to 425° (220° C). Combine beaten egg white and 1 tablespoon (15 ml) water. In shallow bowl, combine breadcrumbs, parsley, cheese and salt and pepper to taste.

- Dip each piece of chicken in egg white and dredge in crumb mixture. Place in heavy skillet with a little oil and saute chicken until golden on both sides, about 5 minutes.

- Transfer to greased baking dish and bake, uncovered for 15 minutes. Saute shallots in a little oil in saucepan.

- Add wine, cream and chicken broth. Simmer until reduced by half. Stir in butter and sage. Serve over parmesan chicken.

Fowl Fact

Cooked chicken should not be left out of the refrigerator longer than two hours.

Party Chicken Breasts

6 - 8 boneless, skinless chicken breast halves
8 strips bacon
1 (2.5 ounce) jar dried beef   70 g
1 (10 ounce) can cream of chicken soup   280 g
1 (8 ounce) carton sour cream   227 g

- Wrap each chicken breast with 1 strip bacon and secure with toothpicks.

- Place dried beef in bottom of large, shallow baking pan and top with chicken.

- Heat soup and sour cream, just enough to pour over chicken.

- Bake uncovered at 325° (162° C) for 1 hour.

Peachy Chicken

½ cup Italian dressing   120 ml
2 teaspoons ground ginger   10 ml
4 boneless, skinless chicken breast halves
⅓ cup peach preserves   80 ml

- In large plastic bag, combine Italian dressing and ginger. Place chicken in bag and turn several times to coat chicken.

- Marinate in refrigerator, turning occasionally, 4 hours or overnight. When ready to bake, remove chicken and discard marinade. Save ⅓ cup (80 ml) marinade.

- In small saucepan bring saved marinade to boil for 1 minute. Remove from heat, stir in preserves and set aside.

- In oven, broil chicken until juices run clear and brush with mixture last 5 minutes of cooking.

Picante Chicken

4 boneless, skinless chicken breast halves
1 (16 ounce) jar salsa   .5 kg
4 tablespoons brown sugar   60 ml
1 tablespoon prepared mustard   15 ml
Hot cooked rice

- Place chicken in shallow sprayed baking dish.

- In small bowl, combine salsa, brown sugar and mustard and pour over chicken.

- Bake uncovered at 375° (190° C) for 45 minutes or until chicken juices run clear and serve over rice.

Pimento Cheese-Stuffed Fried Chicken

4 boneless, skinless chicken breast halves
½ cup milk   120 ml
1 large egg, beaten
2 cups seasoned breadcrumbs   480 ml
1 (16 ounce) carton prepared pimento cheese   .5 kg

- Preheat oven to 350° (176° C). Dry chicken breasts with paper towels and sprinkle well with salt and pepper.

- Combine milk and beaten egg in shallow bowl and mix well. Place breadcrumbs in second shallow bowl.

- Dip chicken in milk mixture and dredge in breadcrumbs.

- In large skillet over medium to high heat, pour oil to ⅛-inch (.4 cm) depth and cook chicken about 10 to 12 minutes on each side. Transfer to baking sheet.

- Hold chicken with tongs and cut slit in 1 side of each chicken breast to form pocket. Spoon about ¼ cup (60 ml) pimento cheese into each pocket and bake about 3 minutes or until cheese melts.

Pimento-Chicken Enchilada Bake

10 corn tortillas
1 (10 ounce) can cream of mushroom soup   280 g
1 (10 ounce) can cream of chicken soup   280 g
1 cup milk   240 ml
1 small onion, chopped
2 (4 ounce) cans diced, green chilies   2 (114 g)
2 (4 ounce) jars diced pimentos, drained   2 (114 g)
5 boneless, skinless chicken breast halves,
  cooked
1 (12 ounce) package shredded cheddar cheese 340 g

- Preheat oven to 350° (176° C).

- Cut tortillas into 1-inch (2.5 cm) strips and lay half of them in sprayed baking dish. Mix mushroom soup, chicken soup, milk, onion, green chilies and pimentos in saucepan and heat just enough to mix.

- Chop cooked chicken and place half on top of tortilla strips. Pour half of sauce on top of chicken, repeat tortilla layer and sauce layer.

- Cover and bake for 45 minutes. Sprinkle cheese over casserole, return to oven and bake another 5 minutes.

TIP: If you want to make this dish in advance, top with cheese and chill overnight. Bake the next day when you need it.

Pineapple-Teriyaki Chicken

6 boneless, skinless chicken breast halves
½ red onion, sliced
1 green bell pepper, seeded, sliced
1 cup teriyaki marinade   240 ml
1 (15 ounce) can pineapple rings with juice   425 g

- Place chicken in sprayed 9 x 13-inch (23 x 33 cm) baking dish and arrange vegetables over chicken. Mix teriyaki with juice from pineapple. Pour over vegetables and chicken.

- Bake uncovered at 350° (176° C) for 45 minutes. Spoon juices over chicken once during baking.

- About 10 minutes before chicken is done, place pineapple slices over chicken and return to oven.

Fowl Fact

Avoid cross-contamination of utensils used on raw chicken and avoid packages that leak.

Real Easy Baked Chicken

1 (2 - 3 pound) chicken	1 kg
Oil	
2 teaspoons paprika	10 ml
Fresh cracked black pepper	

- Preheat oven to 350° (176°C). Wash and dry chicken and place in sprayed baking pan. Rub outside with oil. Sprinkle paprika, lots of black pepper and a little salt over chicken.

- Bake for 1½ to 2 hours or until juices run clear.

Prairie Spring Chicken

2 pounds chicken thighs	1 kg
Oil	
¾ cup chili sauce	180 ml
¾ cup packed brown sugar	180 ml
1 (1 ounce) packet dry onion soup mix	28 g
⅛ teaspoon cayenne pepper	.5 ml
Cooked rice	

- Preheat oven to 325° (162° C). Brown chicken pieces in skillet with a little oil and place in sprayed 9 x 13-inch (23 x 33 cm) baking dish. Combine chili sauce, brown sugar, dry soup mix, cayenne pepper and ½ cup (120 ml) water and pour over chicken.

- Cover and bake for 20 minutes. Remove cover and bake another 15 minutes. Serve over hot, cooked rice.

Ranch Chicken

½ cup parmesan cheese	120 ml
1½ cups corn flakes	360 ml
1 (1 ounce) package dry ranch-style salad dressing mix	28 g
2 pounds chicken drumsticks	1 kg
½ cup (1 stick) butter, melted	120 ml

- Combine cheese, corn flakes and dressing mix.

- Dip washed, dried chicken in melted butter and dredge in corn flake mixture.

- Bake uncovered at 350° (176° C) for 50 minutes or until golden brown.

Reuben Chicken

4 boneless, skinless chicken breast halves
4 slices Swiss cheese
1 (15 ounce) can sauerkraut, drained   425 g
1 (8 ounce) bottle Catalina salad dressing   227 g

- Arrange chicken breasts in greased, shallow baking pan.

- Place cheese over chicken and spread sauerkraut next. Cover with dressing.

- Bake covered at 350° (176° C) for 30 minutes. Uncover and cook another 15 minutes.

Ritzy Chicken

6 boneless, skinless chicken breast halves
1 (8 ounce) carton sour cream   227 g
⅓ (12 ounce) box round buttery crackers,
    crushed   340 g

- Dip chicken in sour cream and roll in cracker crumbs with ¼ teaspoon (1 ml) pepper. Place chicken in greased, shallow baking dish.

- Bake uncovered at 350° (176° C) for 55 minutes.

Roasted Chicken

1 (3 - 4 pound) chicken	1.3 kg
3 tablespoons butter, softened	45 ml

- Preheat oven to 350° (176° C).

- Wash and dry chicken with paper towels. Remove giblets package from cavity. Spread butter over breasts, legs and wings. Salt and pepper liberally.

- Place chicken on back in deep, roasting pan. Bake for 20 to 30 minutes per pound or until juices run clear.

- Baste frequently, add water if necessary. Turn bird occasionally to brown evenly.

TIP: Basting with pan juices will make a glazed coating on chicken. For a crusted topping on chicken, sprinkle flour over bird after spreading butter on outside.

Roasted Chicken and Vegetables

2 pounds boneless chicken breasts	1 kg
1 cup lemon pepper marinade with lemon juice, divided	240 ml
1 (16 ounce) package frozen mixed vegetables, thawed	.5 kg
¼ cup olive oil	60 ml

- Preheat oven to 375° (190° C).

- Arrange chicken skin-side down in sprayed 9 x 13-inch (23 x 33 cm) baking pan. Pour ⅔ cup (160 ml) marinade over chicken. Bake uncovered for 30 minutes.

- Turn chicken over and baste with remaining ⅓ cup (80 ml) marinade.

- Toss vegetables with oil and 1 tablespoon (15 ml) salt. Arrange vegetables around chicken and cover with foil. Return pan to oven and bake additional 20 to 30 minutes, or until juices run clear.

Roasted Chicken Supreme

This is such an easy recipe and good for any meal.

1 (3 pound) whole chicken	**1.3 kg**
1 rib celery	
1 onion	
Vegetable oil	
Paprika	

- Preheat oven to 325° (162° C). Wash chicken and dry with paper towels. Cut celery in half. Insert celery and onion into chicken cavity. Tie legs together, rub chicken with oil and sprinkle with paprika.

- Roast in open pan for 20 to 30 minutes per pound of chicken, or until juices run clear. Baste every 40 minutes. To serve, remove onion and celery. (You can save and reuse for soup or stew.) Chicken will be extra juicy and moist with no onion flavor.

Rosemary Chicken

½ cup flour	**120 ml**
1 tablespoon dried rosemary, divided	**15 ml**
½ cup Italian salad dressing	
4 - 5 boneless, skinless chicken breast halves	

- Preheat oven to 350° (176° C).

- Combine flour and half rosemary. Pour a little Italian dressing in shallow bowl and dip chicken breasts in dressing.

- Dredge chicken in flour mixture. Place in sprayed 9 x 13-inch (23 x 33 cm) baking dish.

- Bake uncovered for 40 minutes. Remove from oven and sprinkle remaining rosemary over breasts and cook additional 10 minutes.

Saucy Chicken

5 - 6 boneless, skinless chicken breast halves
2 cups thick, chunky salsa   480 ml
1/3 cup packed light brown sugar   80 ml
1½ tablespoons dijon-style mustard   22 ml
Hot cooked rice

- Place chicken breasts in greased 9 x 13-inch (23 x 33 cm) baking dish.

- Combine salsa, sugar and mustard and pour over chicken.

- Cover and bake at 350° (176° C) for 45 minutes. Serve over rice.

Sunday Chicken

5 - 6 boneless, skinless chicken breast halves
½ cup sour cream   120 ml
¼ cup soy sauce   60 ml
1 (10 ounce) can French onion soup   280 g

- Place chicken in greased 9 x 13-inch (23 x 33 cm) baking dish.

- In saucepan, combine sour cream, soy sauce and soup and heat just enough to mix well. Pour over chicken breasts.

- Bake covered at 350° (176° C) for 55 minutes.

Saucy Chicken Breasts

This sauce really makes a delicious chicken dish!

1½ cups mayonnaise	360 ml
½ cup cider vinegar	120 ml
¼ cup lemon juice	60 ml
⅓ cup sugar	80 ml
3 tablespoons white wine Worcestershire sauce*	45 ml
5 boneless, skinless chicken breast halves	

- In saucepan, combine mayonnaise, vinegar, lemon juice, sugar and white Worcestershire sauce and mix well with wire whisk until mixture is smooth. Pour half mixture into plastic bag with chicken breasts and marinate for 4 to 6 hours. Move chicken around a couple of times to make sure marinade covers chicken.

- Preheat oven to 350° (176° C). When ready to cook, place chicken breasts in sprayed 9 x 13-inch (23 x 33 cm) pan (so each breast does not touch). Pour remaining half of marinade from bag over chicken. Sprinkle pepper generously over breasts.

- Cook uncovered for 50 to 60 minutes. If chicken breasts are not slightly brown, place under broiler for 3 to 4 minutes, but watch closely.

- Do not let sauce between chicken breasts get brown. It is done when sauce is just light brown, or until juices run clear.

TIP: White wine Worcestershire sauce gives this dish a pleasing color and flavor.

Savory Oven-Fried Chicken

2 cups crushed corn flakes	480 ml
½ cup grated parmesan cheese	120 ml
1 tablespoon rosemary	15 ml
1 tablespoon thyme leaves	15 ml
1 teaspoon oregano	5 ml
1 tablespoon parsley flakes	15 ml
½ teaspoon garlic powder	2 ml
½ cup (1 stick) butter, melted	120 ml
8 boneless, skinless chicken breast halves	

- Preheat oven to 325° (162° C). In medium bowl, mix corn flakes, parmesan cheese, rosemary, thyme, oregano, parsley, garlic powder, ½ teaspoon (2 ml) salt and 1 teaspoon (5 ml) pepper.

- Place melted butter in small bowl and dip chicken in butter and corn flake mixture.

- Place in sprayed 11 x 14-inch (30 x 36 cm) baking dish. Do not crowd pieces. Bake uncovered for 1 hour.

Springy Chicken

4 - 5 boneless, skinless chicken breast halves	
1 tablespoon oregano	15 ml
¾ teaspoon garlic powder	4 ml
½ cup (1 stick) butter, melted	120 ml

- Preheat oven to 325° (162° C).

- Place chicken breasts in plastic bag and add oregano and garlic. Marinate in refrigerator for 3 or 4 hours.

- Place chicken and butter in sprayed 9 x 13-inch (23 x 33 cm) baking dish. Bake covered for 1 hour.

Sesame Chicken

½ cup flour	120 ml
½ teaspoon chili powder	2 ml
¼ teaspoon paprika	1 ml
½ teaspoon onion salt	2 ml
½ teaspoon celery salt	2 ml
1 teaspoon lemon pepper	5 ml
1 teaspoon garlic powder	5 ml
8 boneless, skinless chicken breast halves	
½ cup (1 stick) butter, melted	120 ml
1 cup sesame seeds, lightly toasted	240 ml

- Preheat oven to 350° (176° C). Thoroughly mix flour, chili powder, paprika, onion salt, celery salt, lemon pepper and garlic powder. Roll chicken breasts in flour mixture and continue to roll chicken until all flour mixture is used.

- Dip floured chicken in butter and roll in sesame seeds. Place chicken breasts in greased 9 x 13-inch (23 x 33 cm) baking dish. Pour any extra butter in baking dish and bake for 1 hour.

Real Simple Cornish Game Hens

4 (2 pound) Cornish game hens	4 (1 kg)
Oil	
2 teaspoons paprika	10 ml
Fresh cracked black pepper	

- Preheat oven to 350° (176°C). Wash and dry hens and place in sprayed baking pan. Rub outside with oil. Sprinkle paprika, lots of black pepper and a little salt over each.

- Bake for 1½ to 2 hours or until juices run clear.

Soft Chicken-Taco Bake

6 boneless, skinless chicken breast halves	
1 (1 ounce) package taco seasoning	28 g
1 (15 ounce) can kidney beans, rinsed, drained	425 g
1 large onion, chopped, divided	
12 corn tortillas	
1 cup half-and-half cream	240 ml
3 large tomatoes, chopped	
1 tablespoon minced cilantro	15 ml
1 (12 ounce) package shredded cheddar cheese, divided	340 g
1 (5 ounce) package Fiesta Sides Spanish rice	143 g

- Preheat oven to 325° (162° C). Boil chicken in just enough water to cover. When chicken cooks and is tender, season with taco seasoning and 1 tablespoon (15 ml) salt. Cool and chop or shred chicken.

- Place several tablespoons meat, several tablespoons beans and 1 teaspoon (5 ml) onion in middle of each tortilla, roll and place side by side in sprayed 9 x 13-inch (23 x 33 cm) baking dish. Pour cream over rolled tortillas.

- Combine tomatoes, remaining onion and cilantro and sprinkle evenly over rolled tortillas. Spread cheese over top of tomatoes and bake uncovered for 20 minutes or until cheese melts. Serve hot with Spanish rice.

Chicken-on-the-Border

8 boneless, skinless chicken breast halves	
1 cup grated Monterey Jack cheese	240 ml
½ cup grated cheddar cheese	120 ml
1 (4 ounce) can chopped green chilies, drained	114 g
1 teaspoon cilantro	5 ml
3 tablespoons onion flakes	45 ml
⅓ cup (⅔ stick) butter	80 ml
2 teaspoons cumin	10 ml
1 teaspoon chili powder	5 ml
1 cup crushed tortilla chips	

- Preheat oven to 350° (176° C). Pound chicken breasts to about ¼-inch (.6 cm) thick. In bowl, mix cheeses, chilies, cilantro and onion.

- Place 2 to 3 tablespoons (30 ml) cheese mixture on each chicken breast and roll and place seam-side down in sprayed 9 x 13-inch (23 x 33 cm) baking dish. In saucepan, melt butter, add cumin and chili powder and pour over chicken.

- Bake covered for 30 minutes, uncover and top with crushed chips. Return to oven and bake for 15 more minutes.

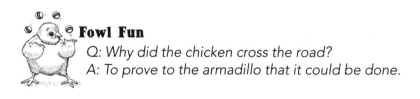

Fowl Fun

Q: Why did the chicken cross the road?
A: To prove to the armadillo that it could be done.

Southern-Stuffed Peppers

6 large green peppers
½ pound chicken livers, chopped   227 g
6 slices bacon, diced
1 cup chopped onion   240 ml
1 cup sliced celery   240 ml
1 clove garlic, crushed
1 (4 ounce) can sliced mushrooms   114 g
2 cups cooked rice   480 ml

- Preheat oven to 375° (190° C). Wash peppers, cut slice from stem end and remove seeds. Cook peppers about 5 minutes in small amount of boiling, salted water. Remove from water and drain.

- Cook chicken livers, bacon, onion, celery, garlic, 1 teaspoon (5 ml) salt, ¼ teaspoon (1 ml) pepper and a dash of cayenne (if you have it) until vegetables are tender. Add mushrooms and rice. Stuff peppers with mixture.

- Arrange in baking pan, seal and freeze. To serve, thaw and add ½-inch (1.2 cm) water to pan, cover and bake for 20 to 25 minutes.

Southwest-Mexican Pizzas

6 (8-inch) flour tortillas	6 (20 cm)
1 (14 ounce) jar Mexican roasted ranchero sauce	396 g
1½ cups shredded, cooked chicken	360 ml
1 green bell pepper, finely diced or 1 fresh poblano chile, roasted, peeled, chopped	
4 fresh green onions, finely diced	
1 (8 ounce) package shredded Monterey Jack cheese	227 g

- Preheat oven to 425° (220° C).

- Butter 1 side of tortilla and place tortillas, butter side up, on baking sheets. Bake 4 to 5 minutes, just enough to crisp tortillas.

- Spread each tortilla with about ¼ to ⅓ cup (60 ml) ranchero sauce, shredded chicken, bell pepper and green onions. Top with shredded cheese.

- Return to oven and bake just until cheese melts. Cut into wedges to serve.

Fowl Language

A "free-range" chicken is one that is given twice as much room as mass produced chickens and they are free to roam indoors and outdoors. This is supposed to enhance the "chicken" flavor because they are "happy" chickens.

Spiced-Spanish Chicken

2 cups instant rice, uncooked	480 ml
4 boneless, skinless, cooked chicken breast halves, cut into strips	
1 (15 ounce) can Mexican-style stewed tomatoes with juice	425 g
1 (8 ounce) can tomato sauce	227 g
1 (15 ounce) can whole kernel corn, drained	425 g
1 (4 ounce) jar diced pimentos, drained	114 g
1 teaspoon chili powder	5 ml
1 teaspoon ground cumin	5 ml

- Grease 3-quart (3 L) baking dish and spread rice evenly over dish. Place chicken strips over top of rice.

- In large bowl, combine stewed tomatoes, tomato sauce, corn, pimentos, chili powder, cumin, ½ teaspoon (2 ml) each of salt and pepper or cayenne pepper and mix well.

- Slowly and easily pour this mixture over chicken and rice. Bake covered at 350° (176° C) for 1 hour.

Spicy Chicken and Rice

3 cups cooked, sliced chicken	710 ml
2 cups cooked brown rice	480 ml
1 (10 ounce) can fiesta nacho cheese soup	280 g
1 (10 ounce) can chopped tomatoes and green chilies	280 g

- Combine chicken, rice, cheese soup, tomatoes and green chilies and mix well.

- Spoon mixture into buttered 3-quart (3 L) baking dish.

- Cook covered at 350° (176° C) for 45 minutes.

Succulent Pecan-Chicken Breasts

⅓ cup (⅔ stick) butter	80 ml
1 cup flour	240 ml
1 cup finely ground pecans	240 ml
¼ cup sesame seeds	60 ml
1 tablespoon paprika	15 ml
1 egg, beaten	
1 cup buttermilk*	240 ml
6 - 8 boneless, skinless chicken breast halves	
⅓ cup coarsely chopped pecans	80 ml
Fresh parsley	

- Preheat oven to 350° (176° C). Melt butter in large 9 x 13-inch (23 x 33 cm) baking dish and set aside. Combine flour, finely ground pecans, sesame seeds, paprika, 1 teaspoon (5 ml) salt and ¼ teaspoon (1 ml) pepper.

- Combine egg and buttermilk in separate bowl. Dip chicken in egg mixture, dredge in flour mixture and coat well.

- Place chicken in baking dish and turn once to coat with butter. Sprinkle with chopped pecans and bake for 40 minutes or until golden brown. Garnish with fresh parsley.

TIP: Chicken may be cut into strips, prepared the same way and used as an appetizer. A honey-mustard dressing would be nice for dipping. This recipe could also be used for fish, like orange roughy, if cooking time is reduced to half.

*TIP: To make buttermilk, mix 1 cup (240 ml) milk with 1 tablespoon (15 ml) lemon juice or vinegar and let milk rest for about 10 minutes.

Sunshine Chicken

1 chicken, quartered	
Flour	
1 cup barbecue sauce	240 ml
½ cup orange juice	120 ml

- Place chicken in bowl of flour and coat well.

- In skillet, brown chicken and place in greased, shallow baking pan.

- Combine barbecue sauce and orange juice. Pour over chicken.

- Bake covered at 350° (176° C) for 45 minutes. Remove from oven, spoon sauce over chicken and bake uncovered another 20 minutes.

Sweet-and-Sour Chicken

6 - 8 boneless, skinless chicken breast halves	
Oil	
1 (1 ounce) package dry onion soup mix	28 g
1 (6 ounce) can frozen orange juice concentrate, thawed	168 g

- Brown chicken in a little oil or butter and place chicken in greased 9 x 13-inch (23 x 33 cm) baking dish.

- Combine onion soup mix, orange juice and ⅔ cup (160 ml) water in small bowl. Mix well and pour over chicken.

- Bake uncovered at 350° (176° C) for 45 to 50 minutes.

Super Cheese Chicken

1 (10 ounce) can cream of chicken soup	280 g
1 cup regular brown rice	240 ml
4 - 6 boneless, skinless chicken breast halves	
1 (8 ounce) package shredded Colby-Jack cheese	227 g

- Preheat oven to 350° (176° C). Combine soup, rice, 1½ cups (360 ml) water and salt and pepper to taste.

- Place in 9 x 13-inch (23 x 33 cm) baking dish.

- Sprinkle chicken with additional pepper and place in baking dish with rice-soup mixture.

- Cover and bake for 50 minutes. Uncover, sprinkle cheese over chicken and serve.

Tangy Chicken

1 (2 pound) broiler-fryer chicken, cut up	1 kg
3 tablespoons butter	45 ml
½ cup steak sauce	120 ml

- Brown chicken pieces in skillet with butter and place in shallow pan.

- Combine sauce and ½ cup (120 ml) water and pour over chicken.

- Cover with foil and bake at 350° (176° C) for 45 minutes. Remove foil last 10 minutes of cooking time so chicken browns.

Tasty Turkey Crunch

1 (8 ounce) package noodles	227 g
2½ cups diced, cooked turkey	600 ml
1 (10 ounce) package chicken gravy, prepared	280 g
2 cups round, buttery cracker crumbs	480 ml

- Boil noodles according to package directions and drain.

- Arrange alternating layers of noodles, turkey and gravy in greased 2-quart (2 L) baking dish and cover with cracker crumbs.

- Bake, uncovered, at 350° (176° C) for 35 minutes.

Turkey Burgers

2 pounds ground turkey	1 kg
1 (16 ounce) jar hot chipotle salsa, divided	.5 kg
8 slices Monterey Jack cheese	
Sesame seed hamburger buns	

- In large mixing bowl, combine ground turkey with 1 cup (240 ml) salsa. Mix well and shape into 8 patties.

- Place patties on broiler pan and broil 12 to 15 minutes. Turn once during cooking. Top each patty with cheese slice and grill just long enough to melt cheese.

- Place burgers on buns, spoon heaping tablespoon (15 ml) salsa over cheese and top with half of bun.

Winey Chicken

6 - 8 boneless, skinless chicken breast halves	
1 (10 ounce) can cream of mushroom soup	280 g
1 (10 ounce) can cream of onion soup	280 g
1 cup white wine	240 ml

- In skillet, brown chicken in little bit of oil. Place in 9 x 13-inch (23 x 33 cm) baking dish.

- Combine soups and wine and pour over chicken.

- Bake covered at 325° (162° C) for 35 minutes. Uncover and bake another 25 minutes.

Notes

Birds of a Feather Frys, Grills and Sautes

Q: Which day of the week do chickens hate most?

A: Fry-day!

American Chicken Chop

2 cups cold, cooked chicken	480 ml
1 cup sliced celery	240 ml
1½ cups cooked rice	360 ml
1 tablespoon butter	15 ml
2 tablespoons flour	30 ml
1½ cups chicken broth	360 ml

- Cut chicken and mix with celery, rice, 1 teaspoon (2 ml) salt and ⅛ teaspoon (.5 ml) pepper. Melt butter in skillet and make into smooth paste with flour.

- Add stock slowly and stir constantly. Bring to a boil and continue stirring.

- Add chicken and rice mixture and heat thoroughly.

Asparagus Chicken

1 (1 ounce) packet hollandaise sauce mix	28 g
2 large boneless skinless chicken breasts, cut into strips	
1 tablespoon lemon juice	15 ml
1 (8 ounce) package egg noodles, cooked	227 g
1 (15 ounce) can asparagus spears	425 g

- Prepare hollandaise sauce according to package directions.

- In large skillet with a little oil, cook chicken strips for 12 to 15 minutes or until brown and stir occasionally.

- Add hollandaise sauce and lemon juice. Cover and cook another 10 minutes, stirring occasionally.

- When ready to serve, place chicken over noodles and add hot asparagus spears.

Asparagus-Cheese Chicken

1 tablespoon butter	15 ml
4 boneless, skinless chicken breast halves	
1 (10 ounce) can broccoli-cheese soup	280 g
1 (10 ounce) package frozen asparagus cuts	280 g
⅓ cup milk	80 ml

- In skillet, heat butter and cook chicken 10 to 15 minutes or until brown on both sides. Remove chicken and set aside.

- In same skillet, combine soup, asparagus and milk. Heat to boiling. Return chicken to skillet and reduce heat to low.

- Cover and cook another 25 minutes until chicken is no longer pink and asparagus is tender.

Cheesy Chicken and Potatoes

1 (20 ounce) package frozen hash browns with peppers and onions, thawed	567 g
1 tablespoon minced garlic	15 ml
2 - 2½ cups bite-size chunks rotisserie chicken	480 ml
1 bunch green onions, sliced	
1 cup shredded cheddar cheese	240 ml

- Add a little oil to large skillet over medium-high heat, cook potatoes for 7 minutes and turn frequently.

- Add garlic, chicken, green onions and ⅓ cup (80 ml) water and cook 5 to 6 minutes. Remove from heat and stir in cheese. Serve immediately right from skillet.

Chicken and Sauerkraut

6 large, boneless, skinless chicken breast halves
1 (16 ounce) can sliced potatoes, drained   .5 g
1 (16 ounce) can sauerkraut, drained   .5 g
¼ cup pine nuts or ½ teaspoon caraway seeds   60 ml

- Season chicken in prepared large skillet with a little black pepper and cook over medium heat for 15 minutes or until chicken browns on both sides.

- Add potatoes to skillet and spoon sauerkraut over potatoes. Cover and cook over low heat for 35 minutes or until chicken is done.

- Toast pine nuts in dry skillet on medium heat until golden brown. Stir constantly. Sprinkle chicken and sauerkraut with toasted pine nuts or caraway seeds and serve.

   TIP: This is good served with sour cream.

Chicken and Shrimp Curry

2 (10 ounce) cans cream of chicken soup   2 (280 g)
⅓ cup milk   80 ml
1½ teaspoons curry powder   7 ml
1 (12 ounce) can boned chicken   340 g
1 (6 ounce) can shrimp, drained, veined   168 g

- In saucepan, heat soup, milk and curry powder. Stir in chicken pieces and shrimp.

- Serve over hot cooked, buttered rice.

Chicken and the Works

6 boneless, skinless chicken breast halves
2 (10 ounce) cans cream of chicken soup   2 (280 g)
2 cups instant white rice   480 ml
1 (10 ounce) package frozen green peas,
  thawed   280 ml

- Sprinkle chicken with black pepper and paprika and brown in large, 12-inch (32 cm) skillet with a little oil. Reduce heat, cover and simmer about 15 minutes. Transfer chicken to plate and keep warm.

- Add soup, 2 cups (480 ml) water and mix well. Heat to boiling and stir in rice and green peas. Top with chicken breasts, cover and simmer over low heat about 10 minutes.

Chicken and Wild Rice Special

1 (6 ounce) package long grain and wild
  rice mix   168 g
4 - 5 boneless, skinless chicken breast halves
2 (10 ounce) cans French onion soup   2 (280 g)
1 red and 1 green bell pepper, julienned

- In saucepan, cook rice according to package directions and keep warm. In large skillet with a little oil over medium to high heat, brown chicken breasts on both sides.

- Add soups, ¾ cup (180 ml) water and bell peppers. Reduce heat to low or medium, cover and cook 15 minutes.

- To serve, place rice on serving platter with chicken breasts on top. Serve sauce in gravy boat to pour over chicken and rice.

TIP: For a thicker sauce, spoon 2 or 3 tablespoons (30 ml) sauce in small bowl and stir in 2 tablespoons (30 ml) flour. Mix well and stir in onion soup. Heat and stir constantly until sauce thickens.

Chicken Cacciatore

Chicken:
1 (2½ pound) frying chicken	1.1 kg
2 onions, sliced	

Sauce:
1 (15 ounce) can stewed tomatoes	425 g
1 (8 ounce) can tomato sauce	227 g
1 teaspoon dried oregano	5 ml
1 teaspoon celery seed	5 ml

- Quarter chicken and sprinkle with plenty of salt and black pepper. Place in large skillet on medium to high heat with a little oil. Add sliced onions and cook until chicken is tender, about 15 minutes.

- Add stewed tomatoes, tomato sauce, oregano and celery seed. Bring mixture to boiling, reduce heat and simmer uncovered for about 20 minutes.

TIP: This is great over hot cooked noodles or spaghetti.

Chicken Couscous

1 (5.6 ounce) package toasted pine nut couscous, cooked	160 g
1 rotisserie chicken, boned, cubed	
1 (15 ounce) can baby green peas, drained	425 g
⅓ cup golden raisins	80 ml

- Combine couscous, chicken, peas and raisins in microwave-safe dish. Heat on medium about 2 minutes or until mixture is warm and stir once.

Chicken Curry

2 (10 ounce) cans cream of mushroom soup	2 (280 g)
2 teaspoons curry powder	10 ml
⅓ cup chopped almonds, toasted	80 ml
4 boneless, skinless chicken breast halves, cooked, cubed	

- In large saucepan combine soup, 1 soup can water, curry powder, almonds and cubed chicken.

- Heat and stir frequently.

- When ready to serve, spoon over cooked white rice.

Chicken Marseilles

3 tablespoons butter	45 ml
5 - 6 boneless, skinless chicken breast halves	
1 (1 ounce) package vegetable soup-dip mix	28 g
½ teaspoon dill weed	2 ml
½ cup sour cream	120 ml

- Melt butter in skillet, brown chicken about 10 to 15 minutes and turn occasionally.

- Stir 2 cups (480 ml) water, soup mix and dill into skillet and bring to boil.

- Reduce heat, cover and simmer, stirring occasionally, for 25 to 30 minutes or until chicken is tender.

- Remove chicken to heated plate, add sour cream to skillet and stir until creamy.

- Place chicken on hot brown rice and spoon sauce over chicken.

Chicken Elegant

This is rich, but worth the calories!

3 tablespoons butter	45 ml
3 tablespoons flour	45 ml
1¾ cups milk	420 ml
½ cup shredded sharp American cheese	120 ml
½ cup shredded Swiss cheese	120 ml
½ teaspoon Worcestershire sauce	2 ml
1 cup cooked, diced chicken or turkey	240 ml
1 cup cooked, diced ham	240 ml
1 (3 ounce) can sliced mushrooms, drained	84 g
2 tablespoons chopped pimiento	30 ml
Toast points or hot, cooked noodles	

- Melt butter in saucepan and blend in flour. Add milk all at once, cook and stir until sauce is thick and bubbly. Remove from heat, add cheeses and stir until they melt.

- Stir in Worcestershire sauce, chicken or turkey, ham, mushrooms and pimiento. Heat thoroughly and serve over toast points or hot, cooked noodles.

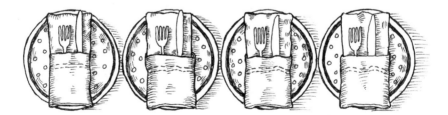

Chicken Fajitas

2 pounds boneless, skinless chicken breast halves	1 kg
1 onion, thinly sliced	
1 sweet red bell pepper, seeded, sliced	
1 teaspoon ground cumin	5 ml
1½ teaspoons chili powder	7 ml
1 tablespoon lime juice	15 ml
½ cup chicken broth	120 ml
8 - 10 warmed flour tortillas	
Guacamole	
Sour cream	
Lettuce and tomatoes	

- Cut chicken into diagonal strips and place in large skillet. Add onion, bell pepper, cumin, chili powder, lime juice and chicken broth; cover and cook for 25 minutes over medium heat.

- When serving, spoon chicken mixture with sauce into center of each warm tortilla and fold.

- Serve with guacamole, sour cream, lettuce or tomatoes or plain.

Fowl Fun

There is more than one chicken for every human in the world.

Simple Chicken In Wine

¼ cup (½ stick) butter	60 ml
4 large boneless, skinless chicken breast halves	
1 cup diced celery	240 ml
½ cup seeded, diced green or red bell pepper	120 ml
½ cup minced onion	120 ml
1½ cups white wine	360 ml

- Melt butter in large skillet over medium-high heat and brown chicken on all sides. Remove chicken and set aside.

- Saute celery, bell pepper and onion until onion is translucent. Pour in wine and stir. Return chicken to skillet, cover and cook about 1 hour or until juices run clear. Baste with pan juices several times while chicken cooks.

Chicken-Broccoli Skillet

3 cups cooked, cubed chicken	710 ml
1 (16 ounce) package frozen broccoli florets	.5 kg
1 (8 ounce) package cubed Velveeta® cheese	227 g
⅔ cup mayonnaise	160 ml

- In skillet, combine chicken, broccoli, cheese and ¼ cup (60 ml) water.

- Cover and cook over medium heat until broccoli is crisp-tender and cheese melts.

- Stir in mayonnaise and heat through, but do not boil. Serve over hot, cooked rice.

Salsa Grilled Chicken

4 - 5 boneless, skinless chicken beast halves	
1 cup thick-and-chunky salsa	240 ml
¼ cup packed dark brown sugar	60 ml
1 tablespoon dijon-style mustard	15 ml

- Pound chicken to about ½-inch (1.2 cm) thick. Combine remaining ingredients in large bowl. Add chicken to bowl, coat with marinade and marinate for 3 to 4 hours in refrigerator. Grill over hot coals until juices run clear and baste with marinade.

Grilled Chicken with Raspberry-Barbecue Sauce

Sauce:

1 (12 ounce) jar seedless raspberry preserves	340 g
½ cup bottled barbecue sauce	120 ml
2 tablespoons raspberry vinegar	30 ml
2 tablespoons dijon-style mustard	30 ml

Chicken:

1 (2½ pound) chicken, quartered	1.2 kg

- In bowl, combine all sauce ingredients and have ready when chicken quarters are nearly done.

- Season chicken quarters liberally with salt and pepper. Grill chicken, covered, over medium-high heat for about 8 minutes on each side. Baste Raspberry-Barbecue sauce over quarters during last 2 minutes of cooking.

- Serve with remaining sauce.

Chicken-Orzo Supper

1 (5 ounce) box chicken-flavored orzo	143 6
1 (7 ounce) package cooked chicken strips	198 g
1 (10 ounce) package frozen corn	280 g
1 (10 ounce) package frozen cut green beans	280 g
¼ cup extra-virgin olive oil	60 ml
1 teaspoon minced garlic	5 ml

- Cook orzo according to package directions. Add chicken strips, corn, green beans, olive oil, garlic, ¼ cup (60 ml) water and a little salt and pepper and mix well.

- Cook on low heat and stir several times until mixture is hot, about 10 to 15 minutes.

Alfredo-Chicken Spaghetti

1 (8 ounce) package thin spaghetti, broken in thirds	227 g
2 teaspoons minced garlic	10 ml
1 (16 ounce) jar alfredo sauce	.5 kg
¼ cup milk	60 ml
1 (10 ounce) box broccoli florets, thawed	280 g
2 cups cooked, diced chicken	480 ml

- Cook spaghetti according to package directions and drain. Place back in saucepan and stir in garlic, alfredo sauce and milk and mix well.

- Add drained broccoli florets and cook on medium heat about 5 minutes and stir several times or until broccoli is tender.

- Add more milk if mixture gets too dry. Stir in diced chicken and spoon into serving bowl.

Almond Chicken

4 boneless, skinless chicken breasts halves	
3 tablespoons butter	45 ml
1 (6 ounce) can frozen orange juice	
concentrate, thawed	168 g
2 tablespoons bourbon	30 ml
Hot, cooked rice	
½ cup chopped, salted almonds, toasted	120 ml

- In skillet, brown chicken in butter over medium heat and reduce heat to low. Add orange juice, ½ teaspoon (2 ml) salt and ¼ teaspoon (1 ml) pepper.

- Cover and cook over medium heat for 25 minutes. Spoon sauce over chicken twice while it cooks. Remove chicken to serving platter and keep warm.

- Add bourbon to sauce in skillet, stir and heat. Pour mixture over chicken and serve over hot, cooked rice. Sprinkle with almonds.

Creamy Chicken and Broccoli

5 large boneless, skinless chicken breast	
halves, thawed	
2 (10 ounce) cans creamy chicken verde soup	2 (280)
½ cup milk	120 ml
1 (16 ounce) package frozen broccoli florets,	
thawed	.5 kg
2 cups instant brown rice	480 ml

- Sprinkle chicken with salt and pepper and brown breasts with oil in large skillet with lid. On medium heat, add both cans soup and milk. Ladle soup mixture over top of chicken. When mixture is hot, reduce heat, cover and simmer for 20 minutes.

- Place broccoli around chicken and return heat to high until broccoli is hot. Reduce heat and simmer about 10 minutes. Serve chicken and sauce over cooked brown rice.

Grilled Chicken with Broccoli Slaw

Chicken:
1 (3½ pound) chicken, quartered	1.4 g
3 tablespoons olive oil	45 ml
⅔ cup bottled barbecue sauce	160 ml

Slaw:
¼ cup mayonnaise	60 ml
3 tablespoons cider vinegar	45 ml
2 tablespoons sugar	30 ml
1 (12 ounce) package broccoli slaw	340 g

- Brush chicken quarters with oil and sprinkle with salt and pepper. Grill 30 to 35 minutes, turning once or twice or until juices run clear when thigh part is pierced and a meat thermometer inserted registers 170° (76° C). Brush with barbecue sauce and grill just until sauce is brown, but not charred.

- Combine mayonnaise, vinegar and sugar and mix well. Spoon over broccoli slaw and toss. Refrigerate until ready to serve.

Fowl Fact

When grilling out, clean the grill well before each use to prevent bacterial contamination.

Creamy Mushroom Chicken

4 boneless, skinless chicken breast halves	
1 (10 ounce) can cream of mushroom soup	280 g
1 (4 ounce) cans sliced mushrooms, drained	114 g
½ cup milk	120 ml

- Sprinkle chicken liberally with salt and pepper. In skillet over high heat with a little oil, brown chicken on both sides.

- While chicken browns, combine mushroom soup, mushrooms and milk in saucepan and heat jut enough to mix well.

- Pour over chicken breasts, reduce heat to low and simmer covered for 15 minutes.

Crunchy Chip Chicken

1½ cups crushed sour cream potato chips	360 ml
1 tablespoon dried parsley	15 ml
1 egg, beaten	
1 tablespoon Worcestershire sauce	15 ml
4 large boneless, skinless chicken breast halves	
¼ cup oil	60 ml

- In shallow bowl, combine potato chips and parsley. In another shallow bowl, combine beaten egg, Worcestershire and 1 tablespoon (15 ml) water.

- Dip chicken pieces in egg mixture and dredge chicken in potato chip mixture. Heat oil in heavy skillet and fry chicken pieces in skillet for about 10 minutes.

- Turn each piece over and cook another 10 minutes until golden brown or until juices run clear.

Creamy Tarragon Chicken

1½ cups flour	360 ml
6 boneless, skinless chicken breast halves	
2 tablespoons oil	30 ml
1 (14 ounce) can chicken broth	396 g
1 cup milk	240 ml
2 teaspoons dried tarragon	10 ml
1 (4 ounce) can sliced mushrooms, drained	114 g
2 (8 ounce) packages roasted chicken rice	2 (227 g)

- Mix flour and a little salt and pepper on wax paper and coat chicken. Save extra flour.

- Heat oil in large skillet over medium to high heat and cook chicken breasts, turning once, about 10 minutes or until light brown. Transfer to plate.

- In same skillet, stir in 2 tablespoons (30 ml) flour-salt mixture. Whisk in chicken broth, milk and tarragon, heat and stir constantly until bubbly. Add mushrooms and return chicken to skillet.

- Cover and simmer for 10 to 15 minutes or until sauce thickens. Microwave rice in package according to package directions and place on serving platter. Spoon chicken and sauce over rice.

Dad's Best Smoked Chicken

3 whole chickens, cut in half	
½ cup (1 stick) butter	120 ml
2 teaspoons Worcestershire sauce	10 ml
2 dashes hot sauce	
2 tablespoons lemon juice	30 ml
½ teaspoon garlic salt	2 ml
1 (12 ounce) can 7-Up	340 g

- Sprinkle chickens with pepper and leave at room temperature for 1 hour. In small saucepan, melt butter and add Worcestershire sauce, hot sauce, lemon juice and garlic salt and add 7-Up.

- Cook chickens over low charcoal fire with hickory or mesquite chips around sides of fire. Turn often and baste with sauce mixture several times.

- When chicken is done (about 60 minutes), baste once more to keep chicken moist.

Deep-Fried Chicken

1 whole chicken, cut up	
1 cup flour	240 ml
2 eggs	
2 cups milk	480 ml
1 teaspoon lemon juice	5 ml

- Wash and pat dry chicken with paper towels. Season chicken with salt and pepper. In bowl, combine flour, eggs, milk and lemon juice and mix thoroughly.

- Dredge chicken in batter and fry in deep fryer over medium to high heat until golden brown.

Dijon Skillet Chicken

¼ cup prepared ranch salad dressing	60 ml
1 tablespoon dijon-style mustard	15 ml
4 boneless, skinless chicken breast halves	
2 tablespoons (¼ stick) butter	30 ml
3 tablespoons white wine or chicken broth	45 ml

- Combine salad dressing and mustard in salad bowl and set aside.

- In skillet, cook chicken in butter and simmer for 10 to 15 minutes.

- Add wine or broth and simmer another 20 minutes.

- Whisk in mustard mixture, cook and stir until it blends and heats through. Serve over rice.

Easy Green Chile Chicken

6 - 8 boneless, skinless chicken breast halves	
Flour	
Oil	
1 onion, chopped	
2 ribs celery, chopped	
3 tablespoons white wine vinegar	45 ml
4 tablespoons Worcestershire sauce	60 ml
1 cup white wine	240 ml
1 (7 ounce) cans chopped green chilies	198 g

- Season chicken with salt and pepper. Dredge chicken in flour, brown in hot oil in skillet and remove from heat.

- Combine onion, celery, vinegar, Worcestershire, wine and green chilies and mix well. Pour marinade over chicken in skillet, cover and cook about 30 to 45 minutes.

- Uncover and cook until chicken juices are clear and chicken breasts are slightly brown. Serve over rice.

Fried Chicken Breasts

4 boneless, skinless chicken breast halves
2 eggs, beaten
20 saltine crackers, crushed

- Pound chicken breasts to ¼-inch (.6 cm) thickness.

- Combine eggs, ¼ teaspoon (1 ml) pepper and
  2 tablespoons (30 ml) water.

- Dip chicken in egg mixture and crushed crackers and coat
  well. Deep fry until golden brown and drain well.

Fried Chicken Livers

1 pound chicken livers, washed, dried   .5 kg
2 tablespoons buttermilk*   30 ml
2 eggs, beaten
Flour
Oil

- Season chicken livers with pepper. Add buttermilk to
  beaten eggs and dip livers into egg mixture. Roll in flour
  and coat livers well.

- Heat about ¼-inch (.6 cm) oil in heavy skillet and brown
  livers on both sides. Lower heat and cook until tender,
  about 15 to 20 minutes.

- Remove from skillet, drain on paper towels, salt and
  pepper again and serve immediately.

  *TIP: To make buttermilk, mix 1 cup (240 ml) milk with 1 tablespoon
  (15 ml) lemon juice or vinegar and let milk rest for about 10 minutes.*

Glazed Chicken and Rice

4 boneless, skinless chicken breast halves, cubed
1 (20 ounce) can pineapple chunks with juice   567 g
½ cup honey-mustard grill-and-glaze sauce   120 ml
1 red bell pepper, chopped
1 cup instant rice, cooked   240 ml

- In skillet with a little oil, brown chicken and cook over low heat for 15 minutes. Add pineapple, honey mustard sauce and bell pepper and bring to boil.

- Reduce heat to low and simmer for 10 to 15 minutes or until sauce thickens slightly. Serve over hot cooked rice.

Grilled Chicken Cordon Bleu

6 boneless, skinless chicken breast halves
6 slices Swiss cheese
6 thin slices deli ham
3 tablespoons oil   45 ml
1 cup seasoned breadcrumbs   240 ml

- Flatten chicken to ¼-inch (.6 cm) thickness and place 1 slice cheese and ham on each piece of chicken to within ¼-inch (.6 cm) of edges.

- Fold in half and secure with toothpicks. Brush chicken with oil and roll in breadcrumbs.

- Grill, covered, over medium-hot heat for 15 to 18 minutes or until juices run clear.

Gourmet Chicken

2 medium skinless chickens, quartered	
Flour	
Oil	
1 (16 ounce) can sliced pineapple with juice	.5 kg
1 cup sugar	240 ml
3 tablespoons cornstarch	45 ml
¾ cup vinegar	180 ml
1 tablespoon soy sauce	15 ml
¼ teaspoon ginger	1 ml
2 chicken bouillon cubes	
1 tablespoon lemon juice	15 ml
2 bell peppers, cut in strips	
Rice	

- Preheat oven to 350°.

- Wash chicken and pat dry with paper towel. Coat chicken with salt, pepper and flour. Brown chicken quarters in oil and place in large shallow roasting pan.

- To make sauce, drain pineapple syrup into 2 cups (480 ml) measure. Add water (or orange juice) to make 1½ cups (360 ml).

- In medium saucepan, combine sugar, cornstarch, pineapple syrup, vinegar, soy sauce, ginger, bouillon cubes and lemon juice and bring to boil.

- Stir constantly for about 2 minutes or until sauce thickens and becomes clear. Pour over browned chicken. Bake covered for about 40 minutes,

- Place pineapple slices and bell pepper on top of chicken and bake 10 to 15 minutes longer. Serve on fluffy white rice.

Grilled Chicken Fajitas

6 boneless, skinless chicken breast halves
¼ cup sesame seeds   60 ml
Cayenne pepper
1 red or green bell pepper
1 onion
12 flour tortillas, warmed

- Pound chicken breasts between pieces of wax paper to flatten. Sprinkle both sides of chicken breasts with sesame seeds, cayenne pepper and salt. Slice bell pepper into strips and slice onion twice to make 3 thick slices.

- Grill chicken breasts, bell pepper and onion over charcoal fire. Cook about 5 minutes on each side. Cut chicken breasts into thin strips.

- To assemble, place several strips chicken, bell pepper and onion in center of tortilla. Top with some avocado, salsa or sour cream. Fold over and serve.

  TIP: Traditional fajitas do not include sour cream, guacamole or chopped avocado, but you don't have to be traditional.

Grilled-Lemon Chicken

2 teaspoons garlic salt   10 ml
1 tablespoon freshly grated lemon peel   15 ml
2 teaspoons dried thyme leaves   10 ml
6 boneless, skinless chicken breast halves

- In small bowl, combine garlic salt, lemon peel, thyme leaves and a little pepper. Heat coals and spray grill with cooking spray.

- Sprinkle seasoning mixture over chicken breasts. Grill chicken 20 to 25 minutes or until chicken is no longer pink and juices run clear. Turn once during cooking.

Italian Chicken and Rice

3 boneless, chicken breasts halves, cut into strips	
1 (14 ounce) can chicken broth seasoned with Italian herbs	396 g
¾ cup uncooked rice	180 g
¼ cup grated parmesan cheese	60 ml

- Cook chicken in non-stick skillet until brown, stirring often, and set aside.

- Add broth and rice to skillet and heat to boil. Cover and simmer over low heat for 25 minutes. (Add water if necessary.)

- Stir in cheese and return chicken to pan. Cover and cook for 5 minutes or until done.

Italian Chicken Over Couscous

1 pound frozen chicken tenders, halved	.5 kg
1 onion, chopped	
1 (15 ounce) can Italian stewed tomatoes	425 g
⅔ cup pitted kalamata olives	180 ml
1 (5.8 ounce) box roasted garlic and olive oil couscous	168 g

- Season chicken with a little salt and pepper. Place in large skillet with a little oil.

- Over medium to high heat add onion and chicken, cook about 8 minutes, covered, and turn once. Add tomatoes and olives, cover and cook another 8 minutes.

- Prepare couscous according to package directions.

- Spoon couscous onto serving plates and top with chicken and sauce.

Jambalaya

1 (8 ounce) package jambalaya mix	227 g
1 (6 ounce) package frozen chicken breast strips, thawed	168 g
1 (11 ounce) can mexicorn	312 g
1 (2 ounce) can chopped black olives	57 g
Hot cooked rice	

- Combine jambalaya mix and 2¼ cups (540 ml) water in soup pot or large saucepan. Heat to boiling, reduce heat and cook slowly 5 minutes.

- Add chopped chicken, corn and black olives. Heat to boiling, reduce heat and simmer about 20 minutes. Serve over hot cooked rice.

TIP: You could also add leftover ham or sausage and 1 tablespoon (15 ml) lemon juice to change it up some.

TIP: If you want to serve more than 5 people, just double the recipe.

Fowl Fact

Never partially cook chicken and store to finish later. The heat may simply start cultivating bacteria that will be thriving too strongly to be fully destroyed by the briefer cooking time when you finish the chicken.

Lemony Chicken And Noodles

1 (8 ounce) package wide egg noodles	227 g
1 (10 ounce) package frozen sugar snap peas, thawed	280 g
1 (14 ounce) can chicken broth	396 g
1 teaspoon fresh grated lemon peel	5 ml
2 cups cubed, skinless rotisserie chicken meat	480 ml
½ cup whipping cream	120 ml

- In large saucepan with boiling water, cook noodles according to package directions, but add snap peas to noodles 1 minute before noodles are done. Drain and return to saucepan.

- Add chicken broth, lemon peel, chicken pieces and ½ teaspoon (2 ml) each of salt and pepper. Heat, stirring constantly, until thoroughly hot.

- Over low heat, gently stir in whipping cream. Serve hot.

Lime-Salsa Campsite Chicken

¼ cup oil	60 ml
1 (10 ounce) jar green chile salsa	280 g
1½ tablespoons lime juice	22 ml
½ teaspoon sugar	2 ml
1 teaspoon garlic powder	5 ml
1 teaspoon ground cumin	5 ml
½ teaspoon ground oregano	2 ml
6 boneless, skinless chicken breast halves	

- Combine all ingredients except chicken and mix well. Add chicken breasts and marinate for 3 to 4 hours.

- Cook over hot coals for about 10 to 15 minutes, or until juices run clear. Turn occasionally.

Mandarin Chicken

1 (11 ounce) can mandarin oranges, drained	312 g
1 (6 ounce) can frozen orange juice concentrate	168 g
1 tablespoon lemon juice	15 ml
1 tablespoon cornstarch	15 ml
4 boneless, skinless chicken breast halves	
2 tablespoons garlic-and-herb seasoning	30 ml
2 tablespoons butter	30 ml

- In saucepan, combine oranges, orange juice concentrate, lemon juice, ⅔ cup (160 ml) water and cornstarch. Cook on medium heat, stirring constantly, until mixture thickens. Set aside.

- Sprinkle chicken breasts with seasoning and place in skillet with butter. Cook about 7 minutes on each side until brown.

- Lower heat and spoon orange juice mixture over chicken, cover, simmer about 20 minutes and add a little water if sauce gets too thick.

Maple-Plum Glazed Turkey Breast

2 cups red plum jam	480 ml
1 cup maple syrup	240 ml
1 teaspoon dry mustard	5 ml
¼ cup lemon juice	60 ml
1 (5 pound) bone-in turkey breast	2.2 kg

- In saucepan, combine plum jam, syrup, mustard and lemon juice and bring to boil.

- Turn down heat and simmer for about 20 minutes or until glaze is thick. Reserve 1 cup (240 ml).

- Place turkey breast in roasting pan, pour remaining glaze over turkey and bake according to directions on turkey breast packaging.

- Slice turkey and serve with heated, reserved glaze.

Creamy Chicken and Mushrooms

½ cup (1 stick) butter	120 ml
1 (1½ pound) carton fresh mushrooms, sliced	.7 kg
3 cups cooked, cubed chicken	710 ml
⅓ cup flour	80 ml
2 (14 ounce) cans chicken broth	2 (396 g)
½ cup sherry	120 ml
Cayenne pepper	

- Melt butter in large skillet over medium-high heat and saute mushrooms. Add chicken and cook for 3 to 4 minutes. Add flour, stir well to remove lumps and slowly pour in broth while stirring.

- Reduce heat and simmer for about 10 to 15 minutes. Add sherry and cayenne pepper just before serving. Serves 4 to 5.

Hurry-Up Chicken Enchiladas

2½ - 3 cups cooked, cubed chicken breasts	600 ml
1 (10 ounce) can cream of chicken soup	280 g
1½ cups chunky salsa, divided	360 ml
8 (6-inch) flour tortillas	8 (15 cm)
1 (10 ounce) can fiesta nacho cheese soup	280 g

- In saucepan, combine chicken, soup and ½ cup (120 ml) salsa and heat.

- Spoon about ¼ cup (80 ml) chicken mixture down center of each tortilla and roll tortilla around filling. Place, seam-side down in sprayed 9 x 13-inch (23 x 33 cm) baking dish.

- Mix nacho cheese, remaining salsa and ¼ cup (60 ml) water and pour over enchiladas. Cover with wax paper and microwave on HIGH, turning several times, for 5 minutes.

Mole Con Pollo Y Arroz

Mole is a traditional Mexican sauce well known all over the world. Chocolate is the secret ingredient used to make the sauce rich, but not overly sweet.

1 cup chopped onion	240 ml
2 cloves garlic, chopped	
1 (8 ounce) package slivered almonds	227 g
1 (1 ounce) square bittersweet chocolate	28 g
1 (15 ounce) can tomato sauce	425 g
2 (7 ounce) cans green chile salsa	2 (198 g)
2 cups cooked, chopped chicken	480 ml
1 cup rice, cooked	240 ml
Avocado	
Lime	
Sour cream	

- Heat a little oil in skillet and cook onion, garlic and almonds until onions are translucent. Add ¼ teaspoon (1 ml) pepper and chocolate and heat on low until chocolate melts. Stir constantly.

- Pour tomato sauce, green chile salsa and chocolate mixture into blender and process until smooth. Pour sauce in skillet and add chicken. Stir to mix well and simmer for about 5 to 10 minutes.

- Serve over hot rice and garnish with avocado and lime slices and dollop of sour cream.

TIP: Mole is a smooth, rich, dark red sauce usually containing a blend of garlic, onion and various chiles and seeds, such as pumpkin seeds called pepitas. A small amount of chocolate makes the sauce a richer flavor and color without adding a sweet flavor.

Quick Tex-Mex Supper

12 corn tortillas	
1 (12 ounce) package shredded Mexican	
4-cheese blend, divided	340 g
2 (12 ounce) cans chicken breasts,	
drained, shredded	680 g
1 small onion, chopped	
2 (10 ounce) cans enchilada sauce	2 (280 g)

- Wrap 6 tortillas in slightly damp paper towel. Place between 2 salad plates and microwave on HIGH 30 to 40 seconds.

- On each tortilla, place about ⅓ cup (80 ml) cheese, chicken and 1 tablespoon (15 ml) onion and roll. Repeat steps with remaining tortillas.

- On sprayed 11 x 14-inch (30 x 36 cm) baking dish, place tortillas seam-side down and pour enchilada sauce on top.

- Sprinkle with remaining cheese and onions, cover and microwave on MEDIUM 5 to 6 minutes. (If microwave does not have turntable, turn tortillas once during cooking.)

Skillet Chicken and More

4 boneless, skinless chicken breast halves	
2 (10 ounce) cans cream of chicken soup	2 (280 g)
2 cups instant white rice	480 ml
1 (16 ounce) package broccoli florets	.5 kg

- Brown chicken breasts on both sides in very large skillet with a little oil and simmer 10 minutes. Remove chicken and keep warm.

- Add soup and 2 cups (480 ml) water. Heat to boiling.

- Stir in instant rice and broccoli florets. Use a little salt, pepper on chicken and place on top of rice. Cover dish and cook on low 15 minutes or until liquid evaporates.

Savory Chicken and Mushrooms

1 (16 ounce) package frozen chopped onions and peppers	.5 kg
1 (8 ounce) package fresh mushrooms, sliced	227 g
1 (10 ounce) can cream of mushrooms soup	280 g
1 cup milk	240 ml
1 rotisserie chicken, boned	

- In large skillet with a little oil, cook onions, peppers and mushrooms about 5 minutes or until onions are translucent and stir frequently.

- Stir in mushroom soup and milk, mix well and add chicken pieces and seasonings.

- Boil, reduce heat and cook for about 10 minutes. Serve over hot, cooked rice.

Fowl Fun

A chicken takes 21 days to hatch.

Skillet Chicken and Peas

4 - 5 boneless, skinless chicken breast halves
2 (10 ounce) can cream of chicken soup   2 (280 g)
2 cups uncooked instant rice   480 ml
1 (10 ounce) package frozen green peas   280 g

- Heat a little oil in very large skillet. Add chicken and cook until it browns well. Transfer chicken to plate and keep warm.

- To skillet, add soup, 1¾ cups (420 ml) water and about ½ teaspoon (2 ml) pepper. Heat to boiling, stir in rice and peas and reduce heat. Place chicken on top and cook on low heat for 15 minutes.

Skillet Chicken and Stuffing

1 (6 ounce) box chicken stuffing mix with
  seasoning packet   168 g
1 (16 ounce) package frozen corn   .5 kg
¼ cup (½ stick) butter   60 ml
4 boneless, skinless chicken breast halves,
  cooked

- In large skillet, combine contents of seasoning packet, corn, butter and 1⅔ (400 ml) cups water and bring to a boil.

- Reduce heat, cover and simmer for 5 minutes.

- Stir in stuffing mix just until moist. Cut chicken into thin slices and mix with stuffing-corn mixture. Cook on low heat just until mixture heats well.

Classic Chicken Piccata

5 - 6 boneless, skinless chicken breast halves	
Flour	
Oil	
3 tablespoons butter	45 ml
1 clove garlic, minced	
1 (1 pound) fresh mushrooms, sliced	.5 kg
1 (14 ounce) can chicken broth	396 g
½ cup dry white wine	120 ml
1 lemon	
2 tablespoons capers	30 ml

- Rinse chicken pieces, pat dry and flatten to about ¼-inch (.6 cm) thick with rolling pin. Dredge in flour and coat well.

- Pour a little oil and butter in large skillet and heat over medium-high heat. Place chicken in skillet and brown on all sides. Remove from skillet and keep warm.

- Saute garlic and mushrooms until tender. Add broth, wine and 3 to 4 tablespoons (45 ml) lemon juice and simmer for several minutes.

- Return chicken to skillet and coat with liquid. Add capers and simmer until chicken is done and juices run clear.

Fowl Fact

The best way to tell when chicken is done is to insert a meat thermometer into the thickest parts of the chicken near the bone. The temperature should read no lower than 160° to be safe. Another way to tell when chicken cooked fully is when the juices are clear or there is no pink color next to the bone. If there is pink in the chicken it needs to cook a little longer.

Southern Fried Chicken

1 whole chicken, cut up	
2 eggs, beaten	
2 tablespoons cream	**30 ml**
Flour	
Oil or shortening	
Gravy:	
3 tablespoons flour	**45 ml**
1½ cups whole milk	**360 ml**

- Salt and pepper each piece of chicken. Combine beaten eggs and cream, dip chicken into mixture and roll in flour. Coat chicken well.

- Heat about ¼-inch (.6 cm) oil or shortening in heavy skillet and brown chicken on both sides. Lower heat and cook for 25 minutes or until tender.

- For gravy, remove chicken from skillet and add 3 tablespoons (45 ml) flour and ½ teaspoon (2 ml) each of salt and pepper. Stir and increase heat to high. Add milk and cook. Stir until gravy thickens. Serve hot.

Fowl Language

King Henry IV of France was the first to state that everyone in his realm should "have a chicken in his pot every Sunday". Later President Herbert Hoover paraphrased the saying with "a chicken in every pot".

Spaghetti Toss

1 (10 ounce) package thin spaghetti	280 g
1 (10 ounce) package frozen sugar snap peas	280 g
2 tablespoons butter	30 ml
3 cups rotisserie-cooked chicken	710 ml
1 (11 ounce) can mandarin oranges, drained	312 g
⅔ cup stir-fry sauce	160 ml

- Cook spaghetti according to package directions. Stir in sugar snap peas and cook 1 additional minute.

- Drain and stir in butter until butter melts. Spoon into bowl. Cut chicken into strips and add strips, oranges and stir-fry sauce. Toss to coat.

Stir-Fry Chicken Spaghetti

1 pound boneless, skinless chicken breast halves	.5 kg
1½ cups sliced mushrooms	360 ml
1½ cups bell pepper strips	360 ml
1 cup sweet-and-sour stir-fry sauce	240 ml
1 (16 ounce) package spaghetti, cooked	.5 kg
¼ cup (½ stick) butter	60 ml

- Season chicken with salt and pepper and cut into thin slices. Brown chicken slices in large skillet with a little oil and cook for 5 minutes on low to medium heat. Transfer to plate and set aside.

- In same skillet with a little more oil, stir-fry mushrooms and bell pepper strips for 5 minutes. Add chicken strips and sweet-and-sour sauce and stir until ingredients are hot.

- While spaghetti is still hot, drain well, add butter and stir until butter melts. Place in large bowl and toss with chicken mixture. Serve hot.

Kicky Chicken

Spice Mix:

1 tablespoon paprika	15 ml
1 teaspoon ground cumin	5 ml
½ teaspoon cayenne pepper	2 ml
½ teaspoon coriander	2 ml
½ teaspoon oregano	2 ml

Chicken:
4 - 5 boneless, skinless chicken breasts, halved lengthwise
Extra-virgin olive oil

- In small bowl combine paprika, cumin, cayenne pepper, coriander, oregano and 1 teaspoon (5 ml) salt.

- In large shallow baking dish, place chicken pieces and drizzle with olive oil to coat. Rub each piece with spice mix and let stand about 10 minutes.

- Heat large skillet over medium to high heat and brown chicken pieces. Reduce heat, cover and simmer about 10 minutes on each side. Transfer to serving platter.

Stir-Fry Chicken

1 pound chicken tenders, cut into strips	.5 kg
1 (16 ounce) package frozen broccoli,	
cauliflower and carrots	.5 kg
1 (8 ounce) jar stir-fry sauce	227 g
1 (12 ounce) package chow mein noodles	340 g

- Place a little oil and stir-fry chicken strips in 12-inch (32 cm) wok over high heat for about 4 minutes.

- Add vegetables and stir-fry another 4 minutes or until vegetables are tender. Stir in stir-fry sauce and cook just until mixture is hot. Serve over chow mein noodles.

Sunny Chicken Supper

4 boneless, skinless chicken breast halves	
1½ teaspoons curry powder	7 ml
1½ cups orange juice	360 ml
1 tablespoon brown sugar	15 ml
1 cup rice	240 ml
1 teaspoon mustard	5 ml

- Rub chicken breasts with curry powder and a little salt and pepper. Combine orange juice, brown sugar, rice and mustard in large skillet and mix well.

- Place chicken breasts on top of rice mixture and bring to a boil. Reduce heat, cover and simmer for 30 minutes. Remove from heat and let stand, covered, about 10 minutes until all liquid absorbs into rice.

Sweet 'N Spicy Chicken

1 pound boneless, skinless chicken breast halves	.5 kg
1 (1 ounce) packet taco seasoning	2 (28 g)
1 (11 ounce) jar chunky salsa	312 g
1 cup peach preserves	240 ml
Hot cooked rice	

- Cut chicken into ½-inch (1.2 cm) cubes. Place chicken in large, resealable plastic bag, add taco seasoning and toss to coat.

- In skillet, brown chicken in a little oil. Combine salsa and preserves, stir into skillet and bring mixture to a boil.

- Reduce heat, cover and simmer until juices run clear. Serve over rice or noodles.

Tempting Chicken

3 boneless, skinless chicken breast halves
3 boneless, skinless chicken thighs
1 (16 ounce) jar tomato-alfredo sauce   .5 kg
1 (10 ounce) can tomato-bisque soup   280 g

- In large skillet, brown chicken pieces in little oil.

- Heat tomato-alfredo sauce, tomato-bisque soup and
  ½ cup (120 ml) water in saucepan just enough to mix. Pour
  over chicken.

- Cover and simmer about 30 minutes.

Tasty Skillet Chicken

5 large boneless, skinless chicken breast halves
1 green and 1 red bell pepper, julienned
2 small yellow squash, seeded, julienned
1 (16 ounce) bottle thick and chunky salsa   .5 kg
Hot buttered rice

- Cut chicken breasts into thin strips. With a little oil in large
  skillet, saute chicken for about 5 minutes. Add peppers
  and squash and cook another 5 minutes or until peppers
  are tender-crisp.

- Stir in salsa and bring to boiling, lower heat and simmer for
  10 minutes. Serve over hot, buttered rice.

Tequila-Lime Chicken

6 boneless, chicken breast halves with skin

Marinade:	
½ cup lime juice	120 ml
¼ cup tequila	60 ml
1½ teaspoons chili powder	7 ml
1½ teaspoons minced garlic	7 ml
1 teaspoon seeded jalapeno pepper	5 ml

- In large plastic bag, combine all marinade ingredients. Add chicken breasts, seal bag and turn to coat. Refrigerate 10 hours or overnight.

- Remove breasts from marinade and sprinkle chicken with a little salt and pepper. Discard marinade.

- Grill skin side down 5 to 7 minutes. Turn and grill 10 minutes or until it cooks thoroughly. Remove to platter, cover and let stand 5 minutes before serving.

Turkey and Asparagus Alfredo

1 bunch fresh asparagus	
1 red bell pepper, julienned	
1 (16 ounce) jar alfredo sauce	.5 kg
½ pound deli smoked turkey, cut into strips	227 g

- In large skillet bring ½ cup (120 ml) water to boiling. Cut off woody ends of asparagus and cut into thirds. Add asparagus and bell pepper to skillet, cook on medium to high heat for 4 minutes or until tender-crisp and drain.

- Stir in alfredo sauce and turkey strips. Bring to boiling, reduce heat and simmer until mixture is thoroughly hot.

Texas Chicken Fajitas

2 pounds skirt steak or 6 boneless, skinless
   chicken breast halves
Flour tortillas

Marinade:	
1 cup salsa	240 ml
1 cup Italian salad dressing	240 ml
2 tablespoons lemon juice	30 ml
2 tablespoons chopped green onions	30 ml
1 teaspoon garlic powder	5 ml
1 teaspoon celery salt	5 ml

Filling for Fajitas:
Salsa
Guacamole
Grilled onions
Chopped tomatoes
Grated cheese
Sour cream

- Combine all marinade ingredients with 1 teaspoon (5 ml) pepper and mix well. Remove fat from meat and wipe dry with paper towels.

- Place meat in shallow dish and pour marinade over meat. Marinate overnight or for at least 6 hours in refrigerator.

- Drain liquid and cook over hot charcoal. Cut meat diagonally. Place few meat strips on warmed flour tortilla, choose fillings, roll and eat!

Tortellini Supper

1 (9 ounce) package refrigerated cheese tortellini	255 g
1 (10 ounce) package frozen green peas, thawed	280 g
1 (8 ounce) carton cream cheese with chives and onion	227 g
½ cup sour cream	120 ml
1 (9 ounce) package frozen cooked chicken breasts	255 g

- Cook cheese tortellini in saucepan according to package directions. Place peas in colander and pour hot pasta water over green peas. Return tortellini and peas to saucepan.

- Combine cream cheese and sour cream in smaller saucepan and heat on low, stirring well, until cheese melts. Spoon mixture over tortellini and peas and toss with heat on low.

- Heat cooked chicken in microwave according to package directions. Spoon tortellini and peas in serving bowl and place chicken on top. Serve hot.

Turkey Croquettes

*These are very easy to make. Make several batches
and freeze them for another meal.*

1½ cups chopped, cooked turkey	360 ml
1 (10 ounce) can cream of chicken soup	280 g
1 cup turkey stuffing mix	240 ml
2 eggs	
1 tablespoon minced onion	15 ml
Flour	
Oil	

• Mix all ingredients in bowl and chill for several hours.
  Shape into patties or rolls. Dredge in flour and fry in deep
  fat until brown.

Wild Rice and Chicken

1 (6 ounce) package long grain and wild rice mix	168 g
4 boneless, skinless chicken breast halves	
½ cup (1 stick) butter, divided	120 ml
1 large red pepper, chopped	

• Prepare rice according to package directions.

• In large skillet, cook chicken in 2 tablespoons (30 ml) butter
  and make sure each chicken breast browns on both sides.
  Remove chicken and keep warm.

• Add remaining butter to pan drippings and saute red
  pepper until tender. Add to rice. Serve with cooked
  chicken breasts.

Turkey and Rice Olé

*This may be served as a 1-dish meal or as a sandwich
wrap in flour tortillas.*

1 pound ground turkey	.5 kg
1 (5.5 ounce) package Mexican rice mix	155 g
1 (15 ounce) can black beans, rinsed, drained	425 g
1 cup thick, chunky salsa	240 ml

- Brown turkey in large skillet and break up large pieces with fork. Add rice mix and 2 cups (480 ml) water.

- Bring to boiling, reduce heat and simmer about 8 minutes or until rice is tender. Stir in beans and salsa and cook just until mixture is hot.

Yummy Barbequed-Grilled Chicken

6 boneless, skinless chicken breast halves	
3 cups ketchup	710 ml
½ cup packed brown sugar	120 ml
¼ cup Worcestershire sauce	60 ml
2 tablespoons vinegar	30 ml
1 teaspoon hot sauce	5 ml

- Wash and dry chicken breasts with paper towels. In saucepan, combine ketchup, brown sugar, Worcestershire sauce, vinegar, 2 teaspoons (10 ml) salt, hot sauce and ½ teaspoon (2 ml) pepper and mix well. Bring to boil, reduce heat to low and cook for 15 minutes.

- Fire up grill and smoke chicken over mesquite wood, if possible. Baste chicken frequently with barbeque sauce. Turn chicken periodically and cook chicken 8 to 10 minutes per side or until juices are clear. Any leftover barbeque sauce keeps well in refrigerator.

Texas-Pecan Chicken

1 cup buttermilk*	240 ml
1 egg, beaten	
1 cup flour	240 ml
1 cup very finely grated pecans	240 ml
2 tablespoons sesame seeds	30 ml
2 teaspoons paprika	10 ml
6 - 8 boneless, skinless, chicken breast halves	
¼ cup (½ stick) butter	60 ml
¼ cup chopped pecans	60 ml

- Preheat oven to 350° (176° C).

- In shallow bowl, combine buttermilk and egg. In larger shallow bowl, combine flour, grated pecans, sesame seeds, paprika, 1 teaspoon (5 ml) salt and ¼ teaspoon (1 ml) pepper.

- Dip chicken breasts in egg-milk mixture and coat well in flour-pecan mixture.

- Melt butter in large baking pan and place breaded chicken in pan. Sprinkle chopped pecans over chicken breasts.

- Bake for 30 to 35 minutes or until flour mixture is light brown.

TIP: To make buttermilk, mix 1 cup (240 ml) milk with 1 tablespoon (15 ml) lemon juice or vinegar and let milk rest for about 10 minutes.

 **Fowl Fun**

The record for laying the most eggs in a day is seven eggs.

Chicken Tarragon

Tarragon works wonders for this chicken.

1 (8 ounce) package egg noodles	227 g
1 cup dry white wine	240 ml
1 teaspoon dried tarragon leaves	5 ml
1 (1 ounce) packet dry vegetable soup mix	28 g
4 boneless, skinless chicken breast halves	
1 (8 ounce) carton sour cream	227 g

- Cook noodles according to package directions, drain and set aside. Pour 2 cups (480 ml) water to large skillet. Over medium heat add wine and tarragon and bring to boil. Stir in dry soup mix and boil 5 minutes.

- Add chicken and reduce heat. Cover and simmer for 15 minutes or until juices run clear. Arrange noodles on serving dish. Use slotted spoon to remove chicken; place on top of noodles and cover with foil.

- Boil juices in skillet for about 5 to 10 minutes or until liquid reduces to ½ cup (120 ml). Turn heat to low and stir constantly while adding sour cream. Heat 3 to 4 minutes more and pour over chicken.

Slow Clucker

Q: What do you get if you cross a chicken with a cow?

A: Roost beef.

Arroz Con Pollo

3 pounds chicken thighs	1.3 kg
2 (15 ounce) cans Italian stewed tomatoes	2 (425 g)
1 (16 ounce) package frozen green peas, thawed	.5 kg
2 cups long grain rice	480 ml
1 (3 ounce) packet yellow rice seasoning mix	10 g
2 (14 ounce) cans chicken broth	2 (396 g)
1 heaping teaspoon minced garlic	5 ml
1 teaspoon dried oregano	5 ml

- Combine all ingredients plus ¾ cup (180 ml) water in sprayed slow cooker and stir well. Cover and cook on LOW for 7 to 8 hours or on HIGH for 3½ to 4 hours.

Artichoke-Chicken Pasta

1½ pounds boneless chicken breast tenders	.7 kg
1 (15 ounce) can artichoke hearts, quartered	425 g
¾ cup roasted red peppers, chopped	180 ml
1 (8 ounce) package American cheese, shredded	227 g
1 tablespoon white wine Worcestershire sauce	15 ml
1 (10 ounce) can cream of chicken soup	280 g
1 (8 ounce) package shredded cheddar cheese	227 g
4 cups hot, cooked bow-tie pasta	1 L

- In slow cooker, combine chicken tenders, artichoke, roasted peppers, American cheese, Worcestershire sauce and soup and mix well.

- Cover and cook on LOW for 6 to 8 hours. About 20 minutes before serving, fold in cheddar cheese, hot pasta, salt and pepper to taste.

Bacon-Wrapped Fiesta Chicken

1 (2.5 ounce) jar dried beef	70 g
6 boneless, skinless chicken breast halves	
6 slices bacon	
2 (10 ounce) cans golden mushroom soup	2 (280 g)
1 (6 ounce) package parmesan-butter rice, cooked	168 g

- Place dried beef sliced in 5-quart (5 L) slow cooker. Roll each chicken breast in slice of bacon and place over dried beef.

- Pour mushroom soup and ⅓ cup (80 ml) water in saucepan, heat just enough to mix and pour over chicken. Cover and cook on LOW for 7 to 8 hours. Serve over hot cooked rice.

Broccoli-Rice Chicken

1¼ cups rice	300 ml
2 pounds boneless, skinless chicken breast halves	1 kg
1 teaspoon dried parsley	5 ml
1 (1.8 ounce) packet cream of broccoli soup mix	45 g
1 (14 ounce) can chicken broth	396 g

- Place rice in lightly sprayed slow cooker. Cut chicken into slices and put over rice. Sprinkle with parsley.

- In saucepan, combine soup mix, chicken broth and 1 cup (240 ml) water. Heat just enough to mix well. Pour over chicken and rice.

- Cover and cook on LOW for 6 to 8 hours.

Chicken Alfredo

1½ pounds boneless chicken thighs	.7 kg
2 ribs celery, sliced diagonally	
1 red bell pepper, julienned	
1 (16 ounce) jar alfredo sauce	.5 kg
3 cups fresh broccoli florets	710 ml
1 (8 ounce) package fettuccine or linguine	227 g
1 (5 ounce) package shredded parmesan cheese	143 g

- Cut chicken into strips. In 4 to 5-quart (4 L) slow cooker, layer chicken, celery and bell pepper. Pour alfredo sauce evenly over vegetables. Cover and cook on LOW for 5 to 6 hours.

- About 30 minutes before serving, turn heat to HIGH and add broccoli florets to chicken-alfredo mixture. Cover and cook another 30 minutes.

- Cook pasta according to package directions and drain. Just before serving pour pasta into cooker, mix and sprinkle parmesan cheese on top.

Chicken and Everything Good

2 (10 ounce) cans cream of chicken soup	2 (280 g)
⅓ cup (⅔ stick) butter, melted	80 ml
3 cups cooked, cubed chicken	710 ml
1 (16 ounce) package frozen broccoli, corn, red peppers	.5 kg
1 (10 ounce) package frozen green peas	280 g
1 (8 ounce) package cornbread stuffing mix	227 g

- Combine soup, melted butter and ⅓ cup (80 ml) water in large saucepan and heat just enough to mix well.

- Add chicken, vegetables and stuffing mix and stir well. Spoon mixture into sprayed slow cooker. Cover and cook on LOW for 5 to 6 hours or on HIGH for 2½ to 3 hours.

Chicken Meets Italy

1 (16 ounce) package frozen whole green beans, thawed	.5 kg
1 onion, chopped	
1 cup halved fresh mushrooms	240 ml
3 boneless, skinless chicken breast halves	
1 (15 ounce) can Italian stewed tomatoes	425 g
1 teaspoon chicken bouillon granules	5 ml
1 teaspoon minced garlic	5 ml
1 teaspoon Italian seasoning	5 ml
1 (8 ounce) package fettuccine	227 g
1 (5 ounce) package parmesan cheese	143 g

- Place green beans, onion and mushrooms in sprayed 4 to 5-quart (4 L) slow cooker. Cut chicken into 1-inch (2.5 cm) pieces and place over vegetables.

- In small bowl, combine stewed tomatoes, chicken bouillon, garlic and Italian seasoning. Pour over chicken. Cover and cook on LOW for 5 to 6 hours.

- Cook fettuccine according to package directions and drain. Serve chicken over fettuccine and sprinkle with parmesan cheese.

TIP: For added flavor, you can add ¼ cup (60 ml) butter.

Stuffy Chicken

This is a great recipe for leftover chicken.

1 (10 ounce) can cream of chicken soup	280 g
2 ribs celery, sliced	
½ cup (1 stick) butter, melted	120 ml
3 cups cooked cubed chicken	710 ml
1 (16 ounce) package frozen broccoli, corn	
and bell peppers	.5 kg
1 (8 ounce) box cornbread stuffing mix	227 g

- In large saucepan, combine chicken soup, celery, butter, cubed chicken, vegetables, stuffing mix and ⅓ cup (80 ml) water and heat just enough to mix well.

- Mix well and transfer to sprayed 5 or 6-quart (5 L) slow cooker. Cover and cook on LOW for 5 to 6 hours.

Chicken-in-the-Garden

4 - 5 boneless, skinless chicken breast halves	
1 (16 ounce) package frozen broccoli,	
cauliflower and carrots, thawed	.5 kg
1 (10 ounce) can cream of celery soup	280 g
1 (8 ounce) package shredded	
cheddar-Jack cheese, divided	227 g

- Cut chicken into strips and place chicken strips sprinkled with 2 teaspoons (10 ml) salt in sprayed slow cooker.

- In saucepan, combine vegetables, celery soup and half cheese and heat just enough to mix well. Spoon over chicken breasts.

- Cover and cook on LOW for 4 to 5 hours. About 10 minutes before serving, sprinkle remaining cheese on top of casserole.

Chicken Breast Deluxe

4 slices bacon	
5 - 6 boneless, skinless chicken breast halves	
1 cup sliced celery	240 ml
1 cup sliced red bell pepper	240 ml
1 (10 ounce) can cream of chicken soup	280 g
2 tablespoons white wine or cooking wine	30 ml
6 slices Swiss cheese	
2 tablespoons dried parsley	30 ml

- In large skillet, cook bacon, drain, crumble and reserve drippings. Place chicken in skillet with bacon drippings and lightly brown on both sides.

- Transfer chicken to sprayed slow cooker and place celery and red bell pepper over chicken.

- In same skillet, combine soup and wine and heat just enough to mix well, and spoon over vegetables and chicken. Cover and cook on LOW for 3 to 4 hours.

- Top with slices of cheese over each chicken breast, sprinkle with parsley and cook for additional 10 minutes. When serving, sprinkle crumbled bacon over each serving.

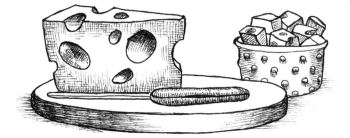

Chicken Coq Vin

Oil
4 chicken quarters
10 - 12 small white onions, peeled
½ pound whole button mushrooms   227 g
1 teaspoon minced garlic   5 ml
½ teaspoon dried thyme leaves   2 ml
10 - 12 small new potatoes with peels
1 (10 ounce) can chicken broth   280 g
1 cup burgundy wine   240 ml
6 bacon slices, cooked, crumbled

- In skillet with oil, brown chicken quarters on both sides and set aside. Place white onions, whole mushrooms, garlic and thyme in bottom of oblong slow cooker. Add chicken quarters, potatoes, chicken broth and a little salt and pepper.

- Cover and cook on LOW for 8 to 10 hours or on HIGH for 3 to 4 hours. During last hour, turn heat to HIGH, add burgundy and continue cooking. Sprinkle crumbled bacon over chicken before serving.

Chicken Curry Over Rice

3 boneless, skinless chicken breast halves
½ cup chicken broth   120 ml
1 (10 ounce) can cream of chicken soup   227 g
1 onion, coarsely chopped
1 sweet red bell pepper, cut into strips
¼ cup golden raisins   60 ml
1½ teaspoons curry powder   7 ml
¼ teaspoon ground ginger   1 ml

- Cut chicken into thin strips.

- Combine chicken strips, broth, soup, onion, bell pepper, raisins, curry powder and ginger in saucepan and heat just enough to mix well. Pour into sprayed 5 to 6-quart (5 L) slow cooker, cover and cook on LOW for 3 to 4 hours. Serve over hot, cooked rice.

Chicken Sherry

5 to 6 boneless skinless chicken breast halves
1 (16 ounce) package frozen broccoli florets,
   thawed   .5 kg
1 sweet red bell pepper, julienne
1 (16 ounce) jar Ragu parmesan mozzarella
   cheese creation sauce   .5 kg
3 tablespoons sherry   45 ml

- In skillet, brown chicken breasts and place in sprayed oval 5 to 6-quart (5 L) slow cooker.

- Place broccoli florets on plate, remove much of stem and discard stems.

- In bowl combine broccoli florets, bell pepper, cheese sauce and sherry and mix well. Spoon over chicken breasts.

- Cover and cook on LOW for 4 to 5 hours. Serve over hot buttered noodles.

Chicken-Celery Delight

¾ cup white cooked rice	180 ml
1 (14 ounce) can chicken broth	396 g
1 (1 ounce) packet dry onion soup mix	28 g
1 sweet red bell pepper, seeded, chopped	
2 (10 ounce) cans cream of celery soup	2 (280 g)
¾ cup white cooking wine	180 ml
4 - 6 boneless, skinless chicken breasts halves	
1 (5 ounce) package grated parmesan cheese	143 g

- In saucepan, combine rice, broth, soup mix, bell pepper, celery soup, ¾ cup (180 ml) water, wine and several sprinkles of black pepper and heat just enough to mix well.

- Spray 6-quart (6 L) oval slow cooker and place chicken breasts in cooker. Pour rice-soup mixture over chicken breasts. Cover and cook on LOW for 4 to 6 hours.

- One hour before serving, sprinkle parmesan cheese over chicken.

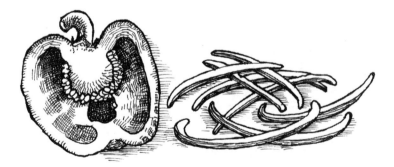

Whole Lotta Chicken Dinner

1 cup rice	240 ml
1 tablespoon chicken seasoning	15 ml
1 (1 ounce) packet dry onion soup mix	28 g
1 green bell pepper, seeded, chopped	
1 (4 ounce) jar diced pimentos, drained well	114 g
¾ teaspoon dried basil	4 ml
1 (14 ounce) can chicken broth	396 g
1 (10 ounce) can cream of chicken soup	280 g
5 - 6 boneless, skinless chicken breast halves	

- In saucepan, combine rice, chicken seasoning, onion soup mix, bell pepper, pimentos, basil, broth, ½ cup (120 ml) water and chicken soup and heat just enough to mix well.

- Place chicken breasts in sprayed slow cooker and cover chicken with rice mixture. Cover and cook on LOW for 6 to 7 hours.

Veggie-Chicken for Supper

5 - 6 boneless, skinless chicken breasts halves	
6 carrots, cut in (1 inch) lengths	2.5 cm
1 (15 ounce) can cut green beans, drained	425 g
1 (15 ounce) can whole new potatoes, drained	425 g
2 (10 ounce) cans cream of mushroom soup	2 (280 g)
Shredded cheddar cheese	

- Wash, dry chicken breasts with paper towels and place in bottom of sprayed oblong slow cooker.

- In saucepan, combine, carrots, green beans, potatoes and mushroom soup, heat just enough to mix well and pour over chicken in cooker.

- Cover and cook on LOW for 8 to 10 hours. When ready to serve, sprinkle cheese on top.

Chicken for the Gods

1¾ cups flour	420 ml
Scant 2 tablespoons dry mustard	30 ml
6 boneless, skinless chicken breast halves	
2 tablespoons oil	30 ml
1 (10 ounce) can condensed chicken and	
rice soup	280 g

- Place flour and mustard in shallow bowl and dredge chicken breasts.

- In skillet, brown chicken breasts in oil. Place all breasts in oblong 6-quart (6 L) slow cooker.

- Pour chicken and rice soup over chicken and add about ¼ (60 ml) cup water.

- Cover and cook on LOW for 6 to 7 hours.

Stuffy Chicken-Ready Supper

1 (6 ounce) package stuffing mix	168 g
3 cups cooked, chopped chicken breast halves	710 ml
1 (16 ounce) package frozen whole green	
beans, thawed	.5 kg
2 (12 ounce) jars chicken gravy	2 (340 g

- Prepare stuffing mix according to package directions and place in oblong slow cooker.

- Follow with layer of chopped chicken or leftover turkey breasts and place green beans over chicken. Pour chicken gravy over green beans.

- Cover and cook on LOW for 3½ to 4½ hours.

Happy Hearty Chicken

4 - 5 carrots, peeled	
6 medium new potatoes with peels, quartered	
4 - 5 boneless, skinless chicken breast halves	
1 tablespoon chicken seasoning	15 ml
2 (10 ounce) cans cream of chicken soup	2 (280 g)
⅓ cup white wine or cooking wine	80 ml

- Cut carrots into ½-inch (1.2 cm) pieces. Place potatoes and carrots in slow cooker. Sprinkle chicken breasts with chicken seasoning and place over vegetables.

- Heat soups with ¼ cup (60 ml) water and wine in saucepan, heat just enough to mix well and pour over chicken and vegetables. Cover and cook on LOW for 5 to 6 hours.

TIP: For a tasty change, use 1 (10 ounce/280 g) can chicken soup and 1 (10 ounce/280 g) can mushroom soup instead of cream of chicken soup.

Chicken with Orange Sauce

1 whole chicken, quartered	
½ cup plus 2 tablespoons flour	120 ml/30 ml
½ teaspoon ground nutmeg	2 ml
½ teaspoon cinnamon	2 ml
2 large sweet potatoes, peeled, sliced	
1 (8 ounce) can pineapple chunks with juice	227 g
1 (10 ounce) can cream of chicken soup	280 g
⅔ cup orange juice	160 ml

- Wash and dry chicken quarters with paper towels. In bowl combine ½ cup (120 ml) flour, nutmeg and cinnamon and coat chicken. Place sweet potatoes and pineapple in large sprayed slow cooker. Arrange chicken on top.

- In saucepan, combine chicken soup, orange juice and remaining flour, heat just enough to mix well and pour over chicken. Cover and cook on LOW for 7 to 9 hours or on HIGH for 3 to 4 hours. Serve over hot buttered rice.

Chow Mein Chicken

4 boneless, skinless chicken breast halves	
2 - 3 cups sliced celery	
1 onion, coarsely chopped	
¼ cup soy sauce	80 ml
¼ teaspoon cayenne pepper	
1 (14 ounce) can chicken broth	396 g
1 (15 ounce) can bean sprouts, drained	425 g
1 (8 ounce) can water chestnuts, drained	227 g
1 (6 ounce) can bamboo shoots	168 g
¼ cup flour	60 ml
1 (6 ounce) package chow mein noodles	168 g

- Combine chicken, celery, onion, soy sauce, cayenne pepper and chicken broth in sprayed slow cooker. Cover and cook on LOW for 3 to 4 hours.

- Add bean sprouts, water chestnuts and bamboo shoots to chicken. Mix flour and ¼ cup (60 ml) water and stir into chicken and vegetables. Cook 1 more hour. Serve over chow mein noodles.

Cream Cheese Chicken

4 boneless, skinless chicken breast halves	
2 tablespoons (¼ stick) butter, melted	30 ml
1 (10 ounce) can cream of mushroom soup	280 g
1 (1 ounce) packet dried Italian salad dressing	28 g
½ cup sherry	120 ml
1 (8 ounce) package cream cheese, cubed	227 g

- Wash chicken breasts, dry with paper towels, brush melted butter over chicken and place in sprayed slow cooker. Add remaining ingredients to saucepan, heat just enough to mix well and add to slow cooker.

- Cover and cook on LOW for 6 to 7 hours. Serve over hot buttered noodles.

Creamed Chicken and Vegetables

1 (10 ounce) can cream of chicken soup	280 g
4 large boneless, skinless chicken breast halves, sliced thinly	
1 (16 ounce) package frozen peas and carrots, thawed	.5 kg
1 (12 ounce) jar chicken gravy	340 g

- Pour soup and ½ cup (120 ml) water into 6-quart (6 L) sprayed slow cooker. Mix and add chicken slices. Sprinkle a little salt and lots of pepper over chicken and soup. Cover and cook on LOW for 4 to 5 hours.

- Add peas, carrots, chicken gravy and another ½ cup (120 ml) water. Increase heat to HIGH and cook for about 1 hour or until peas and carrots are tender.

TIP: Serve over large, refrigerated buttermilk biscuits or over thick, Texas toast.

Creamed Chicken

4 large boneless, skinless chicken breast halves	
Lemon juice	
1 sweet red bell pepper, chopped	
2 ribs celery, sliced diagonally	
1 (10 ounce) can cream of chicken soup	280 g
1 (10 ounce) can cream of celery soup	280 g
⅓ cup dry white wine	80 ml
1 (4 ounce) package shredded parmesan cheese	114 g

- Wash and pat chicken dry with paper towels, rub a little lemon juice over chicken and sprinkle with salt and pepper. Place in slow cooker and top with bell pepper and celery.

- In saucepan, combine soups and wine and heat just enough to mix thoroughly. Pour over chicken breasts and sprinkle with parmesan cheese.

- Cover and cook on LOW for 6 to 7 hours. Serve over hot buttered rice.

Creamy Chicken and Potatoes

4 boneless, skinless chicken breast halves	
2 teaspoons chicken seasoning	10 ml
8 - 10 small new potatoes with peels	
1 (10 ounce) can cream of chicken soup	280 g
1 (8 ounce) carton sour cream	227 g

- Place chicken breast halves, sprinkled with chicken seasoning, in slow cooker. Arrange new potatoes around chicken.

- Combine soup, sour cream and lots of pepper in saucepan and heat just enough to mix well. Spoon over chicken breast. Cover and cook on LOW for 4 to 6 hours.

Creamy Salsa Chicken

4 - 5 boneless, skinless chicken breast halves	
1 (1 ounce) packet taco seasoning mix	28 g
1 cup salsa	240 ml
½ cup sour cream	120 ml

- Place chicken breasts in bottom of 5 to 6-quart (5 L) oblong slow cooker and add ¼ cup (60 ml) water.

- Sprinkle taco seasoning mix over chicken and top with salsa. Cook on LOW for 5 to 6 hours.

- When ready to serve, remove chicken breasts and place on platter. Stir sour cream into juices and spoon over chicken breasts.

Delicious Chicken Pasta

1 pound chicken tenders	.5 kg
Lemon-herb chicken seasoning	
3 tablespoons butter	45 ml
1 onion, coarsely chopped	
1 (15 ounce) can diced tomatoes	425 g
1 (10 ounce) can golden mushroom soup	280 g
1 (8 ounce) box angel hair pasta	227 g

• Pat chicken tenders dry with several paper towels and sprinkle ample amount of chicken seasoning. Melt butter in large skillet, brown chicken and place in oval slow cooker. Pour remaining butter and seasonings over chicken and cover with onion.

• In separate bowl, combine diced tomatoes and mushroom soup and pour over chicken and onions. Cover and cook on LOW for 4 to 5 hours.

• When ready to serve, cook pasta according to package directions. Serve chicken and sauce over pasta.

Delightful Chicken and Veggies

4 - 5 boneless skinless, chicken breast halves	
1 (15 ounce) can whole kernel corn, drained	425 g
1 (10 ounce) box frozen green peas, thawed	280 g
1 (16 ounce) jar alfredo sauce	.5 g
1 teaspoon chicken seasoning	5 ml
1 teaspoon prepared minced garlic	5 ml

• Brown chicken breasts in skillet and place in sprayed oval slow cooker. Combine corn, peas, alfredo sauce, ¼ cup (60 ml) water, chicken seasoning and minced garlic and pour over chicken breasts.

• Cover and cook on LOW for 4 to 5 hours. Serve over hot cooked pasta.

Easy Slow-Cooked Chicken

5 boneless, skinless chicken breast halves
2 (10 ounce) cans cream of chicken soup   2 (280 g)
1 (6 ounce) box chicken stuffing mix   168 g
1 (16 ounce) package frozen green peas,
  thawed   .5 kg

- Place chicken breasts in 6-quart (6 L) slow cooker and spoon soups over chicken.

- Combine stuffing mix with ingredients according to package directions, include seasoning packet and spoon over chicken and soup. Cover and cook on LOW for 5 to 6 hours.

- Sprinkle drained green peas over top of stuffing. Cover and cook another 45 to 50 minutes.

Farmhouse Supper

1 (8 ounce) package medium noodles   227 g
4 - 5 boneless, skinless chicken breast halves
1 (14 ounce) can chicken broth   396 g
2 cups sliced celery   480 ml
2 onions, chopped
1 green and 1 red bell pepper, seeded,
  chopped
1 (10 ounce) can cream of chicken soup   280 g
1 (10 ounce) can cream of mushroom soup   280 g
1 cup shredded 4-cheese blend   240 ml

- Cook noodles in boiling water until barely tender and drain well. Cut chicken into thin slices.

- In large sprayed slow cooker combine noodles, chicken and broth and mix. (Make sure noodles separate and coat with broth.) Combine remaining ingredients in saucepan, heat just enough to mix well and add to slow cooker. Cover and cook on LOW for 4 to 6 hours.

Golden Chicken Dinner

5 boneless, skinless chicken breast halves
6 medium new potatoes with peels, cubed
6 medium carrots, peeled, quartered
1 tablespoon dried parsley flakes   15 ml
1 (10 ounce) can golden mushroom soup   280 g
1 (10 ounce) can cream of chicken soup   280 g
4 tablespoons dried mashed potato flakes 60 ml

- Cut chicken into ½-inch (1.2 cm) pieces. Place potatoes and carrots in slow cooker and top with chicken breasts. Sprinkle parsley flakes, 1 teaspoon (5 ml) salt and a little pepper over chicken.

- Mix soups and spread over chicken. Cover and slow cook on LOW for 6 to 7 hours. Combine potato flakes and ½ cup water or milk, mix to make gravy and cook another 30 minutes.

Imperial Chicken

1 (6 ounce) box long grain wild rice	168 g
6 boneless, skinless chicken breast halves	
1 (16 ounce) jar roasted garlic-parmesan cheese creation	.5 kg
1 (16 ounce) box frozen French-style green beans, thawed	.5 kg
½ cup slivered almonds, toasted	120 ml

- Pour 2½ cups (600 ml) water, rice and seasoning packet into sprayed oblong slow cooker and stir well.

- Spoon in jar of cheese and mix well. Place chicken breasts in slow cooker and cover with green beans. Cover and cook on LOW for 3 to 5 hours. When ready to serve, sprinkle with slivered almonds.

Orange Russian Chicken

6 boneless, skinless chicken breasts halves	
1 (12 ounce) jar orange marmalade	340 g
1 (8 ounce) bottle Russian salad dressing	227 g
1 (1 ounce) package dry onion soup mix	28 g

- Place chicken breasts in oblong slow cooker. Combine orange marmalade, dressing, soup mix and ¾ cup (180 ml) water and stir well.

- Spoon mixture over chicken breasts. Cover and cook on LOW for 4 to 6 hours.

Italian Chicken

1 small head cabbage	
1 onion	
1 (4 ounce) jar sliced mushrooms, drained	114 g
1 medium zucchini, sliced	
1 red bell pepper, julienned	
1 teaspoon Italian seasoning	5 ml
1½ pounds skinless chicken thighs	.7 kg
1 teaspoon minced garlic	5 ml
2 (15 ounce) cans Italian stewed tomatoes	2 (425 g)

- Cut cabbage into wedges, slice onions and separate into rings. Make layers of cabbage, onion, mushrooms, zucchini and bell pepper in bottom of sprayed 6-quart (6 L) slow cooker.

- Sprinkle Italian seasoning over vegetables. Place chicken thighs on top of vegetables.

- Mix garlic with tomatoes and pour over chicken. Cover and cook on LOW for 4 to 6 hours.

TIP: When serving, sprinkle a little parmesan cheese over each serving.

Lemon Chicken

1 (2½ - 3 pound) chicken, quartered	1.3 kg
1 teaspoon dried oregano	5 ml
2 teaspoons prepared minced garlic	10 ml
2 tablespoons (¼ stick) butter	30 ml
¼ cup lemon juice	60 ml

- Season chicken quarters with salt, pepper and oregano and rub garlic on chicken.

- In skillet, brown chicken quarters on all sides in butter and transfer to sprayed oblong slow cooker.

- Add ⅓ cup (80 ml) water to skillet, scrape bottom and pour over chicken.

- Cover and cook on LOW for 5 to 7 hours.

- Pour lemon juice over chicken and cook additional 1 hour.

Fowl Fact

To truss a whole chicken means to tie the legs, wings and body with string in such a way that it keeps its shape after it is cooked and makes a nice presentation. It should be tied so that the string can be cut without disturbing the chicken.

Mushroom Chicken

4 boneless, skinless chicken breast halves
1 (15 ounce) can tomato sauce | 425 g
2 (4 ounce) cans sliced mushrooms, drained | 2 (114 g)
1 (10 ounce) package frozen seasoning blend
   onions and peppers | 280 g
2 teaspoons Italian seasoning | 10 ml
1 teaspoon prepared minced garlic | 5 ml

- In skillet brown chicken breasts and place in sprayed oval slow cooker.

- In bowl combine tomato sauce, mushrooms, onions, peppers, Italian seasoning, minced garlic and ¼ cup (60 ml) water and spoon over chicken breasts.

- Cover and cook on LOW for 4 to 5 hours.

Quick-Fix Chicken

4 - 6 boneless, skinless chicken breast halves
1 (8 ounce) carton sour cream | 227 g
¼ cup soy sauce | 60 ml
2 (10 ounce) cans French onion soup | 2 (280 g)

- Wash and dry chicken with paper towels and place in oblong slow cooker sprayed with vegetable cooking spray.

- Combine sour cream, soy sauce and onion soup, stir and mix well.

- Cover and cook on LOW for 5 to 6 hours if chicken breasts are large, 3 to 4 hours if breasts are medium.

TIP: Serve chicken and sauce with hot, buttered rice or mashed potatoes.

Perfect Chicken Breasts

1 (2.5 ounce) jar dried beef   70 g
6 small boneless, skinless chicken breast
  halves
6 slices bacon
2 (10 ounce) cans golden mushroom soup   2 (280 g)

- Line bottom of oblong slow cooker with slices of dried beef and overlap some.

- Roll each chicken breast with slice of bacon and secure with toothpick. Place in slow cooker, overlapping as little as possible.

- Combine mushroom soup and ½ cup (120 ml) water or milk in saucepan, heat just enough to mix well and spoon over chicken breasts. Cover and cook on LOW for 6 to 8 hours.

TIP: When cooked, you will have a great "gravy" that is wonderful served over noodles or rice.

Russian Chicken

1 (8 ounce) bottle Russian salad dressing	227 g
1 (16 ounce) can whole cranberry sauce	.5 kg
1 (1 ounce) package dry onion soup mix	28 g
1 whole chicken, skinned, quartered	

- In bowl, combine dressing, cranberry sauce, ½ cup (120 ml) water and soup mix. Stir well. Place 4 chicken pieces in 6-quart (6 L) oval slow cooker and spoon dressing-cranberry mixture over chicken.

- Cover and cook on LOW for 4 to 5 hours. Serve sauce and chicken over hot cooked rice.

TIP: *If you don't want to cut up a chicken, use 6 chicken breasts.*

Chicken Noodle Delight

5 - 6 boneless, skinless chicken breast halves	
1 teaspoon chicken seasoning	5 ml
1 (10 ounce) can cream of chicken soup	280 g
1 (10 ounce) can broccoli-cheese soup	280 g
½ cup white cooking wine	120 ml
1 (12 ounce) package medium noodles, cooked	340 g

- Cut chicken breasts in half if they are unusually large. Place breast halves, sprinkled with pepper and chicken seasoning in sprayed slow cooker.

- In saucepan, combine soups and wine and heat enough to mix well. Pour over chicken. Cover and cook on LOW for 5 to 6 hours. Serve chicken and sauce over hot, cooked noodles.

Saffron Rice and Chicken

1 fryer-broiler chicken, quartered	
½ teaspoon garlic powder	2 ml
1 (14 ounce) can chicken broth	396 g
1 onion, chopped	
1 green bell pepper	
1 yellow bell pepper	
1 (4 ounce) jar pimentos, drained	114 g
⅓ cup prepared bacon bits	80 ml
1 (5 ounce) package saffron yellow rice mix	143 g
2 tablespoons (¼ stick) butter, melted	30 ml

- Sprinkle chicken with garlic powder, salt and pepper. In skillet, brown chicken quarters in little oil. Place chicken in sprayed oblong slow cooker and pour broth in slow cooker.

- Combine, onion, bell peppers, pimentos and bacon bits and spoon over chicken quarters. Cover and cook on LOW for 4 to 5 hours.

- Carefully remove chicken quarters from cooker, stir in rice mix and butter and return chicken to cooker. Cover and cook 1 hour or until rice is tender.

Fowl Language

A broiler is a young, tender chicken weighing 2 to 3 pounds when sold whole. Most popular cuts are packaged from these chickens.

Savory Chicken Fettuccine

2 pounds boneless, skinless chicken thighs, cubed	1 kg
½ teaspoon garlic powder	2 ml
1 sweet red bell pepper, seeded, chopped	
2 ribs celery, chopped	
1 (10 ounce) can cream of celery soup	280 g
1 (10 ounce) can cream of chicken soup	280 g
1 (8 ounce) package cubed Velveeta® cheese	227 g
1 (4 ounce) jar diced pimentos	114 g
1 (16 ounce) package spinach fettuccine	.5 kg

- Place chicken in sprayed slow cooker. Sprinkle with garlic powder, ½ teaspoon (2 ml) pepper, bell pepper and celery. Mix soups (no water) and pour on chicken.

- Cover and cook on HIGH for 4 to 6 hours or until chicken juices are clear. Stir in cheese and pimentos. Cover and cook until cheese melts.

- Cook fettuccine according to package directions and drain. Place fettuccine in serving bowl and spoon chicken over fettuccine. Serve hot.

Slow-Cook Arroz Con Pollo

This is a classic Southwest chicken and rice dinner, but cooked conveniently in a slow cooker.

3 - 4 pounds boneless, skinless chicken breasts and thighs	
1 (15 ounce) can Mexican-stewed tomatoes	425 g
1½ cups long grain rice	360 ml
1 (3 ounce) package yellow rice with seasoning mix	84 g
2 (14 ounce) cans chicken broth	2 (396 g)
1 clove garlic, minced	
1 teaspoon oregano	5 ml
1 teaspoon chili powder	5 ml

- In large sprayed slow cooker, combine all ingredients plus ¾ cup (180 ml) water and stir well.

- Cover and cook on LOW for 7 to 8 hours or on HIGH for 3½ to 4 hours.

Slow-Cooker Cordon Bleu

4 boneless, skinless chicken breast halves	
4 slices cooked ham	
4 slices Swiss cheese, softened	
1 (10 ounce) can cream of chicken soup	280 g
¼ cup milk	60 ml

- Place chicken breasts on cutting board and pound until breast halves are thin. Place ham and cheese slices on chicken breasts, roll and secure with toothpick.

- Arrange chicken rolls in 4-quart (4 L) slow cooker. Thin chicken soup with milk in saucepan, heat just enough to mix well and pour over chicken rolls.

- Cover and cook on LOW for 4 to 5 hours. Serve over hot cooked noodles and cover with sauce from soup.

Slow-Cook Chicken Fajitas

This is a convenient way to have a popular one-pot dinner.

2 pounds boneless, skinless chicken breast halves	1 kg
1 onion, thinly sliced	
1 red bell pepper, julienne	
1 teaspoon ground cumin	5 ml
1½ teaspoons chili powder	7 ml
1 tablespoon lime juice	15 ml
½ cup chicken broth	120 ml
8 - 10 warmed flour tortillas	

- Cut chicken into diagonal strips and place in sprayed slow cooker. Top with onion and bell pepper.

- In bowl, combine cumin, chili powder, lime juice and chicken broth and pour over chicken and vegetables. Cover and cook on LOW for 5 to 7 hours.

- When serving, spoon several slices of chicken mixture with sauce into center of each warm tortilla and fold. Serve with guacamole, sour cream, lettuce or tomatoes.

Chicken Little Slow-Cook

4 boneless, skinless chicken breast halves	
1 (10 ounce) can French onion soup	280 g
2 teaspoons chicken seasoning	10 ml
1 (4 ounce) jar sliced mushrooms, drained	114 g
1 cup shredded mozzarella cheese	240 ml
Chopped green onions	

- In skillet brown each chicken breast and place in oblong slow cooker. Pour onion soup over chicken and sprinkle pepper and chicken seasoning over chicken breasts.

- Place mushrooms and cheese over chicken breasts. Cover and cook on LOW for 4 to 5 hours.

    TIP: To make this chicken really festive when ready to serve, sprinkle some chopped green onions over each serving.

So-Good Chicken

4 - 5 boneless, skinless chicken breast halves	
1 (10 ounce) can golden mushroom soup	280 g
1 cup white cooking wine	240 ml
1 (8 ounce) carton sour cream	227 g

- Wash and dry chicken breasts with paper towels and sprinkle a little salt and pepper over each.

- In saucepan, combine mushroom soup, wine and sour cream and heat just enough to mix well. Spoon over chicken breasts. Cover and cook on LOW for 5 to 7 hours.

Southern Chicken

1 cup half-and-half cream	240 ml
1 tablespoon flour	15 ml
1 (1 ounce) package chicken gravy mix	28 g
1 pound boneless, skinless chicken thighs	.5 kg
1 (16 ounce) package frozen stew vegetables, thawed	.5 kg
1 (4 ounce) jar sliced mushrooms, drained	114 g
1 (10 ounce) package frozen green peas, thawed	280 g
1½ cups biscuit baking mix	360 ml
1 bunch fresh green onions, chopped	
½ cup milk	120 ml

- Combine cream, flour, gravy mix and 1 cup (240 ml) water, stir until smooth and pour in large slow cooker. Cut chicken into 1-inch (2.5 cm) pieces and stir in vegetables, mushrooms and peas.

- Cover and cook on LOW for 4 to 6 hours or until chicken is tender and sauce thickens. Stir in peas.

- Combine baking mix, onions and milk in bowl and mix well. Drop dough by tablespoonfuls onto chicken mixture. Change heat to HIGH, cover and cook another 50 to 60 minutes.

Fowl Language

A stewing chicken is a hen or rooster that is past its prime.

Southwestern Chicken Pot

6 boneless, skinless chicken breast halves	
1 teaspoon ground cumin	5 ml
1 teaspoon chili powder	5 ml
1 (10 ounce) can cream of chicken soup	280 g
1 (10 ounce) can fiesta nacho cheese soup	280 g
1 cup salsa	240 ml

- In sprayed oblong slow cooker, place chicken breasts sprinkled with cumin, chili powder and some salt and pepper.

- In saucepan, combine soups and salsa. Heat just enough to mix and pour over chicken breasts. Cover and cook on LOW for 6 to 7 hours. Serve over hot, cooked rice with warmed flour tortillas spread with butter.

Sweet-and-Spicy Chicken

2 pounds chicken thighs	1 kg
¾ cup chili sauce	180 ml
¾ cup packed brown sugar	180 ml
1 (1 ounce) envelope dry onion soup mix	28 g
⅛ teaspoon cayenne pepper	.5 ml

- Arrange chicken pieces in bottom of sprayed 5-quart (5 L) slow cooker.

- Combine chili sauce, brown sugar, dry onion soup mix, cayenne pepper and ¼ cup (60 ml) water and spoon over chicken

- Cover and cook on LOW for 6 to 7 hours. Serve over hot, cooked rice.

Slow-Cook Taco Chicken

3 cups cooked, chopped chicken	710 ml
1 (1 ounce) packet taco seasoning	28 g
1 cup white rice	240 ml
2 cups chopped celery	480 ml
1 green bell pepper, seeded, chopped	
2 (15 ounce) cans Mexican stewed tomatoes	2 (425 g)

- Combine chicken, taco seasoning, rice, celery, bell pepper and stewed tomatoes and mix well. Pour into 5-quart (5 L) slow cooker. Cover and cook on LOW for 3 to 4 hours.

TIP: This is a great recipe for leftover chicken.

Tangy Chicken Legs

12 - 15 chicken legs	
1/3 cup soy sauce	80 ml
2/3 cup packed brown sugar	160 ml
Scant 1/8 teaspoon ground ginger	.5 ml

- Place chicken legs in 5-quart (5 L) slow cooker.
- Combine soy sauce, brown sugar, 1/4 cup (60 ml) water and ginger and spoon over chicken legs.
- Cover and cook on LOW for 4 to 5 hours.

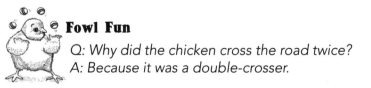

Fowl Fun

Q: Why did the chicken cross the road twice?
A: Because it was a double-crosser.

Tasty Chicken and Veggies

1 (2½ - 3 pound) whole chicken, quartered	1.3 kg
1 (16 ounce) package baby carrots	.5 kg
4 potatoes, peeled, sliced	
3 ribs celery, sliced	
1 onion, peeled, sliced	
1 cup Italian salad dressing	240 ml
⅔ cup chicken broth	160 ml

- Rinse, dry and place chicken quarters in sprayed 6-quart (6 L) slow cooker with carrots, potatoes, celery and onion.

- Pour salad dressing and chicken broth over chicken and vegetables. Cover and cook on LOW for 6 to 8 hours.

  TIP: It's always nice to garnish with sprigs of fresh parsley when you are serving.

Tasty Chicken-Rice and Veggies

4 boneless, skinless chicken breast halves	
2 (10 ounce) jars sweet-and-sour sauce	2 (280 g)
1 (16 ounce) package frozen broccoli,	
cauliflower and carrots, thawed	.5 g
1 (10 ounce) package frozen baby peas, thawed	280 g
2 cups sliced celery	480 ml
1 (6 ounce) package parmesan-butter rice mix	168 g
⅓ cup toasted, slivered almonds	80 ml

- Cut chicken in 1-inch (1.25 cm) strips. Combine chicken, sweet-and-sour sauce and all vegetables in 6-quart (6 L) sprayed slow cooker. Cover and cook on LOW for 4 to 6 hours.

- When ready to serve cook parmesan-butter rice according to package directions and fold in almonds. Serve chicken and vegetables over hot cooked rice.

Tortilla Flats Chicken Bake

6 (6-inch) corn tortillas	6 (15 cm)
3 cups leftover cooked chicken, cubed	710 ml
1 (10 ounce) package frozen whole kernel corn	280 g
1 (15 ounce) can pinto beans with juice	425 g
1 (16 ounce) hot jar salsa	.5 kg
¼ cup sour cream	60 ml
1 tablespoon flour	15 ml
3 tablespoons snipped fresh cilantro	45 ml
1 (8 ounce) package shredded 4-cheese blend	227 g

- Cut tortillas into 6 wedges. In bottom of sprayed slow cooker, place half wedges of tortillas.

- Place remaining wedges on cooking sheet, bake about 10 minutes at 250° (121° C) and set aside. Layer chicken, corn and beans over tortillas in slow cooker.

- In bowl combine salsa, sour cream, flour and cilantro and pour over corn and beans. Cover and cook on LOW for 3 to 4 hours. When ready to serve, place baked tortillas wedges and cheese on top of each serving.

Tom Turkey Bake

1½ pounds turkey tenderloin	.7 kg
1 (6 ounce) package Oriental rice and vermicelli	168 g
1 (10 ounce) package frozen green peas,	
thawed	280 g
1 cup sliced celery	240 ml
¼ cup (½ stick) butter, melted	60 ml
1 (14 ounce) can chicken broth	396 g
1½ cups fresh broccoli florets	360 ml

- Cut tenderloins into strips. In non-stick skillet, saute turkey strips until it is no longer pink.

- In large slow cooker, combine turkey strips, rice-vermicelli mix plus seasoning packet, peas, celery, butter, chicken broth and 1 cup (240 ml) water and mix well.

- Cover and cook on LOW for 4 to 5 hours. Turn heat to HIGH setting, add broccoli and cook another 20 minutes.

Smoked-Turkey Sausage

This is a great recipe for leftover turkey.

2 cups cooked turkey, cubed	480 ml
8 ounces smoked turkey sausage	227 g
3 carrots, sliced	
1 onion, halved, sliced	
1 (15 ounce) can navy bean	425 g
1 (15 ounce) white lima beans	425 g
1 (8 ounce) can tomato sauce	227 g
1 teaspoon dried thyme	5 ml
¼ teaspoon ground allspice	1 ml

- Cut turkey sausage in ½-inch (1.2 cm) pieces. Combine all ingredients in sprayed slow cooker. Cover and cook on LOW for 4 to 5 hours.

Gobble-It-Up Turkey Loaf

2 pounds ground turkey	1 kg
1 onion, very finely chopped	
½ red bell pepper, very finely chopped	
2 teaspoons minced garlic	10 ml
½ cup chili sauce	120 ml
2 large eggs, beaten	
¾ cup Italian seasoned dry breadcrumbs	180 ml

- In large bowl, combine all ingredients plus 1 teaspoon (5 ml) salt and ½ teaspoon (2 ml) pepper and mix well. Shape into round loaf and place on top of foil handles in roasting pan.

- Cover and cook on LOW for 5 to 6 hours. Remove from cooker to serving plate and serve with salsa.

Turkey Sausage and Rice

1 pound turkey sausage	.5 kg
1 (6 ounce) box Rice-a-Roni	168 g
2 (14 ounce) cans chicken broth	2 (396 g)
2 cups sliced celery	480 ml
1 red bell pepper, julienned	
1 (15 ounce) can cut green beans, drained	425 g
⅓ cup toasted slivered almonds	80 ml

- Break up turkey sausage up and brown in skillet. Place in 4 to 5-quart (4 L) slow cooker. Add Rice-a-Roni, 1 cup (240 ml) water, chicken broth, celery, bell pepper and green beans and stir to mix.

- Cover and cook on LOW for 3 to 4 hours. When ready to serve, sprinkle almonds over top.

Turkey Spaghetti

2 pounds ground turkey	1 kg
2 (10 ounce) cans tomato-bisque soup	2 (280 g)
1 (14 ounce) can chicken broth	396 g
1 (15 ounce) can whole kernel corn, drained	425 g
1 (4 ounce) can sliced mushrooms, drained	114 g
¼ cup ketchup	60 ml
2 (7 ounce) boxes ready-cut spaghetti	2 (198 g)

- In non-stick skillet, cook ground turkey and season with a little salt and pepper. Place cooked turkey in sprayed, 5 to 6-quart (5 L) slow cooker.

- Combine soup, broth, corn, mushrooms and ketchup and stir to blend. Add spaghetti to slow cooker and pour soup mixture on top. Cover and cook on LOW for 5 to 7 hours or on HIGH for 3 hours.

Winter Dinner

1 pound chicken tenderloins	.5 kg
1 pound Polish sausage	.5 kg
2 onions, chopped	
1 (28 ounce) can pork and beans with juice	794 g
1 (15 ounce) can ranch-style beans, drained	425 g
1 (15 ounce) can great northern beans	425 g
1 (15 ounce) can butter beans, drained	425 g
1 cup ketchup	240 ml
1 cup packed brown sugar	240 ml
1 tablespoon vinegar	15 ml
6 slices bacon, cooked, crumbled	

- In skillet, brown chicken slices in a little oil and place in large sprayed slow cooker. Cut sausage in 1-inch (2.5 cm) pieces and add to slow cooker. Combine onions, 4 cans beans, ketchup, brown sugar and vinegar, add to slow cooker and stir gently.

- Cover and cook on LOW for 7 to 8 hours or on HIGH for 3 hours 30 minutes to 4 hours. When ready to serve, sprinkle crumbled bacon over top.

Fresh Produce

____ Apples
____ Avocados
____ Bananas
____ Beans
____ Bell Peppers
____ Broccoli
____ Cabbage
____ Carrots
____ Cauliflower
____ Celery
____ Corn
____ Cucumbers
____ Garlic
____ Grapefruit
____ Grapes
____ Lemons
____ Lettuce
____ Lime
____ Melons
____ Mushrooms
____ Onions
____ Oranges
____ Peaches
____ Pears
____ Peppers
____ Potatoes
____ Strawberries
____ Spinach
____ Squash
____ Tomatoes
____ Zucchini
____ _____
____ _____

Deli

____ Cheese
____ Chicken
____ Turkey
____ Ham
____ Main Dish
____ Prepared Salad
____ Sandwich Meat
____ Side Dish
____ _____
____ _____

Fresh Bakery

____ Bagels
____ Bread
____ Cake
____ Cookies
____ Croissants
____ Donuts
____ French Bread
____ Muffins
____ Pastries
____ Pies
____ Rolls

Dairy

____ Biscuits
____ Butter
____ Cheese
____ Cottage Cheese
____ Cream Cheese
____ Cream
____ Creamer
____ Eggs
____ Juice
____ Margarine
____ Milk
____ Pudding
____ Sour Cream
____ Yogurt
____ _____
____ _____

Frozen Foods

____ Breakfast
____ Dinners
____ Ice
____ Ice Cream
____ Juice
____ Pastries
____ Pies
____ Pizza
____ Potatoes
____ Vegetables
____ Whipping Cream
____ Whipped Topping
____ _____
____ _____

Grocery

___ Beans
___ Beer/Wine
___ Bread
___ Canned Vegetables
___ _____
___ _____
___ Cereal
___ Chips/Snacks
___ Coffee
___ Cookies
___ Crackers
___ Flour
___ Honey
___ Jelly
___ Juice
___ Ketchup
___ Kool-Aid
___ Mayonnaise
___ Mixes
___ _____
___ _____
___ Mustard
___ Nuts/Seeds
___ Oil
___ Pasta
___ Peanut Butter
___ Pickles/Olives
___ Popcorn
___ Rice
___ Salad Dressing
___ Salt
___ Seasonings
___ _____
___ _____
___ Sauce
___ Sodas
___ Soups
___ Spices
___ _____
___ _____
___ Sugar
___ Syrup
___ Tea
___ Tortillas
___ Water
___ _____
___ _____

Meat

___ Bacon
___ Chicken
___ Ground Beef
___ Ham
___ Hot Dogs
___ Pork
___ Roast
___ Sandwich Meat
___ Sausage
___ Steak
___ Turkey
___ _____
___ _____

General Merchandise

___ Automotive
___ Baby Items
___ _____
___ Bath Soap
___ Bath Tissue
___ Deodorant
___ Detergent
___ Dish Soap
___ Facial Tissue
___ Feminine Products
___ Aluminum Foil
___ Greeting Cards
___ Hardware
___ Insecticides
___ Light Bulbs
___ Lotion
___ Medicine
___ Napkins
___ Paper Plates
___ Paper Towels
___ Pet Supplies
___ Prescriptions
___ Shampoo
___ Toothpaste
___ Vitamins
___ _____
___ _____

U.S. MEASUREMENT AND METRIC CONVERSION CHART

Teaspoon

¼ teaspoon .... 1 ml
½ teaspoon .... 2 ml
⅓ teaspoon ....
⅔ teaspoon
¾ teaspoon .... 4 ml
1 teaspoon .... 5 ml
1½ teaspoons......... 7 ml
1¾ teaspoons......... 9 ml
2 teaspoons........... 10 ml

Tablespoon

1 tablespoon .... 15 ml
1½ tablespoons...... 22 ml
2 tablespoons........ 30 ml
3 tablespoons........ 45 ml
4 tablespoons........ 60 ml
5 tablespoons .... 75 ml
6 tablespoons........ 90 ml

Volume & Liquid

¼ cup .... 60 ml
⅓ cup..................... 80 ml
½ cup .... 120 ml
⅔ cup..................... 160 ml
¾ cup .... 180 ml
1 cup .... 240 ml
1¼ cup .... 300 ml
1⅓ cup.................. 320 ml
1½ cup .... 360 ml
1⅔ cup................... 400 ml
1¾ cup .... 420 ml
2 cups (1 pint)......... 480 ml
2¼ cups.................. 540 ml
2⅓ cups .... 560 ml
2½ cups.................. 600 ml
2⅔ cups .... 640 ml
2¾ cups.................. 660 ml
3 cups..................... 710 ml
3¼ cups.................. 770 ml
3⅓ cups .... 790 ml

3½ cups   830 ml
3⅔ cups   870 ml
3¾ cups   890 ml
4 cups (32 oz)   960 ml ...... 1.1 L
6 cups (48 oz)   1½ qt........ 1.5 L
8 cups (64 oz) ½ gal 2 qts. .... 1.9 L
16 cups 1 gallon   (4 quarts).. 3.8 L
2 gallons (8 quarts)   7.6 liter

Weight

½ ounce .... 14 g
¾ ounce .... 21 g
1 ounce .... 28 g
1.5 ounce .... 45 g
2 ounces .... 57 g
2.5 ounces .... 70 g
3 ounces .... 84 g
3.5 ounces .... 100 g
4 ounces .... 114 g
4.5 ounces .... 128 g
5 ounces .... 143 g
5.5 ounces .... 155 g
6 ounces .... 170 g
7 ounces .... 198 g
8 ounces .... 227 g
9 ounces .... 255 g
10 ounces .... 280 g
11 ounces .... 312 g
12 ounces .... 340 g
Liquid 12 oz .... 354 ml
13 ounces .... 369 g
14 ounces .... 396 g
15 ounces .... 425 g
16 ounces .... 454 g .... (1 pint)
  or 1 pound .... (.5 kg)
18 ounces .... 510 g
20 ounces .... 567 g
22 ounces .... 624 g
24 ounces .... 680 g
26 ounces .... 737 g
28 ounces .... 794 g
32 ounces .... 1 kg .... 2 pounds

38 ounces .... 1.1 kg
42 ounces .... 1.2 kg
44 ounces .... 1.25 kg
48 ounces .... 1.3 kg 3 pounds
52 ounces .... 1.4 kg
2 pounds................. 908 g or (1 kg)
3 pounds................. 1.3 kg
4 pounds................. 1.8 kg
5 pounds................. 2.2 kg
6 pounds................. 2.7 kg
8 pounds................. 3.6 kg

11 inches .... 30 cm
12 inches................. 32 cm
13 inches................. 33 cm
14 inches................. 36 cm
16 inches................. 40 cm
18 inches .... 45 cm
20 inches................. 50 cm
21 inches................. 53 cm
22 inches................. 56 cm
23 inches .... 59 cm
24 inches................. 62 cm

Temperatures

°F	°C
160°	71°
180°	82°
200°	93°
225°	107°
250°	121°
275°	135°
300°	148°
325°	162°
350°	176°
375°	190°
400°	204°
425°	220°
450°	230°
475°	250°
500°	260°

Pan Sizes

9 x 13-inch .... 23 x 33 cm
7 x 11-inch .... 18 x 28 cm
8 x 8-inch .... 20 x 20 cm
8½ x 11-inch .... 21 x 30 cm
9 x 4-inch .... 23 x 10 cm
9 x 9-inch .... 23 x 23 cm
10 x 4-inch .... 25 x 10 cm
10 x 13-inch
(bundt pan)............. 25 x 23 cm

Quarts

1½-quarts............... 1.51 liters
2-quarts.................. 2.5 liters
3-quarts.................. 3 liters
3½-quarts............... 3.5 liters
4-quarts.................. 4 liters

Lengths

¼ inch .... .60 cm
⅓ inch .... .80 cm
½ inch .... 1.2 cm
¾ inch .... 1.8 cm
1 inch .... 2.5 cm
2 inches.................. 5   cm
3 inches.................. 8   cm
4 inches.................. 10 cm
5 inches.................. 13 cm
6 inches.................. 15 cm
7 inches.................. 18 cm
8 inches.................. 20 cm
9 inches.................. 23 cm
10 inches................. 25 cm

U.S. Measurements

3 teaspoons...................... 1 tablespoon
4 tablespoons.................. ¼ cup .... 2 fluid ounces
8 tablespoons.................. ½ cup .... 4 fluid ounces
12 tablespoons................. ¾ cup .... 6 fluid ounces
16 tablespoons................. 1 cup .... 8 fluid ounces
¼ cup .... 4 tablespoons........................... 2 fluid ounces
⅓ cup.............................. 5 tablespoons + 1 teaspoons ..
½ cup .... 8 tablespoons........................... 4 fluid ounces
⅔ cup.............................. 10 tablespoons + 2 teaspoons
¾ cup .... 12 tablespoons........................ 6 fluid ounces
1 cup .... 16 tablespoons........................ 8 fluid ounces
1 cup .... ½ pint
2 cups............................. 1 pint....................................... 16 fluid ounces
3 cups............................. 1½ pints .... 24 fluid ounces
4 cups............................. 1 quart.................................... 32 fluid ounces
8 cups............................. 2 quarts................................... 64 fluid ounces
1 pint.............................. 2 cups..................................... 16 fluid ounces
2 pints .... 1 quart....................................
1 quart .... 2 pints; 4 cups .... 32 fluid ounces
4 quarts........................... 1 gallon; 8 pints; 16 cups
8 quarts........................... 1 peck
4 pecks........................... 1 bushel

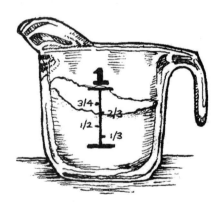

Pan Sizes   **Approx Volume**

Casseroles
8 x 8 x 12 square ....8 cups
11 x 7 x 2 rectangular................................8 cups
9 x 9 x 2 square ....10 cups
13 x 9 x 2 rectangular..............................15 cups
1-quart casserole ....4 cups
2-quart casserole ....8 cups
2½-quart casserole ....10 cups
3-quart casserole ....12 cups

Muffin Pans
1¾ x ¾ mini ....⅛ cup (2 tbsp)
2¾ x 1 1/8 ....¼ cup
2¾ x 1 3/8 ....Scant ½ cup
3 x 1¼ jumbo......................................⅝ cup

Loaf Pans
5½ x 3 x 2½...2 cups
6 x 4½ x 3..3 cups
8 x 4 x 2½..4 cups
8½ x 4¼ x 3..5 cups
9 x 5 x 3..8 cups

Pie Pans
7 x 1¼...2 cups
8 x 1¼...3 cups
8 x 1½...4 cups
9 x 1¼...4 cups
9 x 1½...5 cups
10 x 2..6 cups

Cake Pans
5 x 2 round..2⅔ cups
6 x 2 round..3¾ cups
8 x 1½ round..4 cups
7 x 2 round..5¼ cups
8 x 2 round..6 cups
9 x 1½ round..6 cups
9 x 2 round..8 cups
9 x 3 bundt ....9 cups
10 x 3½ bundt ....12 cups
9 ½ x 2½ springform ....10 cups
10 x 2½ springform ....12 cups
8 x 3 tube..9 cups
9 x 4 tube..11 cups
10 x 4 tube..16 cups

Ingredient Equivalents

Food	Amount	Approximate Equivalent
Apples	1 pound fresh	3 medium; 2¼ cups chopped; 3 cups sliced
Bacon	1 slice, cooked	1 tablespoons crumbled
Bread	1 pound loaf	14-18 regular slices; 7 cups crumbs
	1 slice	½ cup crumbs
Breadcrumbs	8-ounce package	2⅓ cups
Broccoli	1 pound fresh	2 cups chopped
Butter	1 pound regular	4 sticks; 2 cups;
	1 stick	½ cup; 8 tablespoons
Celery	2 ribs	½ cup chopped
Cream Cheese	8 ounces	1 cup
Chicken	3-3½ pounds	3 cups cooked meat
	1 whole breast	1½ cups cooked, chopped
Chocolate	6 ounce chips	1 cup
Chocolate wafers	18-20 cookies	1 cup crumbs
Oreo	22 cookies	1½ cup crumbs
Vanilla wafers	22 cookies	1 cup crumbs
Crackers	15 graham crackers	1 cup crumbs
	28 saltine crackers	1 cup crumbs
Cream	½ pint light	1 cup
	½ pint whipping	1 cup; 2 cups whipped
	½ pint sour cream	1 cup
Garlic	1 clove	½ teaspoon minced

Food	Amount	Approximate Equivalent
Ham	½ pound boneless	1½ cups chopped
Herbs	1 tablespoon fresh, chopped	1 teaspoon dried, crumbled
Ketchup	16-ounce bottle	1⅔ cups
Lemons	4-6	1 cup juice
Limes	6-8	¾ cup juice
Macaroni	8 ounces 1 cup	4 cups cooked 1¾ cups cooked
Marshmallows	6-7 large 85 miniature	1 cup 1 cup
Milk	1 quart	4 cups
Milk, evaporated	5-ounce can	⅔ cup
Mushrooms	1 pound	5 cups sliced; 6 cups chopped
Mustard	1 tablespoon prepared	1 teaspoon dry
Oil	1 quart	4 cups
Onions, green	5 bulbs only 5 with tops	½ cup chopped 1¾ cup chopped
Onions, white	4 medium	3½ cups chopped
Peaches	4 medium	2½ cups chopped or sliced
Peanut Butter	18-ounce jar	1¾ cups
Pecans	1 pound shelled	4 cups chopped
Peppers, bell	2 large 1 medium	2½ cups chopped; 3 cups sliced 1 cup chopped

Food	Amount	Approximate Equivalent
Potatoes, sweet	3 medium	4 cups chopped
Potatoes, white, red, russet	1 pound	4 cups chopped
Rice	1 cup regular 1 cup instant 1 cup brown 1 cup wild	3 cups cooked 2 cups cooked 4 cups cooked 4 cups cooked
Shortening	1 pound	2½ cups
Shrimp	1 pound shelled 1 pound in shell 11-15 jumbo	2 cups cooked 20-30 large
Squash	1 pound summer 1 pound winter	3 cups sliced 1 cup cooked, mashed
Strawberries	1 pint fresh 10 ounces frozen	1½ cups sliced 1½ cups
Sugar	1 pound granulated 1 pound confectioners 1 pound brown	2 cups 3½ cups 2¼ cups packed
Tomatoes	3 medium	1½ cups chopped
Wine	750 ml	3 cups

Ingredient Substitutions

Ingredient	Amount	Substitution
Breadcrumbs, dry	1 cup	¾ cup cracker crumbs
Broth, chicken or beef	1 cup	1 bouillon cube; 1 teaspoon granules in 1 cup boiling water
Butter	1 cup (4 ounces)	⅞ cup vegetable oil or Shortening; 1 cup margarine
Buttermilk	1 cup	1 tablespoon lemon juice or white vinegar plus milk to equal 1 cup (must stand for 5 minutes)
Cottage cheese	1 cup	1 cup ricotta
Cornstarch	1 tablespoon	2 tablespoons flour
Cream, whipping	1 cup	4 ounces frozen whipped topping
Flour	1 cup sifted all-purpose	1 cup minus 2 tablespoons unsifted all-purpose
	1 cup sifted self-rising	1 cup sifted all-purpose flour plus 1½ teaspoon baking powder plus ⅛ teaspoon salt
Garlic	1 small clove	⅛ teaspoon garlic powder
Herbs	1 tablespoon fresh	1 teaspoon dried
Honey	1 cup	1¼ cups granulated sugar plus ⅓ cup liquid in recipe

Ingredient	Amount	Substitution
Lemon juice	1 teaspoon	½ teaspoon vinegar
Mushrooms	½ pound fresh	1 (6 ounce) can, drained
Mustard	1 tablespoon prepared	1 teaspoon dried
Onions	1 small	1 tablespoon instant minced; ½ tablespoon onion powder
Sour cream	1 cup	1 cup plain yogurt; ¾ cup buttermilk; 1 tablespoon lemon juice plus enough evaporated milk to equal 1 cup
Sugar	1 cup light brown	½ cup packed brown sugar plus ½ cup granulated sugar
	1 cup granulated	1¾ cup confections sugar; 1 cup packed brown sugar; 1 cup superfine sugar
Tomato juice	1 cup	½ cup tomato sauce plus ½ cup water
Tomato sauce	1 cup	½ cup tomato paste plus ½ cup water
Yogurt	1 cup	1 cup buttermilk; 1 cup plus 1 tablespoon lemon juice

A

Adobe Chicken 54
After-Thanksgiving Salad 24
Alfredo Chicken 54
Alfredo-Chicken Spaghetti 192
Almond Chicken 193
Almond-Crusted Chicken 125
American Chicken 182
Apache Trail Drum-Sticks 108
Apricot Chicken 118
Apricot-Ginger Chicken 108
Arroz Con Pollo 226
Artichoke-Chicken Pasta 226
Asparagus Chicken 182
Asparagus-Cheese Chicken 183
Aztec Creamy Salsa Chicken 109

B

Bacon-Wrapped Chicken 109
Bacon-Wrapped Fiesta Chicken 227
Baked Chicken Poupon 110
Barbecue-Chicken Salad 27
Barnyard Supper 123
Best-Ever Turkey Loaf 111
Blue Ribbon Chicken 48
Bridge Club Luncheon Chicken 27
Broccoli-Rice Chicken 227
Busy Day Chicken Casserole 34

C

Casseroles
3-Cheese Turkey Casserole 32
Adobe Chicken 54
Alfredo Chicken 54
Busy Day Chicken Casserole 34
Cheesy Chicky Bake 38
Cheesy, Cheesy Chicken 96
Chicken Breasts Supreme 39
Chicken Cashew Bake 77
Chicken Chow Mein 40
Chicken Dish, WOW! 41
Chicken Divan 42
Chicken Martinez 44
Chicken Run Casserole 94
Chicken Spaghetti 45
Chicken Tetrazzini 47
Chicken-Broccoli Deluxe 86
Chicken-Cheese Casserole 45
Chicken-Ham Lasagna 49
Chicken-Ham Tetrazzini 50
Chicken-Noodle Delight 51
Chicken-Orzo Florentine 52
Chicken-Sausage Extraordinaire 53
Chicken-Vegetable Medley 55
Chicky Chicken with Red Peppers 83

Chile-Chicken Casserole 56
Chinese Chicken 57
Chinese Garden 58
Crispy Chicky Chicken 105
Chucky Clucky Casserole 33
Comfort Chicken Plus 59
Creamed Chicken and Rice 60
Curried Chicken Casserole 61
Don't Be Chicken Casserole 75
Easy Chicken Casserole 102
Easy Chicken Enchiladas 34
Eggxellent Chicken Pie 87
Family Chicken Bake 65
Family Night Spaghetti 66
Fluffy Chicken Soufflé 62
Garden Chicken 67
Gobble Gobble Casserole 102
Gobbler Supreme 103
Great Crazy Lasagna 68
Green Chile-Chicken Enchilada
    Casserole 69
Hot-n-Sour Chicky Casserole 35
Jalapeno Chicken 72
Jalapeno Chicken Bark 71
Jazzy Turkey and Dressing 70
Jolly Ole Chicken 73
King Ranch Chicken 74
Manuel's Fiesta Chicken 43
Mexican-Turkey Fiesta 76
Not Just Chicken 78
Old-Fashioned Chicken Spaghetti 79
Orange-Spiced Chicken 80
Pimento-Chicken Enchilada Bake 159
Pollo Delicioso 81
Poppy Seed Chicken 80
Quickie Russian Chicken 106
Red Rock Taco Chicken 83
Rule the Roost Casserole 37
Sassy Chicken over Tex-Mex Corn 84
Sizzling Chicken Pepe 70
Sour Cream Chicken Casserole 87
Sour Cream Chicken Enchiladas 85
Spicy Chicken-Enchilada Casserole 63
Stampede Chicken Enchiladas 89
Supper-Ready Chicken 90
Sweet Pepper Chicken 92
Swiss Chicken 91
Taco Casserole 93
Tempting Chicken and Veggie 62
The Chicken Takes the Artichoke 97
Three-Cheers for Chicken 98
Tomatillo-Chicken Enchiladas 99
Tootsie's Chicken Spectacular 100
Tortilla-Chip Chicken 93
Turkey Perkey Dinner 104
Turkey-Broccoli Bake 35

Zesty Orange Chicken 101
Catalina Chicken 112
Cheese
3-Cheese Turkey Casserole 32
Adobe Chicken 54
Almond-Crusted Chicken 125
Artichoke-Chicken Pasta 226
Asparagus-Cheese Chicken 183
Bacon-Wrapped Chicken 109
Bacon-Wrapped Fiesta Chicken 227
Blue Ribbon Chicken 48
Busy Day Chicken Casserole 34
Cheesy Caesar Pizza 23
Cheesy Chicken and Potatoes 183
Cheesy Chicky Bake 38
Cheesy Crusted Chicken 112
Cheesy, Cheesy Chicken 96
Chicken Alfredo 228
Chicken Breast Deluxe 231
Chicken Breast Eden Isle 118
Chicken Chow Mein 40
Chicken Diablo 114
Chicken Dish, WOW! 41
Chicken Divan 42
Chicken Elegant 188
Chicken for Lunch 15
Chicken Little Slow-Cook 254
Chicken Martinez 44
Chicken Meets Italy 229
Chicken Noodle Delight 249
Chicken Parmesan 117
Chicken Parmesan and Spaghetti 117
Chicken Pockets 119
Chicken Quesadillas 120
Chicken Scarborough Fair 122
Chicken Sherry 233
Chicken Spaghetti 45
Chicken Tetrazzini 47
Chicken-Broccoli Deluxe 86
Chicken-Broccoli Skillet 190
Chicken-Celery Delight 234
Chicken-Cheese Casserole 45
Chicken-Cheese Enchiladas 124
Chicken-Ham Lasagna 49
Chicken-Ham Tetrazzini 50
Chicken-in-the-Garden 230
Chicken-Noodle Delight 51
Chicken-on-the-Border 171
Chicken-Orzo Florentine 52
Chicken-Taco Bake 126
Chicken-Vegetable Medley 55
Chile-Chicken Casserole 56
Chile-Chicken Roll-Ups 127
Chimichangas Con Pollo 11
Chucky Clucky Casserole 33
Cilantro-Chicken Breasts 130

Classic Chicken Marsala 46
Cream Cheese Chicken 238
Creamed Chicken 239
Creamed Chicken and Rice 60
Creamy Chicken Bake 133
Creamy Turkey Enchiladas 134
Day-After-Thanksgiving Turkey Chili 19
Deluxe Dinner Nachos 12
Don't Be Chicken Casserole 75
E Z Chicken 137
Easy Chicken and Dumplings 64
Easy Chicken Casserole 102
Easy Chicken Enchiladas 34
Easy Crispy Chicken Tacos 14
Eggxellent Chicken Pie 87
El Pronto Chicken 138
Family Night Spaghetti 66
Family-Secret Chicken and Noodles 139
Farmhouse Supper 242
Fiesta Chicken 141
Five-Can Soup Bowl 17
Fluffy Chicken Soufflé 62
Garden Chicken 67
Great Crazy Lasagna 68
Green Chile-Chicken Enchilada
    Casserole 69
Grilled Chicken Cordon Bleu 200
Hearty 15-minute Turkey Soup 19
Imperial Chicken 244
Italian Chicken and Rice 203
Jalapeno Chicken 72
Jalapeno Chicken Bark 71
Jazzy Turkey and Dressing 70
King Ranch Chicken 74
Lemon-Almond Chicken 148
Manuel's Fiesta Chicken 43
Mexican-Turkey Fiesta 76
Mozzarella Chicken 151
Nacho Chicken 151
Northern Chili 16
Not Just Chicken 78
Old-Fashioned Chicken Spaghetti 79
Oven-Fried Chicken 153
Oven-Herb Chicken 155
Parmesan Chicken Breasts 114
Parmesan-Crusted Chicken 156
Pasta-Turkey Salad Supper 26
Pimento Cheese-Stuffed Fried
    Chicken 158
Pimento-Chicken Enchilada Bake 159
Pollo Delicioso 81
Pow Wow Chicken 82
Quick Tex-Mex Supper 209
Ranch Chicken 162
Reuben Chicken 163
Rule the Roost Casserole 37

Savory Chicken Fettuccine 251
Savory Oven-Fried Chicken 168
Sizzling Chicken Pepe 70
Slow-Cooker Cordon Bleu 252
So Simple Chicken and Rice 61
Soft Chicken-Taco Bake 170
Sour Cream Chicken Casserole 87
Sour Cream Chicken Enchiladas 85
Southwestern Chicken Pot 256
Southwest-Mexican Pizzas 173
Spicy Chicken-Enchilada Casserole 63
Stampede Chicken Enchiladas 89
Super Cheese Chicken 177
Supper-Ready Chicken 90
Swiss Chicken 91
Taco Casserole 93
Texas Chicken Fajitas 219
The Chicken Takes the Artichoke 97
Three-Cheers for Chicken 98
Tomatillo-Chicken Enchiladas 99
Tortellini Supper 220
Tortilla Flats Chicken Bake 259
Tortilla-Chip Chicken 93
Turkey Burgers 179
Turkey Jerky 13
Turkey Tenders with Honey-Ginger
    Glaze 14
Turkey-Broccoli Bake 35
Veggie-Chicken for Supper 235
White Lightning Chili 22
Cheesy Caesar Pizza 23
Cheesy Chicken and Potatoes 183
Cheesy Chicky Bake 38
Cheesy Crusted Chicken 112
Cheesy, Cheesy Chicken 96
Chicken Alfredo 228
Chicken and Beef Collide 113
Chicken and Everything Good 228
Chicken and Sauerkraut 184
Chicken and Shrimp Curry 184
Chicken and the Works 185
Chicken and Wild Rice Special 185
Chicken Breast Deluxe 231
Chicken Breast Eden Isle 118
Chicken Breasts Supreme 39
Chicken Cacciatore 186
Chicken Cashew Bake 77
Chicken Chow Mein 40
Chicken Coq Vin 232
Chicken Couscous 186
Chicken Crunch 113
Chicken Curry 187
Chicken Curry Over Rice 232
Chicken Diablo 114
Chicken Dipping 115
Chicken Dish, WOW! 41

Chicken Divan 42
Chicken Elegant 188
Chicken for Lunch 15
Chicken for the Gods 236
Chicken Little Slow-Cook 254
Chicken Marseilles 187
Chicken Martinez 44
Chicken Medley Supreme 26
Chicken Meets Italy 229
Chicken Noodle Delight 249
Chicken Oriental 116
Chicken Parmesan 117
Chicken Parmesan and Spaghetti 117
Chicken Pockets 119
Chicken Pot Pie 120
Chicken Quesadillas 120
Chicken Rice Salad Supreme 28
Chicken Run Casserole 94
Chicken Salsa 121
Chicken Scarborough Fair 122
Chicken Sherry 233
Chicken Spaghetti 45
Chicken Tarragon 224
Chicken Tetrazzini 47
Chicken with Orange Sauce 237
Chicken-Broccoli Bake 123
Chicken-Broccoli Deluxe 86
Chicken-Broccoli Skillet 190
Chicken-Celery Delight 234
Chicken-Cheese Casserole 45
Chicken-Cheese Enchiladas 124
Chicken-Ham Lasagna 49
Chicken-Ham Tetrazzini 50
Chicken-in-the-Garden 230
Chicken-Noodle Delight 51
Chicken-Noodle Soup Supper 17
Chicken-on-the-Border 171
Chicken-Orzo Florentine 52
Chicken-Orzo Supper 192
Chicken-Sausage Extraordinaire 53
Chicken-Taco Bake 126
Chicken-Tortilla Dumplings 36
Chicken-Vegetable Medley 55
Chicken-Vegetable Stew Pot 18
Chicken-Waldorf Salad 23
Chicky Chicken with Red Peppers 83
Chile Pepper Chicken 127
Chile-Chicken Casserole 56
Chile-Chicken Roll-Ups 127
Chili-Honeyed Wings 10
Chilly Night's Turkey Bake 128
Chimichangas Con Pollo 11
Chinese Chicken 57
Chinese Chicken Salad 30
Chinese Garden 58
Chip Chicken 128

Chow Mein Chicken 238
Crispy Chicky Chicken 105
Chucky Clucky Casserole 33
Cilantro-Chicken Breasts 130
Classic Chicken Marsala 46
Classic Chicken Piccata 212
Cola Chicken 131
Comfort Chicken Plus 59
Company's Coming Chicken 131
Cracked-Pepper Turkey Breast 15
Cranberry Chicken 132
Cranberry-Glazed Cornish Hens 132
Cream Cheese Chicken 238
Creamed Chicken 239
Creamed Chicken and Rice 60
Creamed Chicken and Vegetables 239
Creamy Chicken and Broccoli 193
Creamy Chicken and Mushrooms 207
Creamy Chicken and Potatoes 240
Creamy Chicken Bake 133
Creamy Mushroom Chicken 195
Creamy Salsa Chicken 240
Creamy Soup Chicken 146
Creamy Tarragon Chicken 196
Creamy Turkey Enchiladas 134
Crispy Herb-Seasoned Chicken 135
Crispy Nutty Chicken 135
Crunchy Chip Chicken 195
Curried Chicken Casserole 61
Curry-Glazed Chicken 136

D

Dad's Best Smoked Chicken 197
Day-After-Thanksgiving Turkey Chili 19
Deep-Fried Chicken 197
Delicious Chicken Pasta 241
Delightful Chicken and Veggies 241
Deluxe Dinner Nachos 12
Dijon Skillet Chicken 198
Don't Be Chicken Casserole 75

E

E Z Chicken 137
Easy Baked Chicken 110
Easy Chicken and Dumplings 64
Easy Chicken Casserole 102
Easy Chicken Enchiladas 34
Easy Crispy Chicken Tacos 14
Easy Green Chile Chicken 198
Easy Slow-Cooked Chicken 242
Easy-Oven Chicken 137
Eggxellent Chicken Pie 87
El Pronto Chicken 138
Elegant Chicken 138

F

Family Chicken Bake 65
Family Night Spaghetti 66
Family-Secret Chicken and Noodles 139
Farmhouse Supper 242
Fiesta Chicken 141
Finger Lickin' BBQ Chicken 111
Five-Can Soup Bowl 17
Flautas de Pollo 10
Fluffy Chicken Soufflé 62
Four-Legged Chicken 142
Fried Chicken Breasts 199
Fried Chicken Livers 199
Fruited Chicken 119

G

Garden Chicken 67
Ginger-Orange Glazed Cornish Hens 143
Glazed Chicken and Rice 200
Glazed Drumsticks 136
Gobble Gobble Casserole 102
Gobble-It-Up Turkey Loaf 261
Gobbler Supreme 103
Golden Chicken 141
Golden Chicken Dinner 243
Gourmet Chicken 201
Great Crazy Lasagna 68
Green Chile-Chicken Enchilada Casserole 69
Grilled Chicken Cordon Bleu 200
Grilled Chicken Fajitas 202
Grilled Chicken with Broccoli Slaw 194
Grilled Chicken with Raspberry-Barbecue
    Sauce 191
Grilled-Lemon Chicken 202

H

Happy Chicken Bake 140
Happy Hearty Chicken 237
Hearty 15-minute Turkey Soup 19
Herb-Roasted turkey 144
Home-Style Southwest Chicken 145
Honey-Baked Chicken 143
Honey-Mustard Chicken 147
Hot Gobble Gobble Soup 21
Hot-n-Sour Chicky Casserole 35
Hurry-Up Chicken Enchiladas 207

I

Imperial Chicken 244
Italian Chicken 245
Italian Chicken Over Couscous 203
Italian Chicken and Rice 203

J

Jalapeno Chicken 72
Jalapeno Chicken Bark 71
Jambalaya 204
Jazzy Turkey and Dressing 70
Jolly Ole Chicken 73

K

Kicky Chicken 215
King Ranch Chicken 74

L

Lemon Chicken 246
Lemonade Chicken 150
Lemon-Almond Chicken 148
Lemon-Chicken Breeze 129
Lemon-Herb Chicken 148
Lemony Chicken And Noodles 205
Lime-Salsa Campsite Chicken 205
Luscious Papaya-Chicken Salad 28

M

Main Dishes
    Alfredo-Chicken Spaghetti 192
    Almond Chicken 193
    Almond-Crusted Chicken 125
    American Chicken 182
    Apache Trail Drum-Sticks 108
    Apricot Chicken 118
    Apricot-Ginger Chicken 108
    Arroz Con Pollo 226
    Artichoke-Chicken Pasta 226
    Asparagus Chicken 182
    Asparagus-Cheese Chicken 183
    Aztec Creamy Salsa Chicken 109
    Bacon-Wrapped Chicken 109
    Bacon-Wrapped Fiesta Chicken 227
    Baked Chicken Poupon 110
    Barnyard Supper 123
    Best-Ever Turkey Loaf 111
    Blue Ribbon Chicken 48
    Broccoli-Rice Chicken 227
    Catalina Chicken 112
    Cheesy Caesar Pizza 23
    Cheesy Chicken and Potatoes 183
    Cheesy Crusted Chicken 112
    Chicken Alfredo 228
    Chicken and Beef Collide 113
    Chicken and Everything Good 228
    Chicken and Sauerkraut 184
    Chicken and Shrimp Curry 184
    Chicken and the Works 185
    Chicken and Wild Rice Special 185
    Chicken Breast Deluxe 231
    Chicken Breast Eden Isle 118

Chicken Cacciatore 186
Chicken Cashew Bake 77
Chicken Coq Vin 232
Chicken Couscous 186
Chicken Crunch 113
Chicken Curry 187
Chicken Curry Over Rice 232
Chicken Diablo 114
Chicken Dipping 115
Chicken Elegant 188
Chicken for the Gods 236
Chicken Little Slow-Cook 254
Chicken Marseilles 187
Chicken Meets Italy 229
Chicken Noodle Delight 249
Chicken Oriental 116
Chicken Parmesan 117
Chicken Parmesan and Spaghetti 117
Chicken Pockets 119
Chicken Pot Pie 120
Chicken Quesadillas 120
Chicken Salsa 121
Chicken Scarborough Fair 122
Chicken Sherry 233
Chicken Tarragon 224
Chicken with Orange Sauce 237
Chicken-Broccoli Bake 123
Chicken-Broccoli Skillet 190
Chicken-Celery Delight 234
Chicken-Cheese Enchiladas 124
Chicken-in-the-Garden 230
Chicken-on-the-Border 171
Chicken-Orzo Supper 192
Chicken-Taco Bake 126
Chile Pepper Chicken 127
Chile-Chicken Roll-Ups 127
Chilly Night's Turkey Bake 128
Chip Chicken 128
Chow Mein Chicken 238
Cilantro-Chicken Breasts 130
Classic Chicken Marsala 46
Classic Chicken Piccata 212
Cola Chicken 131
Company's Coming Chicken 131
Cranberry Chicken 132
Cranberry-Glazed Cornish Hens 132
Cream Cheese Chicken 238
Creamed Chicken 239
Creamed Chicken and Vegetables 239
Creamy Chicken and Broccoli 193
Creamy Chicken and Mushrooms 207
Creamy Chicken and Potatoes 240
Creamy Chicken Bake 133
Creamy Mushroom Chicken 195
Creamy Salsa Chicken 240
Creamy Soup Chicken 146

Creamy Tarragon Chicken 196
Creamy Turkey Enchiladas 134
Crispy Herb-Seasoned Chicken 135
Crispy Nutty Chicken 135
Crunchy Chip Chicken 195
Curry-Glazed Chicken 136
Dad's Best Smoked Chicken 197
Deep-Fried Chicken 197
Delicious Chicken Pasta 241
Delightful Chicken and Veggies 241
Dijon Skillet Chicken 198
E Z Chicken 137
Easy Baked Chicken 110
Easy Chicken Casserole 102
Easy Green Chile Chicken 198
Easy Slow-Cooked Chicken 242
Easy-Oven Chicken 137
El Pronto Chicken 138
Elegant Chicken 138
Family-Secret Chicken and Noodles 139
Farmhouse Supper 242
Fiesta Chicken 141
Finger Lickin' BBQ Chicken 111
Four-Legged Chicken 142
Fried Chicken Breasts 199
Fried Chicken Livers 199
Fruited Chicken 119
Ginger-Orange Glazed Cornish
    Hens 143
Glazed Chicken and Rice 200
Glazed Drumsticks 136
Gobble-It-Up Turkey Loaf 261
Golden Chicken 141
Golden Chicken Dinner 243
Gourmet Chicken 201
Grilled Chicken Cordon Bleu 200
Grilled Chicken Fajitas 202
Grilled Chicken with Broccoli Slaw 194
Grilled Chicken with
        Raspberry-Barbecue Sauce 191
Grilled-Lemon Chicken 202
Happy Chicken Bake 140
Happy Hearty Chicken 237
Herb-Roasted turkey 144
Home-Style Southwest Chicken 145
Honey-Baked Chicken 143
Honey-Mustard Chicken 147
Hurry-Up Chicken Enchiladas 207
Imperial Chicken 244
Italian Chicken 245
Italian Chicken Over Couscous 203
Italian Chicken and Rice 203
Jambalaya 204
Kicky Chicken 215
Lemon Chicken 246
Lemonade Chicken 150

Lemon-Almond Chicken 148
Lemon-Chicken Breeze 129
Lemon-Herb Chicken 148
Lemony Chicken And Noodles 205
Lime-Salsa Campsite Chicken 205
Mandarin Chicken 206
Maple-Plum Glazed Turkey Breast 206
Mole Con Pollo Y Arroz 208
Montezuma Celebration Chicken 150
Mozzarella Chicken 151
Mushroom Chicken 247
Nacho Chicken 151
One-Dish Chicken Bake 152
Onion-Sweet Chicken 152
Orange Russian Chicken 244
Oregano Chicken 153
Oven-Fried Chicken 153
Oven-Fried Ranch Chicken 154
Oven-Fried Turkey 154
Oven-Glazed Chicken 155
Oven-Herb Chicken 155
Party Chicken Breasts 157
Parmesan Chicken Breasts 114
Parmesan-Crusted Chicken 156
Peachy Chicken 157
Perfect Chicken Breasts 248
Picante Chicken 158
Pimento Cheese-Stuffed Fried
        Chicken 158
Pimento-Chicken Enchilada Bake 159
Pineapple-Teriyaki Chicken 160
Prairie Spring Chicken 161
Quick Tex-Mex Supper 209
Quick-Fix Chicken 247
Ranch Chicken 162
Real Easy Baked Chicken 161
Real Simple Cornish Game Hens 169
Reuben Chicken 163
Ritzy Chicken 163
Roasted Chicken 164
Roasted Chicken and Vegetables 164
Roasted Chicken Supreme 165
Rosemary Chicken 165
Russian Chicken 249
Saffron Rice and Chicken 250
Salsa-Grilled Chicken 191
Saucy Chicken Breasts 167
Saucy Chicken 166
Savory Chicken and Mushrooms 210
Savory Chicken Fettuccine 251
Savory Oven-Fried Chicken 168
Sesame Chicken 169
Simple Chicken In Wine 190
Skillet Chicken and More 209
Skillet Chicken and Peas 211
Skillet Chicken and Stuffing 211

Slow-Cook Arroz Con Pollo 252
Slow-Cook Chicken Fajitas 253
Slow-Cook Taco Chicken 257
Slow-Cooker Cordon Bleu 252
Smoked-Turkey Sausage 260
Snazzy Chicken 129
So Simple Chicken and Rice 61
Soft Chicken-Taco Bake 170
So-Good Chicken 254
Southern Chicken 255
Southern Fried Chicken 213
Southern-Stuffed Peppers 172
Southwestern Chicken Pot 256
Southwest-Mexican Pizzas 173
Spaghetti Toss 214
Spiced-Spanish Chicken 174
Spicy Chicken and Rice 174
Springy Chicken 168
Stir-Fry Chicken 215
Stir-Fry Chicken Spaghetti 214
Stuffy Chicken 230
Stuffy Chicken-Ready Supper 236
Succulent Pecan-Chicken Breasts 175
Sunday Chicken 166
Sunny Chicken Supper 216
Sunshine Chicken 176
Super Cheese Chicken 177
Sweet 'N Spicy Chicken 216
Sweet-and-Sour Chicken 176
Sweet-and-Spicy Chicken 256
Tangy Chicken 178
Tangy Chicken Legs 257
Tasty Chicken and Veggies 258
Tasty Chicken-Rice and Veggies 258
Tasty Skillet Chicken 217
Tasty Turkey Crunch 178
Tempting Chicken 217
Tequila-Lime Chicken 218
Texas Chicken Fajitas 219
Texas-Pecan Chicken 223
Tom Turkey Bake 260
Tortellini Supper 220
Tortilla Flats Chicken Bake 259
Turkey and Asparagus Alfredo 218
Turkey and Rice Ole 222
Turkey Burgers 179
Turkey Croquettes 221
Turkey Sausage and Rice 261
Turkey Spaghetti 262
Veggie-Chicken for Supper 235
Whole Lotta Chicken Dinner 235
Wild Rice and Chicken 221
Winey Chicken 179
Winter Dinner 263
Yummy Barbequed-Grilled Chicken 222
Mandarin Chicken 206

Manuel's Fiesta Chicken 43
Maple-Plum Glazed Turkey Breast 206
Mexican-Turkey Fiesta 76
Mole Con Pollo Y Arroz 208
Montezuma Celebration Chicken 150
Mozzarella Chicken 151
Mushroom Chicken 247

N

Nacho Chicken 151
Northern Chili 16
Not Just Chicken 78
Nuts
Almond Chicken 193
Almond-Crusted Chicken 125
Bridge Club Luncheon Chicken 27
Chicken Chow Mein 40
Chicken Curry 187
Chicken Dish, WOW! 41
Chicken Medley Supreme 26
Chicken Run Casserole 94
Chicken-Waldorf Salad 23
Chicky Chicken with Red Peppers 83
Chinese Chicken 57
Chinese Chicken Salad 30
Chinese Garden 58
Chow Mein Chicken 238
Crispy Chicky Chicken 105
Cranberry Chicken 132
Creamy Chicken Bake 133
Crispy Nutty Chicken 135
Gobble Gobble Casserole 102
Gobbler Supreme 103
Golden Chicken 141
Imperial Chicken 244
Lemon-Almond Chicken 148
Luscious Papaya-Chicken Salad 28
Mole Con Pollo Y Arroz 208
Poppy Seed Chicken 80
Raisin-Rice Chicken Salad 25
Strawberry-Chicken Salad 29
Succulent Pecan-Chicken Breasts 175
Supper-Ready Chicken 90
Texas-Pecan Chicken 223
The Chicken Takes the Artichoke 97
Three-Cheers for Chicken 98
Tootsie's Chicken Spectacular 100
Turkey Sausage and Rice 261

O

Old-Fashioned Chicken and Dumplings 20
Old-Fashioned Chicken Spaghetti 79
One-Dish Chicken Bake 152
Onion-Sweet Chicken 152
Orange Russian Chicken 244
Orange-Spiced Chicken 80

Oregano Chicken 153
Oven-Fried Chicken 153
Oven-Fried Ranch Chicken 154
Oven-Fried Turkey 154
Oven-Glazed Chicken 155
Oven-Herb Chicken 155

P

Party Chicken Breasts 157
Parmesan Chicken Breasts 114
Parmesan-Crusted Chicken 156
Pasta-Turkey Salad Supper 26
Peachy Chicken 157
Perfect Chicken Breasts 248
Picante Chicken 158
Pimento Cheese-Stuffed Fried Chicken 158
Pimento-Chicken Enchilada Bake 159
Pineapple-Teriyaki Chicken 160
Pollo Delicioso 81
Poppy Seed Chicken 80
Pow Wow Chicken 82
Prairie Spring Chicken 161

Q

Quick Tex-Mex Supper 209
Quick-Fix Chicken 247
Quickie Russian Chicken 106

R

Raisin-Rice Chicken Salad 25
Ranch Chicken 162
Real Easy Baked Chicken 161
Real Simple Cornish Game Hens 169
Red Rock Taco Chicken 83
Reuben Chicken 163
Rice
  Adobe Chicken 54
  American Chicken 182
  Arroz Con Pollo 226
  Bacon-Wrapped Fiesta Chicken 227
  Broccoli-Rice Chicken 227
  Chicken and the Works 185
  Chicken and Wild Rice Special 185
  Chicken Breast Eden Isle 118
  Chicken Medley Supreme 26
  Chicken Rice Salad Supreme 28
  Chicken Run Casserole 94
  Chicken-Broccoli Bake 123
  Chicken-Sausage Extraordinaire 53
  Chicken-Vegetable Medley 55
  Crispy Chicky Chicken 105
  Creamed Chicken and Rice 60
  Creamy Chicken and Broccoli 193
  Creamy Soup Chicken 146
  Creamy Tarragon Chicken 196
  Curried Chicken Casserole 61
  Curry-Glazed Chicken 136
  E Z Chicken 137
  Easy-Oven Chicken 137
  Elegant Chicken 138
  Glazed Chicken and Rice 200
  Gobbler Supreme 103
  Happy Chicken Bake 140
  Italian Chicken and Rice 203
  Jambalaya 204
  Jolly Ole Chicken 73
  Lemon-Herb Chicken 148
  Not Just Chicken 78
  Orange-Spiced Chicken 80
  Picante Chicken 158
  Pow Wow Chicken 82
  Prairie Spring Chicken 161
  Raisin-Rice Chicken Salad 25
  Red Rock Taco Chicken 83
  Rule the Roost Casserole 37
  Saffron Rice and Chicken 250
  Sassy Chicken over Tex-Mex Corn 84
  Saucy Chicken 166
  Skillet Chicken and More 209
  Skillet Chicken and Peas 211
  Slow-Cook Arroz Con Pollo 252
  Slow-Cook Taco Chicken 257
  So Simple Chicken and Rice 61
  Southern-Stuffed Peppers 172
  Spiced-Spanish Chicken 174
  Spicy Chicken and Rice 174
  Sunny Chicken Supper 216
  Super Cheese Chicken 177
  Sweet 'N Spicy Chicken 216
  Tasty Skillet Chicken 217
  Tootsie's Chicken Spectacular 100
  Turkey and Rice Ole 222
  Turkey Sausage and Rice 261
  Whole Lotta Chicken Dinner 235
  Wild Rice and Chicken 221
  Zesty Orange Chicken 101
Ritzy Chicken 163
Roasted Chicken 164
Roasted Chicken and Vegetables 164
Roasted Chicken Supreme 165
Rosemary Chicken 165
Rule the Roost Casserole 37
Russian Chicken 249

S

Saffron Rice and Chicken 250
Salad
  After-Thanksgiving Salad 24
  Barbecue-Chicken Salad 27
  Chicken-Waldorf Salad 23
  Chinese Chicken Salad 30
  Luscious Papaya-Chicken Salad 28

Strawberry-Chicken Salad 29
Salsa-Grilled Chicken 191
Sassy Chicken over Tex-Mex Corn 84
Saucy Chicken Breasts 167
Saucy Chicken 166
Savory Chicken and Mushrooms 210
Savory Chicken Fettuccine 251
Savory Oven-Fried Chicken 168
Sesame Chicken 169
Simple Chicken In Wine 190
Sizzling Chicken Pepe 70
Skillet Chicken and More 209
Skillet Chicken and Peas 211
Skillet Chicken and Stuffing 211
Slow Cooker
 Arroz Con Pollo 226
 Artichoke-Chicken Pasta 226
 Bacon-Wrapped Fiesta Chicken 227
 Broccoli-Rice Chicken 227
 Chicken Alfredo 228
 Chicken and Everything Good 228
 Chicken Breast Deluxe 231
 Chicken Coq Vin 232
 Chicken Curry Over Rice 232
 Chicken for the Gods 236
 Chicken Little Slow-Cook 254
 Chicken Meets Italy 229
 Chicken Noodle Delight 249
 Chicken Sherry 233
 Chicken with Orange Sauce 237
 Chicken-Celery Delight 234
 Chicken-in-the-Garden 230
 Chow Mein Chicken 238
 Cream Cheese Chicken 238
 Creamed Chicken 239
 Creamed Chicken and Vegetables 239
 Creamy Chicken and Potatoes 240
 Creamy Salsa Chicken 240
 Delicious Chicken Pasta 241
 Delightful Chicken and Veggies 241
 Easy Slow-Cooked Chicken 242
 Farmhouse Supper 242
 Gobble-It-Up Turkey Loaf 261
 Golden Chicken Dinner 243
 Happy Hearty Chicken 237
 Imperial Chicken 244
 Italian Chicken 245
 Lemon Chicken 246
 Mushroom Chicken 247
 Orange Russian Chicken 244
 Perfect Chicken Breasts 248
 Quick-Fix Chicken 247
 Russian Chicken 249
 Saffron Rice and Chicken 250
 Savory Chicken Fettuccine 251
 Slow-Cook Arroz Con Pollo 252

Slow-Cook Chicken Fajitas 253
Slow-Cook Taco Chicken 257
Slow-Cooker Cordon Bleu 252
Smoked-Turkey Sausage 260
So-Good Chicken 254
Southern Chicken 255
Southwestern Chicken Pot 256
Stuffy Chicken 230
Stuffy Chicken-Ready Supper 236
Sweet-and-Spicy Chicken 256
Tangy Chicken Legs 257
Tasty Chicken and Veggies 258
Tasty Chicken-Rice and Veggies 258
Tom Turkey Bake 260
Tortilla Flats Chicken Bake 259
Turkey Sausage and Rice 261
Turkey Spaghetti 262
Veggie-Chicken for Supper 235
Whole Lotta Chicken Dinner 235
Winter Dinner 263
Slow-Cook Arroz Con Pollo 252
Slow-Cook Chicken Fajitas 253
Slow-Cook Taco Chicken 257
Slow-Cooker Cordon Bleu 252
Smoked-Turkey Sausage 260
Snazzy Chicken 129
So Simple Chicken and Rice 61
Soft Chicken-Taco Bake 170
So-Good Chicken 254
Soup
 Chicken-Noodle Soup Supper 17
 Chicken-Tortilla Dumplings 36
 Easy Chicken and Dumplings 64
 Five-Can Soup Bowl 17
 Hearty 15-minute Turkey Soup 19
 Hot Gobble Gobble Soup 21
 Jambalaya 204
Sour Cream Chicken Casserole 87
Sour Cream Chicken Enchiladas 85
Southern Chicken 255
Southern Fried Chicken 213
Southern-Stuffed Peppers 172
Southwestern Chicken Pot 256
Southwest-Mexican Pizzas 173
Spaghetti Toss 214
Spiced-Spanish Chicken 174
Spicy Chicken and Rice 174
Spicy Chicken-Enchilada Casserole 63
Spicy Orange Chicken Over Noodles 88
Springy Chicken 168
Stampede Chicken Enchiladas 89
Stir-Fry Chicken 215
Stir-Fry Chicken Spaghetti 214
Strawberry-Chicken Salad 29
Stuffy Chicken 230
Stuffy Chicken-Ready Supper 236

Succulent Pecan-Chicken Breasts 175
Sunday Chicken 166
Sunny Chicken Supper 216
Sunshine Chicken 176
Super Cheese Chicken 177
Supper-Ready Chicken 90
Sweet 'N Spicy Chicken 216
Sweet Pepper Chicken 92
Sweet-and-Sour Chicken 176
Sweet-and-Sour Chicken and Veggies 91
Sweet-and-Spicy Chicken 256
Swiss Chicken 91

T

3-Cheese Turkey Casserole 32
Taco Casserole 93
Tangy Chicken 178
Tangy Chicken Legs 257
Tasty Chicken and Veggies 258
Tasty Chicken-Rice and Veggies 258
Tasty Skillet Chicken 217
Tasty Turkey Crunch 178
Tempting Chicken 217
Tempting Chicken and Veggie 62
Tequila-Lime Chicken 218
Texas Chicken Fajitas 219
Texas-Pecan Chicken 223
The Chicken Takes the Artichoke 97
Three-Cheers for Chicken 98
Tom Turkey Bake 260
Tomatillo-Chicken Enchiladas 99
Tootsie's Chicken Spectacular 100
Tortellini Supper 220
Tortilla Flats Chicken Bake 259
Tortilla-Chip Chicken 93
Turkey
    3-Cheese Turkey Casserole 32
    Best-Ever Turkey Loaf 111
    Chilly Night's Turkey Bake 128
    Cracked-Pepper Turkey Breast 15
    Day-After-Thanksgiving Turkey Chili 19
    Family Chicken Bake 65
    Gobble Gobble Casserole 102
    Gobble-It-Up Turkey Loaf 261
    Gobbler Supreme 103
    Herb-Roasted turkey 144
    Hot Gobble Gobble Soup 21
    Maple-Plum Glazed Turkey Breast 206
    Oven-Fried Turkey 154
    Pasta-Turkey Salad Supper 26
    Smoked-Turkey Sausage 260
    Tasty Turkey Crunch 178
    Tom Turkey Bake 260
    Turkey and Asparagus Alfredo 218
    Turkey and Rice Ole 222
    Turkey Burgers 179

Turkey Croquettes 221
Turkey Perky Dinner 104
Turkey Sausage and Rice 261
Turkey Tenders with Honey-Ginger
    Glaze 14
Turkey and Asparagus Alfredo 218
Turkey and Rice Ole 222
Turkey Burgers 179
Turkey Croquettes 221
Turkey Jerky 13
Turkey Perky Dinner 104
Turkey Sausage and Rice 261
Turkey Spaghetti 262
Turkey Tenders with Honey-Ginger Glaze 14
Turkey-Broccoli Bake 35

V

Veggie-Chicken for Supper 235

W

White Lightning Chili 22
Whole Lotta Chicken Dinner 235
Wild Rice and Chicken 221
Winey Chicken 179
Winter Dinner 263

Y

Yummy Barbequed-Grilled Chicken 222

Z

Zesty Orange Chicken 101

*A pip is the first small holes
pecked through the eggshell as
a chick gets ready to hatch.*

COOKBOOKS PUBLISHED BY COOKBOOK RESOURCES, LLC

The Ultimate Cooking
with 4 Ingredients

Easy Cooking with 5 Ingredients

The Best of Cooking
with 3 Ingredients

Gourmet Cooking with 5 Ingredients

Healthy Cooking with 4 Ingredients

Diabetic Cooking with 4 Ingredients

4-Ingredient Recipes for
30-Minute Meals

Essential 3-4-5 Ingredient Recipes

The Best 1001 Short, Easy Recipes

Easy Slow-Cooker Cookbook

Easy 1-Dish Meals

Easy Potluck Recipes

Essential Slow-Cooker Cooking

Quick Fixes with Cake Mixes

Casseroles to the Rescue

Easy Casseroles

I Ain't On No Diet Cookbook

Kitchen Keepsakes/
More Kitchen Keepsakes

Old-Fashioned Cookies

Grandmother's Cookies

Mother's Recipes

Recipe Keeper

Cookie Dough Secrets

Gifts for the Cookie Jar

All New Gifts for the Cookie Jar

Gifts in a Pickle Jar

Muffins In A Jar

Brownies In A Jar

Cookie Jar Magic

Easy Desserts

Bake Sale Bestsellers

Quilters' Cooking Companion

Miss Sadie's Southern Cooking

Southern Family Favorites

Classic Tex-Mex and Texas Cooking

Classic Southwest Cooking

The Great Canadian Cookbook

The Best of Lone Star
Legacy Cookbook

Cookbook 25 Years

Pass the Plate

Texas Longhorn Cookbook

Trophy Hunters' Wild Game
Cookbook

Mealtimes and Memories

Holiday Recipes

Little Taste of Texas

Little Taste of Texas II

Southwest Sizzler

Southwest Olé

Class Treats

Leaving Home

Italian Family Cookbook

Sunday Nigh Suppers

365 Easy Meals

365 Easy Chicken

365 Soups and Stews

To Order: **365 Easy Chicken Recipes**

Please send _____ paperback copies @ $16.95 (U.S.) each $ _____

Texas residents add sales tax @ $1.36 each $ _____

Plus postage/handling @ $6.00 (1st copy) $ _____

$1.00 (each additional copy) $ _____

Check or Credit Card (Canada-credit card only) Total $ _____

Charge to: ❏ MasterCard   or   ❏ VISA

Account # _____

Expiration Date _____

Signature_____

Name _____

Address_____

City_____State_____Zip_____

Telephone (day_____(Evening)_____

> Mail or Call:
> Cookbook Resources
> 541 Doubletree Dr.
> Highland Village, Texas 75077
> Toll Free (866) 229-2665
> (972) 317-6404 Fax

To Order: **365 Easy Chicken Recipes**

Please send _____ paperback copies @ $16.95 (U.S.) each $ _____

Texas residents add sales tax @ $1.36 each $ _____

Plus postage/handling @ $6.00 (1st copy) $ _____

$1.00 (each additional copy) $ _____

Check or Credit Card (Canada-credit card only) Total $ _____

Charge to: ❏ MasterCard   or   ❏ VISA

Account # _____

Expiration Date _____

Signature_____

Name _____

Address_____

City_____State_____Zip_____

Telephone (Day)_____(Evening)_____

> Mail or Call:
> Cookbook Resources
> 541 Doubletree Dr.
> Highland Village, Texas 75077
> Toll Free (866) 229-2665
> (972) 317-6404 Fax